STUDIES IN MEDIEVAL AND RENAISSANCE HISTORY

Volume IX

STUDIES IN
Medieval and Renaissance History

History

Volume IX

Edited by
HOWARD L. ADELSON
City University of New York

UNIVERSITY OF NEBRASKA PRESS · LINCOLN
1972

Copyright © 1972 by the University of Nebraska Press

International Standard Book Number 0-8032-0659-3
Library of Congress Catalog Card Number 63–22098

Manufactured in the United States of America

CONTENTS

INTRODUCTION   vii

The Florentine Patriciate in the Transition from Republic to
   Principato, 1530–1609   *Samuel Berner*   3

The Earliest Cardinal-Protectors of the Franciscan Order: A Study
   in Administrative History, 1210–1261   *Williell R. Thomson*   21

Plan and Reality in a Medieval Monastic Economy: The Cistercians
                                                 Richard Roehl   83

Florence, by the Grace of the Lord Pope . . .   *Richard C. Trexler*   115

INTRODUCTION

Studies in Medieval and Renaissance History is a series of annual volumes designed for original major articles and short monographs in all fields of medieval and renaissance history.

The first impetus for the creation of this series came from a belief that there is a need for a scholarly publication to accommodate the longer study whose compass is too large for it to be included regularly in existing media but too small for it to appear in book form. The editors will consider articles in all areas of history from approximately the fourth through the sixteenth centuries—economic, social and demographic, political, intellectual and cultural, and studies that do not fit neatly into a single traditional category of historical investigation.

The editorial board hopes that the *Studies* creates another link between the work of medieval and renaissance scholarship; for many articles pertinent to both disciplines appear in publications consulted almost exclusively by either medieval or renaissance scholars.

While this series is devoted primarily to the publication of major studies it contains occasional bibliographic essays and briefer articles dealing with unpublished archival or manuscript resources. The *Studies* also makes available in translation original articles by scholars who do not write in English.

Studies in Medieval and Renaissance History is not the official organ of any association or institution. Publication in the series is open to all historians whose research falls within its scope and fields of interest.

THE FLORENTINE PATRICIATE IN THE TRANSITION FROM REPUBLIC TO *PRINCIPATO*, 1530–1609

Samuel Berner

University of Virginia

ACKNOWLEDGMENTS

This essay is a highly distilled version of a larger study of the patriciate, the research for which was made possible by a generous two-year fellowship from the Social Science Research Council. I am deeply grateful to the council for its support. In a slightly altered form the essay was delivered at a session of the Eighty-fourth Annual Meeting of the American Historical Association, December 28–30, 1969, Washington, D.C. I particularly acknowledge the helpful criticism of Professor William Bowsky.

THE FLORENTINE PATRICIATE IN THE TRANSITION FROM REPUBLIC TO *PRINCIPATO*, 1530–1609

I

My interest in the Florentine patriciate in the cinquecento has been focused on three central questions. I know of nothing better designed to precipitate an attempt at clarity than that initial confrontation with the vast and intimidating riches of the Archivio di Stato in Florence. There I was immediately made aware of the necessity of precisely defining what I meant by the patriciate. Students of Florentine history are in agreement that the Arno city was an oligarchical society dominated by an urban-centered aristocracy or patriciate. But this all-important group remains elusive. It has not been precisely delimited, the consequence being that some established standard of measurement and limit, so essential for the study of politics and society, has been rendered extremely difficult if not impossible. An exact definition of a social grouping may be analytically convenient but historically unsound, and it is not my intent to reduce the very real complexities of Florentine life to a simplistic schema. However, I do think it is legitimate to claim that the forty-one families represented in the *Senato* of 1532 constitute the heart of the Florentine patriciate—an elite of wealth, political influence and tradition, who enjoyed an elevated social status, and who shared some assumptions about how the Florentine polity should be managed.[1] Thus, to be explicit, I mean two things by the

1. The *Senato*, also known as the *Quarantotto*, was the pivotal institution in the formal change from republic to *Principato* in April, 1532. It replaced the republican *Signoria*; the most important officials in the Tuscan bureaucracy were drawn from it, and tenure was for life. For the provisions of the April reform, see Lorenzo Cantini, *Legislazione Toscana*, 32 vols. (Florence, 1800–1808), I, 5–17. For a list of the original members of the *Senato*, see Archivio di Stato, Florence, Senato de' 48, Vol. I, fols. 2–3; hereafter all manuscript references are to this archive. The basic work on the institutional transition from republic to *Principato* remains Antonio Anzilotti, *La Constituzione interna dello Stato Fiorentino sotto il Duca Cosimo I de' Medici* (Florence, 1910). Elsewhere I have elaborated and documented my definition of the patriciate; see Samuel Berner, "The Florentine Patriciate in the Transition from Republic to *Principato*, 1530–1610" (Ph.D. thesis, University of California, Berkeley, 1969), pp. 5–52. R. Burr Litchfield suggested in Washington that my definition of the patriciate was inadequate. But if we follow his example, where the claim is made that

3

patriciate: (1) the members of the *Senato* of 1532 and their progeny, and (2) members of the families represented in the *Senato* who are not direct descendants of the original senators. Throughout I have tried to test the results of a study of the direct senatorial lines against that of the family as a whole.

My second major concern has been to understand the behavior of the patriciate in the critical first decade of the *Principato*. In 1530–1532 the future shape of the Florentine state was uncertain: it might have become the private patrimony of the Medici, or, the traditional alliance between this great family and the patriciate might have been restored. By 1540 it was clear that the former had happened, and I have been interested in detailing and explaining this process.

Finally, and this is the subject of this essay, I am concerned with the social consequences of the transition from republic to *Principato* through an analysis of the total "life-style" of the second and third generations of the patriciate. The characterization of these two postrepublican generations in terms of a retreat from commerce, a "return to the land," and a growing feudal-aristocratic ethos has appeared with tenacious regularity both in the scholarly and popular literature on cinquecento Florence. The essentials of this characterization may be described through a series of generically related statements:

1.   To win over the old and new nobility, the Medici resuscitated feudal *signorie*. The latifundia were reconstituted, the prevailing emphasis was on "safe" investments, and entailed property multiplied to such an extent that in the seventeenth century three-quarters of Tuscany was in *fidecommisso*.[2]

2.   "Cosimo I de Medici, to avoid trouble, forced the great banking and

---

"the city's ruling class can be identified with some precision" and yet the sample is framed in terms of 700 to 140 families, it seems to me that we are back where we began—with a capacious definition wherein just about every politically active Florentine ranks as a patrician. See R. Burr Litchfield, "Demographic Characteristics of Florentine Patrician Families, Sixteenth to Nineteenth Centuries," *Journal of Economic History*, XXIX (June, 1969), 192–193. This difference of opinion notwithstanding, I want to make it clear that I recognize the significance of Litchfield's contributions to Tuscan studies and that I have great admiration for his work.

2. Carlo Nola, "Politica economica e agricoltura in Toscana nei secoli XV–XIX," *Nuova Rivista Storica*, I (1944–45), 18–19. Emilio Sereni, *Storia del Paesaggio Agrario Italiano* (Bari, 1961), pp. 195–196. Niccolò Rodolico, *Saggi di Storia Medievale e Moderna* (Florence, 1963), p. 340.

trading families to invest their capital in country estates and rewarded them with sonorous titles."[3]

3. The Order of the Knights of Santo Stefano was instituted "to wean the most potent Florentine families from the exercise of trade and thus impede any increase of wealth or power on their part."[4]

4. The fate of the patriciate is incapsulated in the history of one of its principal families, the Acciaiuoli. Few members of the family dedicated themselves to banking; many followed military, diplomatic, or ecclesiastical careers. They were courtiers, Knights of Santo Stefano; they looked after their landed possessions, interested themselves in literature and art, and they collected documents about their family to falsify its past glory.[5]

It is the purpose of this essay to test the validity of these statements and to advance a general portrait of the patriciate more commensurate with reality. It is rather easy to formulate sweeping generalizations, especially difficult to substantiate, refute, or modify them in an area where so little detailed research has been done. However, there is compelling evidence to suggest that the above characterization is at best a gross oversimplification and at worst a serious distortion.

The problem of feudalization, or *refeudalization* as some have termed it,[6] breaks down into two categories: feudalization that sprang from the patriciate itself; feudalization as a consciously pursued component of ducal policy. The question of the extent to which the patriciate purchased and entailed landed property and the degree to which this was done at the expense of commercial investments is clearly relevant to the present study. A satisfactory answer would tell us much and add an important dimension to our portrait of the life-style of this group. But at this juncture in Tuscan studies such an answer cannot be provided, nor will it appear until the thousands of volumes of the *Decima Granducale* (the basic source) are studied systematically.

3. Luigi Barzini, *The Italians* (New York, 1964), p. 301.

4. Cantini, *Legislazione Toscano*, IV, 304. Also, Werner Sombart, *The Quintessence of Capitalism* (New York, 1967), pp. 133–134.

5. Curzio Ugurgieri della Berardenga, *Gli Acciaiuoli di Firenze nella luce dei loro Tempi, 1160–1834*, Vol. II (Florence, 1962), 721. Fernand Braudel's famous discussion of "the failure of the bourgeoisie" opens with Tuscany; see his *Civiltà e imperi del mediterraneo nell'età di Filippo II* (Turin, 1953), pp. 832–833. For the most recent version of these generalizations, see H. G. Koenigsberger and George L. Mosse, *Europe in the Sixteenth Century* (New York, 1968), p. 63.

6. ". . . in Toscana . . . un termine come quello di 'rifeudalizzazione' trova effettivamente il suo uso più appropriato" (Sereni, *Paesaggio Agrari Italiano*, p. 195).

The question is open. However, we do know that "the possession of castles or ville to which great families could periodically retire . . . is a commonplace of Italian municipal history"; that "already before 1260 the ownership of town and country palaces is plainly characteristic of the upper classes generally and not simply of the feudal families of Florence."[7] A study of patrician tax records demonstrates beyond doubt that at the beginning of the cinquecento economic portfolios were diversified, a compound of landed and commercial investments.[8] Finally, it is germane to draw attention to Hans Baron's ignored caveat: "It seems to me that we cannot be cautious enough in our use of the often heard thesis that there was a general 'return' to 'the country' and to agriculture among the urban-commercial classes during the Italian Renaissance. As for Florence, there is not a single generation from the thirteenth to the sixteenth century for which it has not been asserted by some student that such a transformation occurred."[9]

The question of feudalization as a component of ducal policy is more tractable and may be dispensed with in a few words. The evidence makes it difficult to understand why so many writers have insisted that the Medici were intent on transforming the patriciate into a landed aristocracy. In the period 1532–1609 there were only ten feudal grants—not a single patrician family was involved.[10] Most of the grants were in territories formerly belonging to the Sienese republic; their size, economic worth, and jurisdictional scope were such as to hardly deserve the appellation "latifundia."[11]

---

7. P. J. Jones, "Florentine Families and Florentine Diaries," *Papers of the British School at Rome*, XXIV, N.S. XI (1956), 199–200.

8. The basis for this statement is my examination of all patrician assessments in the *Decima* of 1534 (Berner, "The Florentine Patriciate," pp. 5–15). For the diversity of patrician economic conduct, also see Richard A. Goldthwaite, *Private Wealth in Renaissance Florence, a Study of Four Families* (Princeton, 1968).

9. Hans Baron, "The Social Background of Political Liberty in the Early Italian Renaissance," *Comparative Studies in Society and History*, II (1960), 449.

10. "Feudi Concessi da' Serimi Granduchi di Toscana colla descrizione de' medesimi . . . ." (Auditore Reformagioni, Vol. 288). As late as 1737 only six patrician families numbered among Tuscan fief holders; see Antonio Zobi, *Storia civile della Toscana*, Vol. I (Florence, 1850), Appendix XX, pp. 54–55.

11. Here is one concrete example. On October 17, 1605, Duke Ferdinand I granted Giulio Riaro, a Bolognese, Castiglione d'Orcia (or Val d'Orcia) in the state of Siena as a feudal holding. The grant is described (Auditore Reformagioni, Vol. 288, fols. 30–32) in the following terms:

Circuit miles	15
Houses (hearths) in the castle	146

II

The principal source for the study of patrician commercial behavior is the *Tribunale di Mercanzia,* specifically the *accomandita* or limited liability partnership.[12] While the data are by no means a complete, comprehensive index of commercial enterprise, they are sufficiently rich to allow one to grapple with the broad and important question of patrician "withdrawal" from trade, a question implicit in that of the refeudalization thesis. From such a study there is much to be learned about the patriciate: its continued faith in or disillusion with the Florentine and Italian economy; its propensity for safe or adventurous economic conduct; in short, its general relation to the mercantile traditions of renaissance Florence. The immediate aim here is not quantitative certainty, rather it is to understand the psychological and social dimensions of economic enterprise.[13]

In the period 1531–1610 there were 229 patrician *accomandita* investments, and their distribution over this period does not point to a retreat from commerce, for 1570 is the median point in this seventy-nine-year span. Of the total number of investments, one-third appear in the first half, and two-thirds in the second. Of the forty-one families we have defined as patrician, at least one member of thirty-three of them appears in the records. If we isolate the senatorial lines this initial impression of continued investment in commerce is reinforced: twenty-six members of

Houses (hearths) in the territory	96
Population of the castle	555
Population of the territory	522
Soldiers in the whole	32
Income (in scudi)	1042
Expenses (in scudi)	413

12. This source has only been exploited in recent years. See, Maurice Carmona, "Aspects du capitalisme Toscan aux XVIe et XVIIe siècles," *Revue d'Histoire Moderne et Contemporaine,* XI (1964), 81–108; and R. Burr Litchfield, "Les investissements commerciaux des patriciens Florentins au XVIIIe siècle," *Annales Economies Sociétés civilisations,* XXIV, No. 3 (1969), 685–721.

13. The quantitative methods employed by many contemporary historians have yielded some valuable results, but there is something overly seductive, and I would argue even dangerous, about this passion for figures, graphs, and charts. Some have forgotten, if they ever really grasped, the simple but profound truth so well expressed by Gino Luzzatto: "Non bisogna mai dimenticare che l'oggetto principale dell'osservazione di uno storico è sempre l'uomo, con le sue abitudini, le sue passioni, i suoi bisogni, le sue aspirazioni: tutte le cose che ben difficilmente trovano la loro espressione nelle statistiche o nei documenti d'archivio, se non forse in qualche testamento" (Gino Luzzatto, *Per una storia economica d'Italia* [Bari, 1957], p. 97).

the senatorial lines made 71 investments; four belonged to the first generation, eight to the second, and fourteen to the third.[14] With the exception of the last decade of the cinquecento, investments outside of Florence outnumbered those within the city both in number and in the sums invested. The ratio between the two remained fairly constant throughout the century and this suggests a pattern in tune with traditional practice rather than one reflecting a sudden flight of capital from Florence.

A closer look at these investments allows us to get at our central concern: what psychological characteristics may be deduced from an analysis of investment patterns? The data do not permit of more than a crude portrait and it thus seems fitting to frame what follows in terms of two polar characteristics: timidity and aggressiveness.

In October, 1574, Alfonso Carlo Strozzi invested 15,000 Sicilian *scudi* in trade in Palermo "in various kinds of merchandise, exchanges, securities, etc."[15] Over 50 percent of non-Florentine investments bore this vague designation.[16] Vast sums of patrician wealth were poured into ventures clearly intended to provide liquid resources for active partners who had a carte blanche with reference to any opportunities that arose. A second manifestation of this aggressive, adventurous strain is the extent to which patricians did not delimit, in any precise way, the geographical areas in which their funds were to be employed. Often, the *accomandita* simply stated that the recipient would trade in the kingdom of Naples, Flanders, England, or Sicily. In other instances this flexibility was made explicit. Thus investments were made in merchants who were to trade in "Bari and other places in Puglia"; "Messina and other parts of Calabria"; "Seville and other parts of Spain"; "the Maremma of Siena and outside of it"; "Venice and elsewhere"; "Florence and elsewhere"; "Antwerp and the fairs of France"; "Messina and elsewhere"; "Signa and elsewhere"; and "Ancona, the fair of Fuligno and other places within the Papal states."[17] The inclusive dates for these examples are May, 1564–June, 1607; this

14. The source for this and what follows is: *Tribunale di Mercanzia*, 10831, 10832, 10833, 10835, 10838.

15. *Ibid.*, 10833, fol. 23v.

16. *Ibid.*, 10832, fols. 6v–7r, 12r, 26r–v, 70v–71r, 77r, 106r, 125v–127r, 142v, 164v–165r, 190v–191r, 201r–v; 10833, fols. 13v, 19v–20r, 22r–v, 35r, 38r, 52r–53v, 58r–v, 61v–62r, 73v, 96r–v, 112r–v, 122r–123r, 136r–v, 163v–164r, 183r, 185r–186r, 260v; 10835, fols. 1v–2r, 16v–17r, 21r–v, 25r–v, 43r, 58r–v, 60v–61r, 119v–120v, 129v–130r, 134r–v, 142v–143r, 149v–150r, 158r–v, 162r, 167r–168r, 175r–v; 10838, fols. 1r–v, 32v–33r, 35r–v, 40r–v, 42r–43v, 46r–v, 50v–51v, 76v–77r.

17. *Ibid.*, 10832, fols. 164v–165r; 10833, fols. 19v–20r, 66r–v, 75r–v, 185r–v, 191r–v, 260v; 10835, fols. 1v–3v, 9v–10r, 105v–106r, 175r–v; 10838, fols. 40r–v.

is hardly proof of an increasingly less adventurous patriciate on its way to becoming a *rentier* class.

Florentine patrician merchants well knew that immobilized capital was wasted capital. Working through the *Mercanzia* archive one cannot but be impressed by the rapid circulation of patrician capital. The third generation patrician merchant Girolamo Agnolo Guicciardini is a case in point. On June 27, 1583, Girolamo, and his brothers Francesco and Piero, concluded an *accomandita*. The same day they invested 4,500 florins in a Florentine goldworks firm; the following day they put 2,500 ducats into a silk venture. In 1586, 1589, 1593, and 1602 Girolamo was once again recorded as immediately reinvesting his profits from previous investments.[18] He was not an isolated case: Neri Piero Capponi and Andrea Carlo Medici,[19] Alessandro Giovanbatista Gondi and his father,[20] Antonio Jacopo Corsi,[21] Vincenzio Pierfrancesco Ricci[22]—these patrician investors also stand as a vivid testament to a dynamism hardly commensurate with the picture of an ossifying class turning its back on a long mercantile tradition.

Thus far our attention has been focused on investment, the passive dimension of commercial enterprise. But this is only one side of the picture. In 1588 the Venetian ambassador Tomasso Contarini observed that "the wealth of the Florentines is dependent on crafts and mercantile activity: the mercantile activity of the 'nobili' and the crafts of the 'popolo'. However, the 'nobili' are not only superintendents but also with their own hands are involved in the crafts."[23] There is ample evidence to suggest why Contarini came to this conclusion.

Active participation by patricians in commerce took three forms: they were craftsmen or traders, and many of them were *procuratori*, representatives in commercial transactions. For the period 1532–1609, forty-six individual patricians may be identified as craftsmen or traders—that is, recipients of investments who carry on the business in their own name in Florence or elsewhere.[24] If we add all those who were *procuratori* the figure

18. *Ibid.*, 10833, fols. 137*v*–138*v*, 169*v*–170*r*, 196*r*–197*v*; 10835, fols. 43*v*–44*r*, 184*v*–185*v*.

19. *Ibid.*, 10838, fols. 42*r*–*v*, 46*r*–*v*, 62*v*–63*r*.

20. *Ibid.*, 10835, fols. 1*v*–2*r*.

21. *Ibid.*, 10833, fols. 43*r*–*v*, 105*r*–*v*, 106*v*.

22. *Ibid.*, fols. 154*v*–155*r*.

23. Tomasso Contarini, *Relazioni degli Ambasciatore Veneti*, ed. Eugenio Alberi, 3 vols. (Florence, 1839–53), III, 42.

24. *Mercanzia*, 10832, fols. 3*v*, 10*v*, 12*r*, 23*r*, 33*r*, 34*r*, 57*r*, 66*r*, 85*v*–87*r*, 100*v*–101*r*, 125*v*–126*r*, 142*v*, 152*r*, 153*v*–154*r*, 174*v*–175*r*, 182*r*–*v*, 198*v*–199*r*, 202*r*, 209*v*–210*r*; 10833, fols. 1*r*, 2*v*, 4*v*–5*r*, 22*r*–*v*, 23*v*, 38*r*, 86*r*–*v*, 124*v*–125*r*, 132*r*, 147*r*–*v*, 154*v*–155*r*; 10835, fols.

would be closer to seventy-five.[25] All three categories appear throughout the period and there is no diminution in this kind of active participation in commerce. On the contrary, craftsmen and traders increase so that the greatest cluster belong to the second and third generations. The figures are not that great; it would be wrong, I think, to press this argument too far. But no picture of patrician attitudes toward trade and commerce should dispense with the observation that cinquecento Florence was a society in which a Corsini was a goldsmith,[26] a Gondi a shearer of wool,[27] and a Capponi a dyer.[28]

In December, 1553, Mariano Giorgio Ughi was the *procuratore* for the heirs of Restoro Lorenzo Machiavelli. He invested 4,000 florins in their name in Benedetto Lorenzo Machiavelli and Giovanni Ridolfo Lotti. Lotti was present and Taddeo Giovanni dell'Antella represented Benedetto.[29] In September, 1559, Agnolo Girolamo Guicciardini gave 2,000 ducats in a three-year *accomandita* to the goldsmith Giovanbatista Bernardo Bernardi. In January, 1562, when the previous *accomandita* had come to an end, Agnolo invested another 3,000 ducats in Bernardi. Eight years later, Vincenzio Bernardo Bernardi—the goldsmith's brother—was acting as Agnolo Guicciardini's agent.[30]

These two cases point to one of the most significant implications of continued participation in commerce: this activity necessarily involved patricians in a complex of rather close relationships with all segments of Florentine society. Throughout the records one finds examples of patricians and nonpatricians as permanent business partners;[31] of patricians and nonpatricians engaged in trade together;[32] of patricians acting as agents for nonpatricians;[33] of patricians and non-

---

9v–10r, 33v, 34v–35r, 100v–101r, 111r–v, 113v, 129v–130r, 139r–v, 149r–v, 167r–168r; 10838, fols. 55v–56r.

25. Examples of patrician *procuratori* abound: *Mercanzia*, 10832, fols. 3v, 33v–34r, 38r–v, 57r, 70v–71r, 86r–v, 125v–126r, 164v–165r, 182r–v; 10833, fols. 1r–v, 35v–36r, 72v–73v, 86r–v, 110v–111r, 116r–v, 136r–v, 147r–v, 154v–155r, 167v–168r, 185r–v, 191r–v, 193r; 10835, fols. 16v–18r, 28v–29r, 119v–120v, 129v–130r, 142v–143r, 162r; 10838, fols. 35r–v.

26. *Ibid.*, 10832, fol. 202r.

27. *Ibid.*, 10835, fols. 138v–139r.

28. *Ibid.*, fol. 113v.

29. *Ibid.*, 10832, fols. 100v–101r.

30. *Ibid.*, fols. 127v–128r, 155r, 219v.

31. *Ibid.*, fols. 90r–91r, 198v; 10833, fols. 23v, 48r–v, 52r–v, 66r–v, 95r, 260v.

32. *Ibid.*, 10832, fols. 209v–210r; 10833, fols. 3r, 92v–93r; 10835, fols. 111r–v, 167r–168r.

33. *Ibid.*, 10833, fols. 2r, 10r.

patricians investing together;[34] and of nonpatricians investing in patricians.[35]

One of the great merchants in cinquecento Florence was Simone Jacopo Simoni Corsi (1508–1587), who was admitted to the *Senato* in 1556. Prior to that date his name appears only once in the *mercanzia* records; his business career really begins in 1557 and from then on he appears regularly as an investor, at times alone, at times with his brothers. By September, 1560, he is recorded as "cittadino et mercante fiorentino."[36] Clearly, no stigma was attached to commerce in sixteenth-century Florence. How could there be in a society where a Pucci was investing 130 ducats in a druggist shop in San Miniato,[37] a Guicciardini 175 *scudi* in a man who would operate a kiln beside the San Frediano gate,[38] a Rucellai 40 *scudi* in a haberdasher,[39] a Salviati 250 florins in a pork butcher in Pisa,[40] a Strozzi 100 florins in a feed dealer outside the Porta a la Croce,[41] and when all of this was a matter of public record?

III

The life-style of the patriciate, the extent to which it was becoming an aristocratic caste divorced from the rest of society, may be further explicated in relation to two other essential ingredients of the traditional characterization with which we began: the Medici court and the Order of Santo Stefano.

One of the salient dimensions of the territorial state in sixteenth-century Europe was the highly developed court. It is not necessary to attach as much importance to the court as does H. Trevor-Roper in order

34. *Ibid.*, 10832, fols. 11r, 125v–126r; 10833, fols. 1r–v; 10835, fols. 26v–27r; 10838, fols. 50r–v.

35. *Ibid.*, 10832, fols. 86r–v; 10835, fols. 100v–101r. An analysis of marriage patterns reinforces the "open" character of the patriciate. See Berner, "The Florentine Patriciate," pp. 226–232.

36. Domenico Maria Manni, *Il Senato Fiorentino* (Florence, 1771), p. 42. For Corsi's investments, see *Mercanzia*, 10832, fols. 70v–71r, 116r–v, 119v, 125v–126r, 134r, 151r–v, 153v–154r, 208r–v; 10833, fols. 1r–v, 10v, 13v–14r, 43r–v, 71r–v, 74v–75r, 79r, 105r–v, 106v, 136r–v, 147r–v, 153r, 180v–181r, 183r; 10835, fols. 9v–10v, 25r–v, 99r–v, 175r–v; 10838, fols. 35r–v, 53r–v, 76r–77r.

37. *Ibid.*, 10832, fol. 95v.

38. *Ibid.*, fol. 129v.

39. *Ibid.*, fols. 83r–v.

40. *Ibid.*, fols. 44r–v.

41. *Ibid.*, fol. 37v.

to maintain that it was indeed an influential political institution.[42] At court men competed for grace and privilege at a time in European history when monarchs and princes were increasingly more able to dispense or withhold these precious commodities. Proximity to the fountain of honor mattered a great deal since the nature of policy and procedure was more often shaped by royal personality and idiosyncrasy than by predetermined, established norms. The court, in the crisp language of P. S. Lewis, was a "power-complex of influence and favor."[43] But it was also a political tool to be used in a variety of ways to tame the aristocratic elites who had held sway in the fifteenth century. Broadly speaking, two contrary models may be discerned. The first was the French model which came into being in the late fifteenth and early sixteenth centuries and reached its apotheosis in the reign of Louis XIV. Here the court became a centripetal instrument used to cluster the powerful near the monarch so that they might be carefully observed and, through an elaborate etiquette, reduced to quiescent marionettes.[44] The second model is found in Spain, and, at a later date, in Brandenburg—Prussia. Here an effort was made to remove the most powerful class from proximity to the ruler. Most historians have assumed that the French model developed in Tuscany, but the evidence points to precisely the opposite conclusion.

In his *Relazione* of 1588, the Venetian ambassador Tomasso Contarini observed that Duke Ferdinand "was far from wanting the services of Florentines at his court. . . . Perhaps he concluded that to have them so close to him was dangerous and that all would benefit if they attended to their mercantile affairs."[45] The ambassador's assessment was correct. In the Archivio di Stato there is a document entitled "a listing of the Duke's pages from the accession of Duke Ferdinand to the present day [1626]."[46] In all, there are 260 names. The first 18 consist of a guard of honor. These men had served Duke Ferdinand before he became duke, and they were added to his staff in 1587. Only one, Cosimo dell'Antella, was a patrician; of the 18, 7 were Florentines. Of the remaining 242 pages, only 19 were Florentines; of these, 9 were patricians. In this, as in many other respects, Duke Ferdinand was simply following the pattern established by his

42. H. Trevor-Roper, "The General Crisis of the Seventeenth Century," in *Crisis in Europe*, ed. Trevor Aston (New York, 1967), pp. 63–102.

43. P. S. Lewis, *Late Medieval France* (New York, 1968), p. 122.

44. Cardinal Richelieu gave succinct expression of this policy when he wrote "that the frivolousness and unreliability of the French can generally be overcome only by their master's presence . . ." (*The Political Testament of Cardinal Richelieu*, trans. H. B. Hill [Madison, 1965], p. 39).

45. Contarini, *Relazioni*, III, 74.

46. Miscellanea medicea, Vol. 29, No. 18.

predecessors. The data for the earlier part of the cinquecento tell the same story. A series of documents from the ducal exchequer provide a list of courtiers in the period 1551–1555; patricians are few and far between.[47] For example, for the year 1551 all one finds is two members of the Medici family and Giovanni Ricci—the latter employed in the wardrobe and the recipient of an annual stipend of 83 florins.[48]

This should not be construed as proof of the complete alienation of the patriciate from the court. Clearly, the study of Tuscan politics and society requires its own conception of space; the town-country or court-society dichotomy, perhaps useful in understanding France, England, or Spain, is not really applicable to this miniature state—especially since patricians were predominantly urban dwellers. Indeed, the wives, daughters, and widows of patricians found ample representation among those invited to attend special celebrations. In the period 1555–1560, 187 ladies from the quarter of Santo Spirito were called to court; of these, 60 were patricians. For the quarter of Santa Maria Novella, the figures are 57 patricians out of a total of 185 invited guests.[49] But the important point is that the Palazzo Pitti was not Versailles and the Florentine patriciate was not traveling the same road as the French nobility.

In conclusion we return to Lorenzo Cantini's assertion that the Order of Santo Stefano was instituted in 1562 "to wean the most potent families from the exercise of trade and thus impede any increase of their wealth and power."[50] If it can be demonstrated that patricians embraced this institution, then our portrait of this group would require some modification. This is so because membership in the order implied a social posture, a "style" hardly in accord with that which we have argued characterized the second and third generations of the patriciate. Members of the order were forbidden to engage in manual trade on pain of exclusion;[51] they had a highly developed sense of their own importance and made certain that they were appropriately separated and distinguished from other segments of Florentine society;[52] and they were required to prove their "nobility" for entrance and to establish fixed incomes.[53]

---

47. Depositeria Generale, Vols. 391, 392, 393, 394.

48. Depositeria Generale, 391, fols. 25r, 27r, 28r. For other evidence to the same effect, see Guardaroba, 68, fols. 20–24; 279, fols. 45r–v. Here, out of 115 names only 8 are patricians.

49. Manoscritti, Vol. 453, fols. 1–8, 15–23.

50. Cantini, *Legislazione Toscana*, IV, 304.

51. See the legislation of March 29, 1590, in *ibid.*, XIII, 109; and Joannis Bonaventurae Neri Badia, *Decisiones et responsa juris*, Vol. II (Florence, 1776), 606.

52. Manoscritti, Vol. 129, fol. 133v; 130, fols. 70r–71r.

53. Riguccio Galluzzi, *Storia del Granducato di Toscana*, Vol. II (Florence, 1823),

The evidence does not support Cantini's assertion. Francesco Setti-manni, never one to be kind to the Medici, was probably correct when he wrote that Duke Cosimo I created the order "to honor God, defend the Catholic faith, secure the Mediterranean from infidels and ornament his posterity."[54] The proponents of the argument that the order was designed to reduce the Florentine patriciate have not followed Riguccio Galluzzi's lead. In his masterful history of Tuscany, first published in 1781 and still our best guide to this period, he wrote that "Tuscans were not in the majority among the members of the Order."[55] It is possible to statistically verify his statement. Between 1562 and 1609, 305 Florentines were ad-mitted to the order. This figure did not greatly exceed that of the major Tuscan towns: Siena had 106 members;[56] Pistoia, 56;[57] Pisa, 53;[58] Volterra, 40;[59] Cortona, 13;[60] and Borgo San Sepolcro, 9.[61] In the first instance, then, the founding of the order may be understood in terms of a desire to integrate members of important Tuscan families into the newly established *Principato*. In this connection the clear numerical priority of recently conquered Siena is instructive. But non-Tuscans also loom large in the membership rolls, in which we find 73 Spaniards,[62] 40 Bolognese,[63] 38 men from Milan,[64] and 28 from Perugia.[65] And these figures reflect the pursuit for status and prestige by a dynasty not yet securely established in the select circle of European monarchy.

The Florentine patriciate was not beating at the gates for admission. In the first decade of its existence, the order admitted 118 Florentines; of these, 35 were patricians. And the following decades saw no significant change in this distribution. The fact that over a span of forty-seven years only 90 patricians became Knights of Santo Stefano and that of these 90 only 14 belonged to the senatorial lines does little to jeopardize our portrait.

I do not know when the Florentine patriciate took on all those charac-teristics which I have rejected for the cinquecento. What is the significance

---

191–193. Contarini, *Relazioni*, III, 64. The basic work on the order is G. G. Guarnieri, *Storia della marina Stefaniana* (Livorno, 1935).

54. Manoscritti, Vol. 128, fol. 207r.

55. Galluzzi, *Granducato di Toscano*, II, 193.

56. Manoscritti, Vol. 656, fols. 286–289.

57. *Ibid.*, fols. 204–205.

58. *Ibid.*, fols. 231–232.   59. *Ibid.*, fols. 327–328.

60. *Ibid.*, fol. 58.   61. *Ibid.*, fol. 30.

62. *Ibid.*, fols. 259–262.   63. *Ibid.*, fols. 21–22.

64. *Ibid.*, fols. 173–174.   65. *Ibid.*, fols. 22–23.

of the fact that Duke Ferdinand I's death in 1609 brings to an end the personal involvement of this family in commerce, or, that the famous Ordinances of Justice were repeated in 1622?[66] And what were the social consequences of the serious economic decline which set in in the 1620s? These questions, and many more could be suggested, stand as an invitation to other historians to join in the dual task of combatting the entrenched view that after 1530 nothing of interest occurred in Florence, and in rethinking the problem of continuity and change in the transition from republic to *Principato*.

66. Riguccio Galluzzi, *Storia del Granducato di Toscano*, Vol. VI, 1st ed. (Livorno, 1781), 105. Neri Badia, *Decisiones et responsa juris*, p. 599.

THE EARLIEST CARDINAL-PROTECTORS OF THE FRANCISCAN ORDER: A STUDY IN ADMINISTRATIVE HISTORY, 1210–1261

Williell R. Thomson

University of Utah

ABBREVIATIONS

AFH	*Archivum Franciscanum Historicum*
ALKG	*Archiv für Literatur und Kirchengeschichte*
AnalFranc	*Analecta Franciscana*
ArchRSocRom	*Archivio della Reale Società Romana di Storia, Patria*
BF	5 vols. J. H. Sbaralea, *et al.* (eds.) *Bullarium Franciscanum*, (Rome, 1759–1908)
BiblEcCh	*Bibliothèque de l'école des chartes*
BKG	*Beiträge zur Kulturgeschichte des Mittelalters und der Renaissance*
BSFS	British Society of Franciscan Studies
CollFr	*Collectanea Franciscana*
CUA Studies	*Catholic University of America Canon Law Studies*
DDC	*Dictionnaire de Droit Canonique*
Denifle-Chatelain, *CUP* I	H. Denifle and E. Chatelain, *Chartularium Universitatis Parisiensis*, Vol. I (Paris, 1889)
DissHistIHFP	*Dissertationes Historicae, Institutum Historicum Fratrum Praedicatorum ad Sanctam Sabinam*
EHR	*English Historical Review*
EtFranc	*Etudes franciscaines*
Eubel, *BFEp*	C. Eubel, *Bullarii Franciscani Epitome, sive summa Bullarum in eiusdem Bullarii quattuor prioribus tomis relatorum addito supplemento in quo tum gravissima illorum quattuor voluminum diplomata verbotenus recepta tum nonnulla quae in eis desiderantur documenta sunt inserta.* (In *BF*, V)

19

Eubel, *HCMA* I	C. Eubel, *Hierarchia Catholica Medii Aevi*, Vol. I, 2nd ed. (Münster, 1913)
FFDoc	*La France Franciscaine: Documents*
FrFranc	*La France Franciscaine: Mélanges*
FrzStud	*Franziskanische Studien*
Golubovich, *BB*	G. Golubovich, *Biblioteca Bio-Bibliografica della Terra Santa e dell'Oriente Francescano*, Vol. I: *1215–1300* (Quaracchi, 1906); Vol. II: *Addenda al secolo XIII, e fonti nel Sec. XIV* (Quaracchi, 1913)
HistJahrb	*Historisches Jahrbuch*
HistStud	*Historische Studien*
MGH. SS.	*Monumenta Germaniae Historica. Scriptores*
Migne, *PL* CCXV	J. P. Migne, *Patrologiae Cursus Completus. Serie latinae* (Paris, 1855)
MIÖG	*Mitt[h]eilungen des Instituts für österreichische Geschichte*
MiscFr	*Miscellanea Francescana*
Potthast, *Regesta*	A. Potthast, *Regesta Pontificum Romanorum . . .*, 2 vols. (Berlin, 1873, 1875)
QFItArch	*Quellen und Forschungen aus italienischen Archiven*
Reg	Any of several of the *Registres* edited by the Bibliothèque des Écoles françaises d'Athènes et de Rome. L. Auvray ed. Gregory IX in 3 vols.; E. Berger collated Innocent IV in 4; C. Bourel de la Roncière, J. de Loye and P. de Cenival, and A. Coulon, ed. respectively, Alexander IV in 3 vols.
RQ	*Römische Quartalschrift für christliche Alterthumskunde und für Kirchengeschichte*
STF	*Studi e Testi Francescani*, Rome
Wadding, *AnnMin*	L. Wadding, *Annales Minorum seu Trium Ordinum a S. Francisco institutorum*, 3rd ed., 32 vols. (Quaracchi, 1931)

THE EARLIEST CARDINAL-PROTECTORS OF THE FRANCISCAN ORDER: A STUDY IN ADMINISTRATIVE HISTORY, 1210–1261

INTRODUCTION: THE SCENE IN 1210

When Francis of Assisi and his dusty companions presented themselves before the throne of Peter in the late summer or early fall of 1210,[1] the Roman church was caught up in the flux of transition. It was thus against a background of momentous change that the order secured papal approval.

1. The majority of informed opinion inclines to this year. See above all D. Mandić, *De Protoregula Ordinis Fratrum Minorum* (Mostar, 1923), 22–29 (Mandić prefers May or June); and then M. Maccarrone, "Riforma e sviluppo della vita religiosa con Innocenzo III," *Rivista di Storia della Chiesa in Italia*, XVI (1962), 56; H. Boehmer, *Analekten zur Geschichte des Franciscus von Assisi* (Tübingen and Leipzig, 1904), p. 124; Golubovich, *BB*, I, 86; M. D. Knowles, *The Religious Orders in England*, Vol. I (Cambridge, 1948), 128; Wadding, *AnnMin*, I, 73 f.; M. de la Bedoyère, *Francis. A Biography of the Saint of Assisi* (Garden City, 1964), pp. 90 ff.; H. Felder, *Geschichte der wissenschaftlichen Studien im Franziskanerorden bis um die Mitte des 13. Jahrhunderts* (Freiburg-im-Breisgau, 1904), p. 5; A. MacDonell, *Sons of Francis* (London, 1902), p. 30; V. Kybal, *Die Ordensregeln des Heiligen Franz von Assisi und die ursprüngliche Verfassung des Minoritenordens*, BKG, XX (Leipzig, 1905), 5; H. Holzapfel, *The History of the Franciscan Order* (Teutopolis, Ill., 1948), p. 5; J. R. H. Moorman, *The Sources for the Life of S. Francis of Assisi* (Manchester, 1940), p. 27; A. G. Little, "The Mendicant Orders," in *Cambridge Medieval History*, Vol. VI (1929), 729; Gratien de Paris, *Histoire de la Fondation et de l'évolution de l'ordre des Frères Mineurs au XIIIᵉ siècle* (Paris, 1928), p. 7; E. Martire, "San Francesco e Roma," in *L'Italia Francescana nel settimo centenario della morte di S. Francesco* (Santa Maria degli Angeli, 1927), p. 324. The most systematic, but still unconvincing, defense of 1209 is P. Robinson, "Quo Anno Ordo Fratrum Minorum inceperit," *AFH*, II (1909), 181–196; see also V. da Clusone, "Quando ebbe la tonsura S. Francesco d'Assisi?" *L'Italia Francescana*, IX (1934), 15–28; L. M. Patrem, "Appunti critici sulla cronologia della vita di S. Francesco," *L'Oriente Serafico*, VII (1895), 301; A. Ghinato, "De Ordinis agendi ratione ad Regulam S. Francisci," *Antonianum*, XXXV (1960), 5 n. (reprinted in his *Regula S. Francisci in Evolutione O.F.M.*, *STF*, XVI [Rome, 1960], 17 n.), and L. C. Landini, *The Causes of the Clericalization of the Order of Friars Minor 1209–1260 in the Light of Early Franciscan Sources* (Chicago, 1968), pp. 4, 29.

There is in some of the literature a failure to distinguish between the year in which

Before we can fully appreciate the rationale of Innocent's assent, and the conjoined imposition of a cardinal-protector on the order, we have to understand the nature of that change.[2]

The fate of the empire hung still in the balance. Philip had died in June, 1208, but only after fifteen months could Innocent bring himself to crown sly Otto, and barely seven weeks later the new emperor was excommunicated for his incursion into Capua. No one was quite sure what ought to be done with young Frederick in Sicily, and so for several years he remained the protégé of the Curia, learning the subtle lessons of diplomacy and statecraft which he would turn with such devastating effect against the successors of Innocent.

Philip Augustus and John of England stood poorly with Rome in 1210, but both persisted in their wrongheadedness and mutual excoriations. In

---

Francis began to attract followers (1209) and possibly also formulated the *Protoregula*, and the year of the oral approbation by Innocent. Such, for example, are F. Ehrle, "Controversen über die Anfänge des Minoritenordens," *Zft. für Katholische Theologie*, XI (1887), 726, and Fr. Cuthbert, "La Règle Primitive des Frères Mineurs de Saint François (1209)," *EtFranc*, XXIX (1913), 140–153. Among those who say "1209/1210" are K. Esser, *Anfänge und ursprüngliche Zielsetzungen des Ordens der Minderbrüder* (Leiden, 1966), p. 27 n.; L. Oliger, "S. Francesco a Roma e nella Provincia Romana," in *L'Italia Francescana nel settimo centenario*, p. 65; A. Matanić, "Papa Innocenzo di fronte a San Domenico e San Francesco," *Antonianum*, XXXV (1960), 523. The chronicles are tantalizingly vague; Albert of Stade (*Annales Stadenses, MGH. SS.*, XVI [1859], 355) says, for example, *sub anno* 1209: "Circa idem tempus coepit Ordo Praedicatorum [*sic*!] et Minorum Fratrum." A judicious summary *pro et contra* 1210 is in H. Grundmann, *Religiöse Bewegungen im Mittelalter. Untersuchungen über die geistlichen Zusammenhänge zwischen der Ketzerei, den Bettelorden und der religiösen Frauenbewegung im 12. und 13. Jahrhundert . . .*, *HistStud*, CCLXVII (Berlin, 1935), 118, 127 n. But Grundmann did not know Robinson or Ehrle.

It will only be possible to fix the date beyond cavil when we can trace with more exactness the movements of Bishop Guido and Cardinal John of St. Paul. (Potthast, *Regesta*, I, 462, shows that the latter subscribed several bulls at the Lateran between November 25, 1209, and August 11, 1210. The Arch. comunale, Assisi, does not shed light on Guido's whereabouts in 1209 or 1210. [Perg. ser. M1, fols. 4, 14.]) Most narratives agree in placing these two prelates with the Curia when Francis arrived in Rome. For a general overview of the dating problems from 1182 to 1226, see P. Robinson, "Some Chronological Difficulties in the Life of St. Francis," *AFH*, I (1908), 23–30; Patrem, "Appunti critici," pp. 101–107, 135–139, 166–174, 196–199, 228–236, 261–269, 299–308, 327–335, 356–364.

2. S. R. Packard, *Europe and the Church under Innocent III* (New York, 1927); A. Luchaire, *Innocent III*, 6 vols. (Paris, 1904–8); and H. Tillmann, *Papst Innozenz III* (Bonn, 1954) all provide good summaries of the historical context. Knowles, *The Religious Orders in England*, I, 3, believes that the years between 1205 and 1215 were "a watershed in religious history," and that no other decade was so crucial to the future development of the church until the Reformation.

four years Bouvines would fix the course of national development in western Europe, and out of that development would come Gallicanism and the Statute of Provisors.

Within the Papal States themselves the strong spirit of communal independence was only temporarily muted by the rectors and legates dispatched by the pope. Short-term truces and makeshift pacts could not eliminate the basic discontent with clerical power which vented itself in sporadic insurrection. The citizens of the Patrimony, now as in the quattrocento, knew better than anyone else the concrete political powers of the supreme pontiff.[3]

The Latin principalities of the East, and especially the Greek territories that had fallen to the Franks in 1204 and 1205, occasioned much anxiety in Innocent III. Initially reluctant to accept responsibility for them, he soon realized that a temperate occupation might open the door to the long-sought-for conversion of the Greeks to the western rite.[4] He knew the harm that could come from a forced and massive imposition of foreign ways on a proud people, and so in the first few years he fostered a tolerant gradualism.[5] Always, however, he had in prospect the ultimate absorption of these garrison states into the Catholic world.[6] Evidently the Greeks suspected this strategy, for they soon began to make up a kind of church-in-exile, centering first around Bishop Theodore of Negropont, and later

---

3. D. Waley, *The Papal State in the Thirteenth Century* (New York, 1961), covers this ground thoroughly. Also useful are G. Salvemini, "Le lotte fra stato e chiesa nei comuni italiani," in his *Studi Storici* (Florence, 1901), pp. 39–90; C. E. Boyd, *Tithes and Parishes in Medieval Italy. The Historical Roots of a Modern Problem* (Ithaca, 1952), pp. 178–195; and, for a slightly later period, W. Gross, *Die Revolutionen in der Stadt Rom 1219–1254*, HistStud, CCLII (Berlin, 1934).

4. On the schism in general, see Y.-M. Congar, *After Nine Hundred Years* (New York, 1959), and P. Sherrard, *The Greek East and the Latin West: A Study in the Christian Tradition* (London, 1959). On the period of the Latin empire, see W. Norden, *Das Papsttum und Byzanz . . .* (Berlin, 1903), pp. 163–383; W. Miller, *Essays in the Latin Orient* (Cambridge, 1921), and *The Latins in the Levant: A History of Frankish Greece (1204–1566)* (London, 1908); R. L. Wolff, "The Latin Empire of Constantinople, 1204–1261," in *The Later Crusades* (Philadelphia, 1955), pp. 186–233; J. Longnon, "The Frankish States in Greece, 1204–1311," in *ibid.*, 234–274; and K. Setton, "The Latins in Greece and the Aegean from the Fourth Crusade to the End of the Middle Ages," in *The Cambridge Medieval History*, Vol. IV, Part 1, 2nd ed. (1966), 388–430.

5. R. L. Wolff, "The Organization of the Latin Patriarchate of Constantinople, 1204–1261: Social and Administrative Consequences of the Latin Conquest," *Traditio*, VI (1948), 33 n.

6. P. L'Huiller, "La nature des relations ecclésiastiques gréco-latines après la prise de Constantinople par les croisées," in *Akten des XI. Internationalen Byzantinisten-Kongresses München 1958*, ed. F. Dölger and H.-G. Beck (1960), p. 315.

around the Greek patriarchs in Nicaea.[7] Negotiations over doctrine in 1206 (and again in 1213) led nowhere.[8] And the Venetians further undermined the papal efforts at conciliation by reserving the prebends of Hagia Sophia for their countrymen, and generally behaving as if all things Greek in matters of religion fell to the private discretion of the patriarch of Grado.[9] The bright hopes of 1205 were flickering low when the *poverello* obtained his audience with Innocent.

Added to these cares was the crisis of heresy.[10] Innocent knew that the contagion of dualism had grown to epidemic proportions in Lombardy, Tuscany, and the south of France in large measure because the Catholic hierarchy in those regions had given honest men ample cause to despair of salvation at their hands. With the Cathari too he tried suasion and cajolery, but the shocking murder of Peter of Castelnau in January, 1208, made further leniency indefensible. *Rem credulam audivimus* inaugurated the Albigensian Crusade on the tenth of March, and the summer of 1209 was filled with the preparations that led to the bloody sack of Béziers. Faith was not, to Catholic or Cathar, a mere matter of opinion; the articles of a man's creed were more important than anything else. For that reason alone the "perfect" could not be allowed to coexist with Christianity. Moreover the dualists not only propagated a dangerous doctrine but they possessed too a formidable organization and a subversive apparatus as well oiled as any since the first Christian communities. In France, the archbishop of Narbonne and the bishops of Auch, Béziers, Carcassone, and

7. Wolff, "Organization," pp. 36 f.

8. L'Huiller, "La nature des relations," pp. 316–319. Cf. canon 4 of Lateran IV, "De superbia Graecorum contra Latinos," in J. Alberigo *et al.*, *Conciliorum Oecumenicorum Decreta* (Basel, 1962), pp. 211 f., *et alibi*.

9. A. Palmieri, "I vicarii patriarcali di Costantinopoli," *Bessarione*, 2nd ser., VII (1904), 43; Wolff, "Organization," p. 41.

10. J. B. Russell, *Dissent and Reform in the Early Middle Ages* (Berkeley, 1965), presents a sophisticated typology of heterodoxy that has found a favorable response among scholars. S. Runciman, *The Medieval Manichee: A Study of the Christian Dualist Heresy* (Cambridge, 1947), is still of value, particularly with reference to the eastern origins of the Cathars. The new standard work, however, is A. Borst, *Die Katharer*, Schriften der *MGH*, XII (Stuttgart, 1953), which includes (pp. 1–58) a comprehensive list of historical works from the eleventh century to 1950. The bibliography since that time is given in H. Grundmann, *Bibliographie zur Ketzergeschichte des Mittelalters (1900–1966)*, Sussidi Eruditi, XX (Rome, 1967), 33–45. Cf. also Grundmann, *Religiöse Bewegungen*, pp. 14–69; J. Guiraud, *Histoire de l'Inquisition au Moyen Âge*, Vol. I (Paris, 1935), xi–xv, xxi–xxix, xxxviii–xl, 79–234; G. Volpe, *Movimenti religiosi e setti ereticali nella società medioevale italiana (secoli XI-XIV)* (Florence, 1922); B. Marthaler, "Forerunners of the Franciscans: The Waldenses," *Franciscan Studies*, XVIII (1958), 133–142; E. S. Davison, *Forerunners of St. Francis of Assisi and Other Studies* (London 1928), pp. 199–283.

Toulouse were in notorious collusion with the heretics.[11] In Italy, Assisi had a Patarine podesta in 1203;[12] the populace of Orvieto, aroused by a heretic, put to death their papal governor in May, 1209;[13] there may even have been Cathari of some sort in the Eternal City itself in the same year.[14] The church was battered and beleaguered, but it was about to be relieved from an unexpected quarter.

Francis tells us in his testament[15] that he wrote out a rule, went to Rome of his own accord, and obtained Pope Innocent's consent to continue as he and his *socii* had been, preaching penance and following in their own lives the example of Christ. The *Vita prima* of Thomas of Celano[16] and virtually all later accounts add that Bishop Guido of Assisi and Cardinal John of St. Paul, the bishop of Sabina, intervened on his behalf with the pope and persuaded him of Francis's worth. Beyond this we are in the realm of inference and conjecture.[17] Yet before we move on to consider the central issue of the cardinal-protector, instituted as a direct result of the encounter (or encounters) between Francis and Innocent, we have to set forth alternative hypothetical reconstructions of the episode as a whole.

First, the matter of timing: did Francis simply conclude, after the brethren had returned from Spain[18] and France[19] and the rest of Italy,

11. Runciman, *Medieval Manichee*, p. 134; cf. H. K. Mann, *The Lives of the Popes in the Middle Ages* (London, 1925), XII, 224.

12. K. Esser, "Franziskus von Assisi und die Katharer seiner Zeit," *AFH*, LI (1958), 239.

13. A. Bergamino, "Francescanesimo, Chiesa e Impero nella prima metà del secolo XIII," *Nuova Rivista Storica*, XIII (1929), 557.

14. Volpe, *Movimenti religiosi*, p. 92; but cf. Waley, *Papal State*, p. 52: "Viterbo [was] the southernmost point of dualist advance."

15. "Et postquam dominus dedit michi de fratribus, nemo ostendebat michi, quid deberem facere, sed ipse Altissimus revelavit michi, quod deberem vivere secundum formam sancti Evangelii. Et ego paucis verbis et simpliciter feci scribi, et dominus Papa confirmavit michi" (K. Esser, *Das Testament des heiligen Franziskus von Assisi. Eine Untersuchung über seine Echtheit und seine Bedeutung*, Vorreformationsgeschichtliche Forschungen, XV [Münster, 1949], 101).

16. *Vita Prima*, *AnalFranc*, X (1926), 26; Bonaventure, *Legenda Maior*, *ibid.*, p. 570.

17. Reinhold Schneider has written a play, *Innozenz und Franziskus* (Wiesbaden, 1952), centering about this fateful meeting. It does not pretend to be historical, but the subtle nuances of personality are communicated very well.

18. A. López, *La Provincia de España de los Frailes Menores* . . . (Santiago, 1915), p. 10.

19. Fr. Thomas, "Le mouvement franciscain dans la région lyonnaise au XIIIe siècle," *EtFranc*, XLVII (1955), 547–559, marshals some little-known evidence to show that two or three friars went to Villefranche (near Lyon) in 1209, and returned to Assisi in time for

that the protection of one bishop in one diocese was insufficient? Had he been told by someone that it was impermissible to preach without a higher sanction? Did he go knowing that Guido would bespeak his cause among the cardinals?[20] Had the bishop in fact discouraged him from going, fearing the likelihood of rejection?[21] An affirmative answer, or a negative one, is possible for all of these questions. The period following the entrance of Giles into the order (April 16, 1209) and the audience with the pope is one of the most obscure in the entire history of the order, and at the same time one most pregnant with decisions.

We may be firmer in establishing the likely sequence of events after the friars arrived in Rome. Surely they soon discovered that it was no easy thing to see the Lord Pope: lodging had to be secured (with Guido? or where he had stayed on his pilgrimage in 1206?[22]), a convenient time arranged, and perhaps funds tapped to placate the bureaucracy.[23] After

the trip to Rome. If Giles and Bernard of Quintavalle used the same period to journey to Spain and back, it is scarcely conceivable that Francis could have appeared with them at the Curia before midsummer of 1210.

20. As suggested by Grundmann, *Religiöse Bewegungen*, p. 129 n.

21. De la Bedoyère, *Francis*, p. 103. A phrase in the *Vita prima* hints that the bishop was quite surprised to see Francis at Rome: "Cumque vidisset sanctum Franciscum et fratres eius, *causam nesciens*, ipsorum adventum graviter tulit; timebat enim ne patriam propriam vellent deserere, in qua Dominus per servos suos iam coeperat maxime operari" (*AnalFranc*, X, 26; italics mine). Cf. the very similar phrase in the *Legenda Trium Sociorum* (1246), ed. M. Faloci-Pulignani, *MiscFr*, VII (1898), 98 f. Guido receives no mention in the account of Julian of Speier, *Vita S. Francisci, AnalFranc*, X, 344 f.

22. Mrs. A. Strong, "St. Francis in Rome," in *St. Francis of Assisi, 1226–1926: Essays in Commemoration* (London, 1927), p. 270.

23. All sources agree on the mercenary character of most of the business transacted at the Curia. See, e.g., A. Fliche, "Innocent III et la réforme de l'église," *Revue d'histoire ecclésiastique*, XLIV (1949), 91–97, 111 f.; E. Nitz, *Die Beurteilungen der römischen Kurie* (Berlin, 1930), p. 42 f.; R. von Heckel, "Beiträge zur Kenntnis des Geschäftsgang der päpstlichen Kanzlei im 13. Jahrhundert," in *Festschrift Albert Brackmann . . .* (Weimar, 1933), p. 442. But it was still customary for service charges in the chancery (and presumably in other departments too) to be waived in cases of charity, of which Francis was plainly one. (Von Heckel, "Das päpstliche und sizilische Registerwesen in vergleichender Darstellung, mit besonderer Berücksichtigung der Ursprünge," *Archiv für Urkundenforschung*, I [1908], 502–510; W. E. Lunt, *Papal Provisions in the Middle Ages*, Vol. I [New York, 1934], 125 f.) Even so, I cannot imagine that the son of a man who made his living by hard bargaining would have completely forgotten in four years the technique of crossing palms with silver, when the need arose. Cardinal Eudes de Châteauroux, for one, saw parallels between Francis's merchant beginnings and his later zeal: "Fuit ergo negociator fervens et promptus, et sicut negociatores merces suos deferunt ad diversas mundi partes . . ." (Gratien de Paris, "Sermons franciscains du Cardinal Eudes de Châteauroux," *EtFranc*, XXX [1913], 308).

seeing to the mechanical details, they must have realized that prestigious friends were needed to improve their chances of success. Every day great prelates in silk and satin and fine nobles wearing velvet capes entered the papal chambers and came out empty-handed, and everywhere there appeared notaries and procurators at one's elbow, prophesying frustration.[24] We suspect that all of this proved somewhat disturbing for Francis; certainly Guido, always watchful but never overly solicitous, would have suggested to his protégé that it might be opportune for him to put in a word with someone close to the Holy Father. That someone, as it turned out, was the venerable Cardinal John of St. Paul, who must now engage us.

JOHN OF ST. PAUL, 1210–1214[?]

Recent scholarship has assembled a fairly complete picture of the man that was to be the first cardinal-protector of the Franciscan order, at least so far as his activities before 1210 are concerned.[25] His first career was that of a professor of medicine in the distinguished faculty at Salerno. In that capacity he wrote a number of treatises, including a *Practica* or *Breviarium* which displays a wide and surprisingly clinical familiarity with pathological symptoms.[26] Of considerable interest in this handbook are his dispassionate remarks on leprosy.[27] The temptation is very strong to construct

24. Cf. R. von Heckel, "Das Aufkommen der ständigen Prokuratoren an der päpstlichen Kurie im 13. Jahrhundert," in *Miscellanea Francesco Ehrle* . . . II, Studi e Testi, XXXVIII (1924), 290–321.

25. Specific studies devoted to him include B. Altaner, "Zur Biographie des Kardinals Johannes von St. Paul," *HistJahrb*, XLIX (1929), 304–306; M. Bihl, "De Iohanne de S. Paolo, cardinale episcopo Sabinensi, primo S. Francisci in Curia Romana an. 1209 fautore," *AFH*, XIX (1926), 282–285; P. Paschini, "Il Cardinale Giovanni di San Paolo," in *Studi di Storia e Diritto in onore di Carlo Calisse*, Vol. III (Milan, 1940), 109–118; K. Wenck, "Die Römischen Päpste zwischen Alexander III. und Innocenz III. und der Designationsversuch Weihnachten 1197," in *Papsttum und Kaisertum . . . Paul Kehr . . . dargebracht*, ed. A. Brackmann (Munich, 1926), pp. 456–474; S. Majarelli, "Giovanni di S. Paolo," *Enciclopedia Cattolica*, Vol. VI (Vatican City, 1951), 606 f.

26. The known MSS of his works are listed in L. Thorndike and P. Kibre, *A Catalogue of Incipits of Mediaeval Scientific Writings in Latin*, Mediaeval Academy of America Publications, XXIX 2nd ed. (London, 1963), cols. 114, 153, 195, 229 f., 235, 269, 644, 691, 1543. See also G. Sarton, *Introduction to the History of Science*. Vol. II, Part 1: *From Rabbi ben Ezra to Ibn Rushd* (Baltimore, 1931), 439 f., where his activity at Salerno is assigned to the third quarter of the twelfth century. As cardinal he built "un ampio, e magnifico spedale" at Amalfi (L. Cardella, *Memorie Storiche de' Cardinali della Santa Romana Chiesa* [Rome, 1792], Vol. I, Part 2, p. 183).

27. British Museum, Add. MS 16385, fols. 14v–15v. (Four other thirteenth-century MSS are known.) The text of the *Breviarium* has been edited, with a critical introduction,

an imaginary initial dialogue between the beggar and the cardinal, one which soon turned to the topic of Francis's encounter with the leprous wretch outside Assisi and his subsequent commitment to toil in the midst of these pitiful outcasts. How could John help but respond favorably to this gifted practitioner of the art of healing?

For some reason, however, the instruction of men's minds and the training of their diagnostic senses was insufficient for him. Religion called, and he answered; for several years before Celestine III conferred the cardinalate on him, John (his name *in seculo* may have been Johannes Castalius[28]) led the life of a Benedictine monk in the quiet convent of San Paolo fuori le mura.[29] Whether he found it entirely to his liking we cannot say, but without doubt he acquired in the monastic milieu a taste for meditation as well as the aptitude for administration which marked his later years. Francis possessed likewise the power to dwell on things eternal, and his aim in coming to Rome was to facilitate the governance of his followers. A firm basis for rapport lay in the cardinal's own experiences.

So impressive was John's performance as cardinal priest of San Prisca and the pope's vicar-general that Celestine personally preferred him as his successor.[30] But it was no longer usual for the *collegium* to feel itself bound by a deathbed wish of this sort.[31] A younger man ascended to the

---

by G. H. Kroemer, *Johanns von Sancto Paulo: "Liber de simplicis medicinarum virtutibus" und ein anderer Salernitaner Traktat* . . . (Leipzig, 1920). The *Flores Dietarum*, his other principal treatise, was also edited at Leipzig in the previous year by H. J. Ostermuth (*"Flores Diaetarum," Eine salernitanische Nahrungsmitteldiätetik aus dem XII. Jahrhundert, verfasst vermutlich von Johannes de Sancto Paulo*). I have not been able to see either of these editions.

28. Sarton, *Introduction*, Vol. II, Part 1, p. 439. Paschini, "Il Cardinale," p. 109, doubts that he was a Colonna; Altaner, "Zur Biographie," p. 305, suggests he may have come from the south of France.

29. Wenck, "Die Römischen Päpste," p. 457. The usual assumption is that he was abbot or at least rector there before he was elevated to the *collegium*. At any event it is improbable that one of his stature would remain unnoticed for long so close to Rome. The archival materials for this convent are summarized in P. Kehr, *Italia Pontificia* . . . , Vol. I (Rome, 1906), 164.

30. Wenck, "Die Römischen Päpste," p. 459; Paschini, "Il Cardinale," p. 110. Cf. Bonaventure, *Legenda Maior*, p. 570: ". . . omnis sanctitatis amator et adiutor pauperum Christi . . ."; Cardella, *Memorie storiche*, Vol. I, Part 2, p. 181: "illustre per una squisita erudizione, ed eloquenza, non meno, che per una singolare illibatezza . . ."; and a similar eulogy in G. J. Eggs, *Purpura Docta, seu Vitae . . . &c. S. R. E. Cardinalium*, Vol. I (Munich, 1714), p. 109. See a good dense résumé in V. Pfaff, "Die Kardinäle unter Papst Celestin III.," *Zft. der Savigny-Stiftung für Rechtsgeschichte, Kanonistische Abt.* 41 (1955), 86 f.

31. K. Holder, *Die Designation der Nachfolger durch die Päpste* (Fribourg, 1892), pp. 68 f.

Chair of St. Peter, yet he too acknowledged the merits of John, and sent him out almost immediately with legatine authority to quell the agents of Markward of Anweiler in the Patrimony. In 1200 and 1201 he appears in the difficult roles of intermediary to Philip Augustus and conciliator of the Albigensians.[32]

Although John's journeys away from Rome on papal business failed to produce positive results, Innocent continued to rely on him for counsel and direction. Indeed it was his special charge to serve as the pope's penitentiary, hearing confessions and assigning penances to the most eminent churchmen in Europe.[33] With such a man Francis could openly speak his mind.

About the end of 1204[34] John asked to be transferred to the suburbicarian diocese of Sabina. The wish was granted in short order, and within a few months he gave every indication of becoming something rather rare among cardinal bishops—a reformer of his own see.[35] His predecessor, Conrad, had taken up the archbishopric of Mainz in 1183, and died in 1200;[36] the church at Sabina had long been headless and was falling into disrepair. The reassertion of episcopal authority would not be an easy matter: it seems John quarreled over revenue with his chapter and

32. For these missions, see H. Zimmermann, *Die päpstliche Legation in der ersten Hälfte des 13. Jahrhunderts* . . . , Görres-Gesellschaft: Veröffentlichungen der Sektion für Rechts- und Sozialwissenschaft, XVII (Paderborn, 1913), 21–31; and A. Ciacconius and A. Oldoinus, *Vitae, et Res Gestae Pontificium Romanorum et S. R. E. Cardinalium* (Rome, 1677), cols. 1161 f.

33. The indisputable evidence is in Gerald of Wales's *Libri de Invectionibus*, Bk. VI (Vol. I of *Giraldus Cambrensis Opera*, ed. J. S. Brewer, Rolls Series [1861]), chap. 26, pp. 188 f. As *electus* of St. David's, Gerald spent many months at the Curia before his election was overturned, and he wrote the *De Invectionibus* in 1204 or 1205. Cf. also E. Göller, *Die päpstliche Pönitentiarie von ihrem Ursprung bis zu ihrem Umgestaltung unter Pius V.*, Vol. I, Bibliothek des kgl. Preussischen Historischen Instituts in Rom 3–4 (1907), 82, 98; Wenck, "Die Römischen Päpste," pp. 469 f.; B. Rusch, *Die Behörden und Hofbeamten der päpstlichen Kurie des 13. Jahrhunderts*, Schriften der Albertusuniversität: Geisteswissenschaftliche Reihe 3 (Leipzig and Berlin, 1936), pp. 39 f.

34. His last subscription as cardinal priest of San Prisca was on December 2, 1204, and his first as cardinal bishop of Sabina on January 9, 1205—both at St. Peter's. (Potthast, *Regesta*, I, 462, 464; Paschini, "Il Cardinale," p. 112.) F. Ughelli and N. Coleti, *Italia Sacra sive de Episcopis Italiae* . . . , I (Venice, 1717), col. 162; G. Cappelletti, *Le Chiese d'Italia dalla loro Origine sino ai nostri giorni*, Vol. I (Venice, 1844), 603; and F. Cristofori *Storia dei Cardinali di Santa Romana Chiesa dal Secolo V. all'anno del Signore MDCCCLXXXVIII* (Rome, 1888), p. 33, all erroneously give 1203 for his translation to the see of Sabina. Eubel, *HCMA* I, 45, and others, have 1205.

35. Cf. Migne, *PL* CCXV, col. 914 (letter of June 27, 1206); Ughelli and Coleti, *Italia Sacra*, I, col. 162; Cappelletti, *Le Chiese d'Italia* I, 603.

36. P. B. Gams, *Series Episcoporum* . . . (Regensburg, 1873), pp. xiii, 289, etc.

possibly also had a clash or two with the secular officials before his rights were acceded to.[37] He could well sympathize in 1210 with the outsider from Assisi who had run up against the entrenched local structures of Roman officialdom.

There were thus many reasons why John of St. Paul, among all the cardinals then in Rome, would have seemed the obvious advocate of Francis's plea. But what did he really say in his open defense before Innocent and in the crucial private conferences afterwards? On what arguments did he base his proposition that yet another unwashed sodality ought to be lifted up by Peter's heir?

On the substance of his case little doubt is possible.[38] With a profound instinct for exposing the pope's fondest aspirations, the cardinal insisted that Francis was orthodox,[39] that he was sincere, that he had come of his own free will, and that his example would lead others down the path of righteousness. Every one of these suggestions was implicit in the most forceful consideration of all: Could the church afford to ignore Francis?

As to the elaborations of this basic theme, the sources do not permit us to set them forth with any confidence. But it is not overly fanciful to imagine that John exploited the pope's preoccupation with heresy to remind him that this bold little penitent might attract his fellow citizens away from their stiff-necked follies,[40] or that he exem-

37. This is the only logical inference to be drawn from Ughelli's general statement: "Hic omnia *iura, opesque* ad Sabinensem Ecclesiam spectantes, quae ex longiori ... absentia Episcopatui illi deperierant, diligentissimum conquisitione in *pristinam ius, potestatemque successorum asseruit*" (*Italia Sacra* Vol. I, Part 2, col. 162; italics mine).

38. The best review of near-contemporary testimony (Thomas of Celano, the Anonymous of Perugia, Bonaventure, and Angelo Clareno) is in Grundmann, *Religiöse Bewegungen*, p. 132 n. As to the story of Matthew Paris (*Chronica Majora* III, ed. H. R. Luard, Rolls Series [1876], 132: Matthew depends here on Roger of Wendover, *Flores Historiarum* II, ed. H. G. Hewlett, Rolls Series [1887], 329 f.) that the *poverello* was roughly expelled from the papal presence on a first attempt at confrontation, I would agree with Mrs. Strong ("St. Francis in Rome," p. 275) that it does not ring true. Francis's deep reverence for sacerdotal dignity would never have allowed him to barge in on the most august priest of Christendom; nor would Innocent be likely to have ejected him without a hearing. Cf. Wadding, *AnnMin*, I, 90–96.

39. Esser, "Franziskus von Assisi und die Katharer," pp. 241–264, gives an excellent picture of Francis's doctrinal views and their incompatibility with the dualist beliefs.

40. Undoubtedly this point would incline the pope to favor Francis, but it cannot be stated that it was decisive, and certainly not that the order was visualized primarily as a weapon against the Waldensians—as is the assertion of G. J. von Eggs, *Pontificium Doctum, seu Vitae ... Pontificum Romanorum ...* (Basel, 1718), p. 422. Cf. the refutation of Tocco in K. Balthasar, *Geschichte des Armutsstreites im Franziskanerorden bis zum Konzil von Vienne*, Vorreformationsgeschichtliche Forschungen, VI (1911), 6 n., and the judicious statement in Tillmann, *Papst Innozenz III*, p. 210.

plified ideally the kind of life Innocent had urged repeatedly on his own clergy.[41]

The machinery of decision ground slowly at the Curia; there may have been several interviews,[42] and we would be overhasty and unjustly condemnatory of the medieval faith in visions if we dismissed out of hand the oft-repeated tale of Innocent's dream. The day of judgment arrived, and from his sovereign goodness the supreme pontiff deigned to grant the beggar's request. Yet he did not direct Francis to have his simple rule[43] transcribed and sealed by the chancery clerks. A time of testing, of indefinite duration, was prescribed for the Friars Minor as it had been for Dominic and Durandus of Huesca. The major privilege granted by Innocent in 1210 was simply to allow the friars to preach penance and practice poverty (mendicancy?) wherever they pleased without infringing diocesan rights, and to conduct their lives in obedience to Francis, and he his in submission to Rome. Whether this meant that he was thereby constituted the first minister-general of the order, as some have claimed,[44] is highly questionable on technical grounds; but his practical headship of the new organization was never in doubt. The tonsure and the request (whose?) that Cardinal John of St. Paul serve as liaison between the order and the Curia[45]—thus inaugurating the office of cardinal-protector—completed the transactions at the Lateran.

41. Cf. especially Migne, *PL* CCXV, cols. 1024 f. (letter of November 17, 1206, to his legate in the Midi, Raoul de Fontfroide, commanding him to select as preachers against the heretics such men as "paupertatem Christi pauperis imitando, in despecto habitu et ardenti spiritu non pertimescant accedere ad despectos ... ut, ad eosdem hereticos festinantes, per exemplum operis et documentum sermonis eos, concedente Domino, sic revocent ab errore ..."). Discussed in Fliche, "Innocent III," p. 143.

42. Constitutionally, the cardinals in consistory were supposed to advise the pope on the reception of new orders (J. B. Sägmüller, *Die Thätigkeit und Stellung der Kardinäle bis Bonifaz VIII* ... [Freiburg-im-Breisgau, 1896], p. 52). But cf. J. Lulvès, "Die Machtbestrebungen des Kardinalkollegiums gegenüber dem Papsttum," *MIÖG*, XXXV (1914), 457: the activities of the consistory were "niemals ... durch päpstliche Konstitutionen umschreiben oder festgelegt worden."

43. For divergent reconstructions of the text of the first rule (Thomas of Celano called it a "propositum conversationis"), see Kybal, *Die Ordensregeln*, p. 16; Fr. Cuthbert, "La Règle Primitive," pp. 142–153; Mandić, *De Protoregula Ordinis Fratrum Minorum*, pp. 45 f.

44. J. J. Nunes (ed.), *Crónica da Ordem dos Frades Menores (1209–1258)* ..., Vol. I (Coimbra, 1918), 9 f.: "E o senhor papa ... estebelleceo a sam Framçisco por ministro geeraal de toda a hordem." Cf. *Secoli Serafici ovvero compendio cronologico della Storia Francescana* ... (Florence, 1757), p. 7.

45. This seems to be the best concise characterization of his functions; he had volunteered after the first interview with Francis to serve as "procurator suum in Curia" (Faloci-Pulignani, "Legenda Trium Sociorum," p. 99).

The deed was done. And what was the brotherhood now? A recent analysis has emphasized its intermediate and even anomalous character:

> The new community, while advancing to the status of a "religion" approved by the Apostolic See, had in actuality an ill-defined structure, preserving still the elements of a *fraternitas* of penitents, which Innocent III strove to uplift by making them clerics and granting them the *licentia ubique praedicandi* . . . . He realized that it was not possible to reduce the paupers of Assisi . . . to the status of the congregations of diocesan preachers; and so he approved them as religious, taking them under his direct surveillance.[46]

The friars were free to go now, and, knowing the sudden resolve of which Francis was capable, we may fairly assume that they left almost immediately for the founder's native city. The fact that they carried away no tangible proof that Innocent had sanctioned them[47] surely occasioned embarrassment several times in the next few years, but no untoward incidents of this kind in Italy are mentioned in the early sources; so we have to conclude that the Franciscans largely made their own way in the world. Before long they would discover that their reputation for humble and effective service preceded them wherever they went, and bishops and barons alike would have a house ready for them when the road-weary messengers of God crossed into their territory.

It was a momentous decision. By embracing this ragtag of spiritual amateurs, the papacy acquired at minimal cost an instrument of unsurpassed adaptability and effectiveness for the extension of its evangel and its power. The year 1210 was a turning point of equal importance for Rome and for Assisi.

Wadding claims that Francis came again to Rome in 1212, and

46. Maccarrone, "Riforma e sviluppo," pp. 58 f., 71; cf. Matanić, "Papa Innocenzo," p. 512.

47. Unless a *bullum* or some such token were affixed to Francis's rule, which we know he had written out. Even that would scarcely satisfy a suspicious bishop inured to forged abbatial exemptions. Or would such a semiofficial document represent a rare variant of the "diplomatic blank" or letter of limited validity which were beginning to make their appearance in this century? Cf. D. E. Queller, "Diplomatic 'Blanks' in the Thirteenth Century," *EHR*, LXXX (1965), 476–491; H. Tillmann, "Über päpstliche Schreiben mit bedingter Giltigkeit im 12. und 13. Jahrhundert," *MIÖG*, XLV (1931), 191–200. All of this seems very unlikely; Francis himself always preferred to accept the pope's word as sufficiently binding, and no indication of anything more formal than the tonsure appears in any of the early sources.

preached there against the prevailing vices of the day.[48] It seems logical to suppose that he would have spent some days at least in the diocese of Sabina, exhorting the people to mend their ways, at the invitation of its venerable bishop. We have, however, no record of any contact between Francis and John in 1212—a fact which may be taken as illustrative of the informal character of John's office. That he saw Innocent again and submitted, as it were, a progress report, is likewise credible.[49] Francis may even have sought some kind of pardon for having illegally accepted Clare's profession—if indeed Guido had not already granted a dispensation,[50] and provided he knew that as a deacon he did not possess the canonical right to receive such a profession,[51] and provided he had in fact taken Clare in before, and not after, he went to Rome.[52] Perhaps on this occasion too he made the acquaintance of "Fra Jacopa," the noblewoman of Settesoli who appeared miraculously in response to his deathbed longing fourteen years later.[53] How we should relate this second trip to his abortive attempt to sail to the Holy Land and the germination of the overland pilgrimage to Spain in the following year are, if possible, even more speculative questions.[54]

The Fourth Lateran Council sat from November 13 to November 30, 1215. Over twelve hundred worthies of the church participated in its deliberations and lent their weighty counsel to the drafting of seventy new laws for Christendom. Of these the thirteenth, "Concerning Prohibited New Orders,"[55] ordained that anyone desiring to found a community of

48. Wadding, *AnnMin*, I, 146–148. Cf. López, *La Provincia de España*, p. 18.

49. Unfortunately we have to ask our sketchy and mainly negative evidence to support a great inferential burden. This is a constant bedevilment to historians of the scientific school, who take a jaundiced view of pyramided opinions. Yet the record of the first two decades of the Franciscan order, as it emerges from the primary sources, is far too fragmentary to sustain a coherent narrative. Sober interpolation is unavoidable.

50. The fact that already in 1212 Bishop Guido entrusted the little church of San Damiano to Clare points to some such related indult. See Grundmann, *Religiöse Bewegungen*, p. 148 f.

51. P. Sabatier, *Life of St. Francis of Assisi* (New York, 1935), p. 151.

52. Clare came to Francis sometime in the spring of 1212. The Curia was at the Lateran from the beginning of the year through mid-June, then at Segni through September 18, and back in Rome again from then until at least July 6, 1213 (Potthast, *Regesta*, I, 375–416).

53. E. d'Alençon, "Jacqueline de Settesoli," *EtFranc*, II (1899), 11; MacDonell, *Sons of Francis*, pp. 113–122; Strong, "St. Francis in Rome," pp. 292–304.

54. Cf. N. Durigan, *L'"Istituzione" dei Missionari nell'Ordine dei Frati Minori (Studio Storico-giuridico)* (Cairo, 1959), 35.

55. "De novis religionibus prohibentis," in Alberigo *et al.*, *Conciliorum Oecumenicorum Decreta*, p. 218.

religious must choose among the approved rules. Within a few years the canon became a dead letter, as lay brotherhoods and military orders continued to proliferate; but in 1216 at any rate it was enforced in the case of Dominic, who had to opt for the Augustinian formula. That Francis was not compelled to follow the same road is a clear indication of some entente with Innocent prior to Lateran IV that the *propositum conversationis* offered in 1210 could stand as an approved rule.[56] Did John of St. Paul perhaps communicate to Francis the pope's assurance? The cardinal was not at Lateran IV,[57] and we infer therefore that he was gravely ill or dead by that time; but the council had been advertised since 1213, and the *poverello* on his return from Spain would surely have had time to seek out the pope and obtain whatever further ratification was needed.[58] We do not have a complete daily record of what transpired in the council's deliberations, and thus the means whereby word of the friars' confirmed status was passed on to the authors of canon 13 are unknown.[59]

There remains the possibility that a hasty arrangement was made only in the first week or so that Lateran IV was in session. Anyone familiar with the bewildering spur-of-the-moment decisions made in twentieth-century political conventions and party conferences will appreciate the odds in favor of analogous whispered consultations and patched-up arrangements during the great ecclesiastical gatherings of the High Middle Ages. The indirect evidence testifying to Francis's presence at Lateran IV has persuaded virtually all recent scholars that he was there,[60] though in

56. Grundmann, *Religiöse Bewegungen*, p. 144; *Secoli Serafici*, p. 9. See the forthcoming review of this tangled question by Christopher and Rosalind Brooke, based chiefly on the Leonine materials.

57. J. Werner, "Die Teilnehmerliste des Laterankonzils vom Jahre 1215," *Neues Archiv der Gesellschaft für ältere deutsche Geschichtskunde*, XXXI (1906), 584.

58. In all likelihood he would also have taken this opportunity to present Innocent, with some reluctance, with Clare's petition for the *privilegium paupertatis*, for which see, *inter alia*, P. Sabatier, "Le privilège de la pauvreté," *Revue d'Histoire Franciscaine*, I (1924), 1–54.

59. S. Kuttner and A. García y García have recently edited the report of a German who wrote home from Rome early in 1216, but this document, valuable as it is in revealing personalities and even direct discourse at several key points in the council's deliberations, says nothing of Francis ("A New Eyewitness Account of the Fourth Lateran Council," *Traditio*, XX [1964], 115–178). See also R. Foreville, "Procédure et Débats des Conciles Médiévaux du Latran (1123–1215)," *Rivista di Storia della Chiesa in Italia*, XIX (1965), 31.

60. Grundmann, *Religiöse Bewegungen*, pp. 144, 147, shows that the sources supporting his presence at Rome in late 1215 are of respectable antiquity. Cf. also L. Oliger, "S· Francesco a Roma," p. 70; K. Esser, "Franziskus von Assisi und die Katharer," p. 240 n.; L. Casutt, *Die älteste franziskanische Lebensform. Untersuchungen zur Regula Prima sine Bulla* (Graz, 1955), pp. 65–68; Strong, "St. Francis in Rome," pp. 281 f.; De la Bedoyère,

exactly what capacity we cannot be sure. Because the order itself was still in the first stages of its structural development (no chapters-general, for example, had yet been convened), he can scarcely have been there on an equal footing with the great abbots of Cîteaux and Prémontré.[61] If, as we have suggested, he had already obtained some signs that he stood well with the Curia and would not come under the new ban, why then would he have gone to Rome again? Perhaps he was concerned to find a new cardinal-protector, after the intervening death of John. Perhaps the pope wished to introduce him and his sodality to the whole assembly and make plain the worth of his endeavors.[62] Perhaps he was simply curious to glimpse the pageantry and brilliance of such a rare spectacle: it might have seemed to him a kind of enormous pilgrimage. All we can state positively is that whatever his reasons, the arrangements he made at Lateran IV fell once again into the category of informal word-of-mouth exchanges. Did an official document resemble too much in his eyes the crafty contracts of the merchant father whose inheritance he had foresworn?

How was the Franciscan order viewed within the Catholic hierarchy from the time of Francis's first appearance at the Lateran until the death of Innocent in 1216? Insofar as it is feasible to answer this question, we will be able to appreciate more concretely the privileges and commissions given the Friars Minor by Innocent's successors, and mediated to them by the cardinal-protectors after John.

That Guido, John of St. Paul, and Innocent came to feel a special attraction to Francis and his *socii* is already evident. Moreover, several sources manifest a bias in favor of the order on the part of other prelates as well. The best-known case is that of Jacques de Vitry, since 1212 bishop of Acre and from 1229 until his death in 1240[63] cardinal bishop of

---

Francis, p. 152; L. Spätling, "Der Anteil der Franziskaner an den Generalkonzilien des Spätmittelalters," *Antonianum*, XXXVI (1961), 300–303; Fr. Franciscus, "Franciscus en het IVe Laterans Concilie," *Franciscaans Leven*, XLV (1962), 79, 137–139; XLVI (1963), 11–20, etc. It strikes me that Franciscus assumes too much; Innocent's opening address could have influenced Francis's eschatology at least as much as Francis influenced the pope!

61. Oliger, "S. Francesco a Roma," p. 71.

62. "Es sprechen gewichtige Gründe dafür, dass Franz von Assisi sein persönliches Anliegen und das seiner jungen Brüderschaft vor dem grossen Innozenz III. und der hohen Konzilsversammlung in eigener Person zwar demütig, aber mannhaft vertreten hat" (Spätling, "Der Anteil der Franziskaner," p. 303).

63. The dates are discussed in P. Funk, *Jakob von Vitry. Leben und Werke, BKG*, III (Leipzig and Berlin, 1909), 31–67. On his connection with other religious establishments, cf. *ibid.*, *passim*; G. Schreiber, "Religiöse Verbände in mittelalterliche Wertung: lateini-

Frascati. Completely aside from his own admiration for the *poverello*, his correspondence [64] provides several *testimonia minora* of the high esteem with which the order was regarded by other prominent churchmen:

> They are held in great reverence by the Lord Pope and the cardinals; yet they are not concerned at all with material things, but strive every day with earnest desire and singleminded zeal to save those mired in the vanities of the world and convert them to their ways.[65]

The *Legend of the Three Companions*, too, relates that John of St. Paul often spoke warmly of Francis and his brethren to the other cardinals, and desired to keep a friar close by him as a constant example of the holy life.[66] (We should like to know who that friar was, and what role he played in the interaction of the Curia and the order.) Rainerio Capocci, cardinal deacon of Santa Maria in Cosmedin, wrote hymns in praise of Francis which may still be found in the order's breviary.[67] And Nicolas de Romanis, bishop of Frascati since 1205 and the papal penitentiary after John of St. Paul relinquished that duty, is believed by some to have worn mendicant garb and even to have tried to enter the order, but Honorius persuaded him to abandon that project.[68] Cardinal Leo Brancaleone provided Francis lodging in 1223 and was warmed by the friars' example.[69] From these indications, both general and specific, we have to affirm the existence of a substantial amount of enthusiasm for the friars

---

scher Westen und griechischer Osten," *HistJahrb*, LXII–LXIX (1949), 288–295; E. McDonnell, *The Beguines and Beghards in Medieval Culture, with Special Reference to the Belgian Scene* (New Brunswick, 1954), pp. 35 ff.

64. Recently assembled by R. B. C. Huygens, *Lettres de Jacques de Vitry: Edition critique* (Leiden, 1960). Cf. also his two "Sermones vulgares ... ad fratres minores" (BN MS lat. 17509, fols. lxvii^a–lxxi^b).

65. Letter I, of indeterminate date (but quite early); a kind of memorandum to himself (Huygens, *Lettres*, p. 75).

66. Faloci-Pulignani, "*Legenda Trium Sociorum*," p. 103.

67. F. Hurter, *Tableau des Institutions et des Moeurs de l'Eglise au Moyen Âge ...* , Vol. I (Paris, 1843), 196. For a full-length biography of this important cardinal, see E. von Westenholz, *Kardinal Rainer von Viterbo* (Heidelberg, 1912). On his liturgical contributions, see S. J. P. Van Dijk and J. H. Walker, *The Origins of the Modern Roman Liturgy: The Liturgy of the Papal Court and the Franciscan Order in the Thirteenth Century* (London, 1960), p. 381.

68. M. Bihl, "Nicolaus de Romanis (+1219) fueritne primus Cardinalis O. F. M.?" *AFH*, XIX (1926), 286. Cf. Wenck, "Die Römischen Päpste," p. 471; Göller, *Die Päpstliche Pönitentiarie*, pp. 82 f.

69. Wadding, *AnnMin*, I, 95; II, 82.

at the very top of the hierarchy. The idea that a strong nucleus of opposition to the order within the *collegium* worked to counteract the reforms inaugurated by Innocent[70] may not be totally untrue, but it would be exceedingly difficult in any case to separate the petty grudges of cardinals who felt put off at the pope's methods from the more principled dissent of the conservative few.

What can we now conclude as to the jurisdiction and activities of John of St. Paul between 1210 and his death in 1214 or 1215, when the order was well on its way to mature organization?

Inference from his former conduct and the largely circumstantial evidence, already reviewed, of Francis's return to Rome in 1212 and probably again before Lateran IV, allows us to fill in a few gaps.[71] His sympathy with the friars' medical and evangelical work ensured that those two aspects of the order's apostolate would receive renewed encouragement every time Francis met the cardinal, and that Innocent for his part would hear from his venerable counselor the most favorable reports of its progress from one commune to the next. Because he possessed a keen sense of the dangers besetting undisciplined enthusiasm, he may have regarded with some misgivings Francis's journey to Spain, especially if the saint had seemed really determined to gain a martyr's laurels from it. That the order received only one formal privilege—and that for Clare, not for the friars[72] —during his four or five years as protector reflects not indifference but a profound appreciation of Francis's own distaste for formalities. For that very reason his precise relationship with the friars in this period remains a mystery: He, like the *poverello*, preferred to keep matters on the level of personal dialogue. And through dialogues with Innocent and the other cardinals he rendered the order his most valuable service—creating an awareness in Rome that the new fraternity was of immense utility to the cause of reform.[73]

70. See, *inter alia*, P. van den Haute, *Breviarium Historicum Ordinis Minorum . . .* (Rome, 1777), p. 202, where John of St. Paul is portrayed as defending Francis "contra varios cardinales."

71. Even so, in the last analysis it remains true that, after 1210, we have no direct documentary support for further specific meetings between the two men (Paschini, "Il Cardinale," p. 113; Bihl, "De Iohanne de S. Paolo," p. 285).

72. See note 58, *supra*.

73. Cf. C. Suyskens, "De S. Francisco Confessore Fundatore Ordinis Minorum Assisii in Umbria Commentarius Praevius," in *Acta Sanctorum . . .* , L (=t. II, October), p. 606e–f.: "Haec satis probant, Cardinalem Joannem concilio et opera sua vere se Ordinis Minorum protectorem exhibuisse; at non talem tamen, quale deinde a summis Ponti-

NICOLAS DE ROMANIS

More than four decades ago Father Bihl examined K. Wenck's idea that Nicolas de Romanis (cardinal bishop of Frascati, 1205–1219) served as a kind of interim protector (*fautor*) of the order between the death of John and the formal appointment of Hugolino in 1220, or at any rate before the Florence meeting of 1217. Since he wrote no one has renewed the inquiry.

Bihl himself was careful to strip away all dubious evidence (for example, references to Nicolas de Casamario, the Cistercian penitentiary of the pope, and Nicolas de Chiaramonte, also of the Cistercian order, bishop of Frascati 1219–1227). He actually concluded that the single weightiest document, the letter of Jacques de Vitry from Perugia on July 31, 1216,[74] does not prove irrefutably that it was in fact the bishop of Frascati who tried to enter the order at the beginning of Honorius's pontificate, only to be recalled insistently into the papal service. So it seems that we are left with very little to go on. Yet the suspicion persists that Cardinal Nicolas did have something to do with the order in the two or three years' hiatus between John and Hugolino. He succeeded John as chief papal penitentiary,[75] and must have known of Francis's visits to the Curia in 1210 and 1212.[76] Certainly Honorius, who soon proved to be a stalwart friend of the friars, would not have objected to Nicolas de Romanis's taking on himself the liaison duties of John of St. Paul. Some such arrangement could have been made even under Innocent, at or shortly before Lateran IV, or in conjunction with the Porziuncula Indulgence at Perugia.[77] The chronicles

---

ficibus cum certis praerogativis et potestate eidem Ordini concessi fuere." (The reference at the beginning is to the pertinent passage of the *Legenda Trium Sociorum*, which Suyskens was the first to edit.)

74. Text in Huygens, *Lettres*, p. 76 and note *ad lineam* 130. Cf. Strong, "St. Francis in Rome," p. 291.

75. Wenck, "Die Römischen Päpste," p. 471.

76. Potthast, *Regesta*, I, 462, alludes to his signature of solemn letters in August, 1210, and March and August, 1212. No signatures, however, are recorded for the interval between November 4, 1213, and February 5, 1216. He was at Lateran IV: cf. Werner, "Die Teilnehmerliste," p. 584. Ughelli and Coleti, *Italia Sacra*, I, col. 321, believe he was also partial to Dominic; Cappelletti, *Le Chiese d'Italia*, I, p. 632, notes that his duties as bishop were necessarily minimal because of the depopulation of his diocese.

77. The existence, nature, and significance of this oral grant have been in dispute for centuries. Recent opinion inclines to accept its historicity, if not all of the extravagant claims made on its behalf. See especially R. M. Huber, *The Portiuncula Indulgence from Honorius III to Pius XI*, Franciscan Studies, XIX (New York, 1938), which, though badly

and the *vitae* of the order are silent, and the most that can be drawn from an *argumentum ex silentio* is that for the crucial period from 1210 to 1217 *nothing* can be said with complete accuracy about Francis's relations with Rome. An open mind to at least the notion of a stopgap protector will enable us to piece together whatever clues turn up in future.

CARDINAL HUGOLINO

If John of St. Paul was informally charged to watch over the order at its modest inception, and if Nicolas de Romanis may have interceded occasionally on its behalf with the Curia, Hugolino, cardinal bishop of Ostia and Velletri since 1206,[78] is universally styled the first *official* cardinal-protector of the order.[79] From 1217 until his consecration as Gregory IX ten years afterwards, the doughty kinsman of Innocent III manifested by numerous acts both his affection for the Franciscans and his commitment to the expanding responsibilities of his position.

We happen to know a good deal about Hugolino's early preparation for a career in the church and about his legations as cardinal. Historians in consequence have been more successful in presenting a coherent account of his relations with Francis and the order than of John's or Nicolas's, although the record is not free of ambiguity. As pope he was to excite both admiration and animosity in his contemporaries, and the turbulent story of his relations with Frederick has proved a tale of greater drama, if of less ultimate significance, than the *Decretals* which bear his name.

Paris inculcated in him theology and a feeling for Scripture; Bologna gave him the rudiments of law.[80] When Innocent raised him to the

---

written, does scan virtually all the literature on the subject; and A. Fortini, *Nova Vita di San Francesco*, II (Assisi, 1959), 427 ff.: he dates the indulgence August 2, 1216.

78. Created cardinal deacon of St. Eustace in 1198, he achieved the highest dignity in the *collegium* eight years later. Cf. P. M. Baumgarten, "Die Translationen der Kardinäle von Innocenz III bis Martin V," *HistJahrb*, XXII (1901), 96.

79. Nunes (ed.), *Crónica da Ordem*, I, 21: "Ugullino . . . foy o primeiro protetor de sua ordem demandado segundo a forma de sua hordem." Cf. also L.-R. Misserez, "Cardinal-Protecteur," *DDC*, II (1937), col. 1340; Suyskens, "De S. Francisco Confessore," p. 695b–c; Sägmüller, *Die Thätigkeit und Stellung der Kardinäle*, p. 112.

80. J. Felten, *Papst Gregor IX* (Freiburg-im-Breisgau, 1886), p. 8; E. Brem, *Papst Gregor IX. bis zum Beginn seines Pontifikats: Ein Biographischer Versuch*, Heidelberger Abhandlungen zur mittleren und neueren Geschichte, XXXII (1911), 2 f.; B. Zöllig, "Kardinal Hugolino und der heilige Franziskus," *FrzStud*, XX (1933), 1 f.

cardinalate he is not likely to have been over thirty[81]—eloquent testimony to the promise he had already shown. For a few months previously he had served as a papal chaplain, exhibiting in this capacity a sensitivity to spiritual needs which led him over the next several years to found Joachimite houses at Velletri and Anagni, and a hospital for the indigent in the latter place as well.[82] The influence on him of a Cistercian abbot, Rainerio, is unquestionable, and may be held in large part accountable for his sustained encouragement of that order over the next four decades. Perhaps there was a kind of congenital piety in the Conti line: Innocent himself, Hugolino, his sister's son[83] Rainaldo (the future Alexander IV, and protector of the Franciscans for thirty-four years), and several lesser-known members of this distinguished family found the austere example of the recluse and the holy gregariousness of the mendicants worth culti-vating.

The cardinal bishop of Ostia and Velletri was by ancient custom *primus inter pares* in the *collegium*.[84] Only he had the right to consecrate new popes. In addition, his participation in diplomatic missions of the utmost delicacy and long duration often meant that he had to neglect his dio-cese.[85] Yet Hugolino was not insensitive to the modest requirements of his flock; in December, 1206, he exhorted the citizens of Velletri to patch up a peace with five of their neighbor communes.[86] He gave the inhabitants of Ostia at least a semblance of security by walling in the town.[87] As pope in 1235 he exempted the Velletri faithful from paying certain levies,[88] and in the same year he wrote of his wearisome struggle to expel the marauding nobles of Sarmineto from that diocese.[89]

But it was as legate to Tuscany, Lombardy, and Germany that he

---

81. The general consensus is that he was born at Anagni around 1170; as the son of one of Innocent's older brothers he surely could not have been born in 1140, as Matthew Paris would have us believe. Cf. Felten, *Papst Gregor IX*, p. 6; Zöllig, "Kardinal Hugolino," p. 1.

82. Felten, *Papst Gregor IX*, pp. 18 f. Cf. Auvray, *Reg*, I, 1007–9/1846.

83. The genealogy is firmly fixed in J. Haller, "Die Herkunft Papst Alexanders IV," *QFItArch*, XXXII (1942), 254–259. S. Sibilia, *Alessandro IV (1254–1261)* (Anagni, 1961), 44 f., relies on Haller, while S. Andreotta, *La Famiglia di Alessandro IV e l'abbazia di Subiaco* (Rome, 1963) carries his inquiries even further.

84. G. Le Bras, *Institutions ecclésiastiques de la chrétienté médiévale*, Vol. II (Tournai, 1964), 345 n., cautions us that his powers were mostly ceremonial, at least in the twelfth century.

85. Capelletti, *Le Chiese d'Italia*, I, 466.

86. Ughelli and Coleti, *Italia Sacra*, I, col. 67.

87. F. Gregorovius and W. Kampf, *Geschichte der Stadt Rom*, Vol. II (Basel, 1963), 354.

88. Potthast, *Regesta*, I, 835 f./9813; cf. Ughelli and Coleti, *Italia Sacra*, I, col. 68 f.

89. Auvray, *Reg*, II, 151/2747 (August 23, 1235).

made a name for himself. Three times he crossed the Alps in single or joint commission to bring a Roman peace between the imperial rivals; by the summer of 1209 he had shown himself an astute negotiator.[90] At the very outset of his pontificate Honorius commissioned him to work out a dignified settlement between Cîteaux and four daughter houses, to avoid further scandal coming to that institute.[91] Success met his efforts, and further enhanced his reputation. Indeed he stands out as one of the major papal diplomats of his time, overshadowed only by William of Modena[92] and Gregory of Montelongo.[93]

In 1217, when he met Francis at Florence, he was once more engaged in a demanding task: to preach a crusade and pacify the troubled politics of central Italy.[94] And from a similar but more extensive legation in 1221, which involved also the adjudication of ecclesiastical disputes throughout Lombardy and the eastern marches, we have preserved his *Register*—a record of inestimable value, as it reveals him in the full flower of his talents.[95]

Cardinal Hugolino had thus become, by the time of the Florence encounter, a man of many abilities: preacher, patron of religious, lawyer, theologian, and diplomat. In the *collegium* itself he was so highly regarded

90. These missions are briefly reviewed in Zimmermann, *Die päpstliche Legation,* pp. 39 f.; more fully in Brem, *Papst Gregor IX.*, pp. 4–70.

91. Brem, *Papst Gregor IX.*, p. 70.

92. For an intensive study of this prelate who journeyed several times to Scandinavia and the Baltic East over a period of twenty years, see G. A. Donner, *Kardinal Wilhelm von Sabina, Bischof von Modena 1222–1234, Päpstlicher Legat in den Nordischen Ländern (1251),* Societas Scientiarum Fennica: Commentationes Humanarum Litterarum, Ser. II, Vol. V (Helsinki, 1929).

93. On Gregory, see H. Frankfurth, *Gregorius de Montelongo. Ein Beitrag zur Geschichte Oberitaliens in den Jahren 1238–1269* (Marburg, 1898); G. Marchetti-Longhi, "La legazione in Lombardia di Gregorio de Monte Longo negli anni 1238–1251," *ArchRSocRom,* XXXVI (1913), 225–285, 585–687; XXXVII (1914), 139–266; XXXVIII (1915), 283–362, 591–675. His patriarchate is reviewed in K. Hampe, "Eine Denkschrift Gregors von Montelongo an das Kardinalkollegium über die finanzielle Zerrüttung seines Patriarchats Aquileia aus dem Jahre 1252," *MIÖG,* XL (1925), 189–204; M. Nicoletti, *Vita del Patriarcha di Aquileia Gregorio di Montelongo* (Udine, 1898). Both William and Gregory figure importantly in the early history of mendicant ascendancy.

94. Potthast, *Regesta,* I, 478/4530, 483/5487 f., etc. Cf. Zimmermann, *Die päpstliche Legation,* 73 f.; Zöllig, "Kardinal Hugolino," pp. 4 f.

95. Edited by G. Levi from BN MS lat. 5152, *Registri dei Cardinali Ugolino d'Ostia e Ottaviano degli Ubaldini* (Rome, 1890), pp. 3–154. Cf. also Levi, "Documenti ad illustrazione del Registro del Cardinale Ugolino d'Ostia, Legato Apostolico in Toscana e Lombardia," *ArchRSocRom,* XII (1889), 241, 326; C. Thouzellier, "La légation en Lombardie du cardinal Hugolin (1221). Un épisode de la Vᵉ Croisade," *Revue d'histoire ecclésiastique,* XLV (1950), 508–542.

as to have been chosen immediately after Innocent's death, with Cardinal Guido of Palestrina, to select a candidate for the papacy *per compromissum*, since the cardinals could not agree among themselves.[96] And it was to his care that Francis—also a preacher, respectful of the older orders, knowing the ways of the law, deferential to the masters of theology, and soon enough initiated into the mysteries of papal diplomacy—was presently to entrust his young brotherhood.

Had Hugolino and the *poverello* faced each other before that celebrated confrontation in the summer of 1217?[97] This question has dogged scholars for generations; it is not possible to answer it definitively.[98] But it hardly seems likely that the cardinal would have been completely ignorant of Francis or his movement, and for his part Francis must surely have known that Hugolino favored the orders and the lay penitential fraternities so prominent then in Italian religious life. Why would Francis have interrupted his journey to France if he did not think that the cardinal, immersed in the thousand details of his legation, would welcome him and have something useful to say to him? There is no chance that the meeting was prearranged. The determination of the chapter-general to organize provinces and send a colony to France crystallized only in mid-May, and the cardinal had no fixed residence in Florence, but was there only in transit.[99] Yet once Francis heard that Hugolino was in town, perhaps from the bishop of Florence,[100] on whom he would have called to obtain

96. O. Joelson, *Die Papstwahlen des 13. Jahrhunderts bis zur Einführung der Conclaveordnung Gregors X.*, HistStud, CLXXVIII (1928), 12.

97. This date has been conclusively established by A. Callebaut, "Autour de la Rencontre à Florence de S. François et du Cardinal Hugolin (en été 1217)," *AFH*, XIX (1926), 530–558.

98. Cf., e.g., Zöllig, "Kardinal Hugolino," pp. 16–22; L. Zarncke, *Der Anteil des Kardinals Hugolino an der Ausbildung der drei Orden des heiligen Franz*, BKG, XLII (1930), 104–106.

99. The chapter was held on May 14. Until June 2 Hugolino was in the vicinity of Genoa; on June 16 he was at Mariano, near Lucca; from then until July 27 he moved about from Livorno to Camaiore to Lucca; August 12–16 found him near Volterra, and on October 10 he was back at the Lateran (Callebaut, "Autour de la Rencontre," p. 535). The itinerary is far from complete, and there is certainly room in July and August for a sojourn of several days in Florence.

100. John of Velletri, 1205–1231 (Eubel, *HCMA* I, 250). His native city (if in fact he was born in Velletri) suggests a prior acquaintance with Hugolino outside the formal perimeters of curial business. Cf. Zöllig, "Kardinal Hugolino," p. 27: "Die Zusammenkunft der beiden Männern ist einzig der schonen Gewohnheit Franziszi zu verdanken, beim Eintritt in eine Stadt oder in ein Land sich den Bischöfen und Priestern vorzustellen." (Clearly based on Thomas of Celano, *Vita prima*, p. 56.)

permission for the work of his friars in that diocese, he seized the opportunity to consult with the eminent churchman. That is the impression conveyed by Thomas of Celano,[101] who must be considered the most authoritative source for this episode, and only a slightly different version appears in the *Legenda Trium Sociorum.*[102]

Thus far we have pursued a logical speculation, reined in by a fair number of chronological and biographical facts. Irresistibly, however, a new sort of dilemma forces itself on our attention: what was the *subject* of those private talks with Hugolino in Florence? Was Francis searching for a new protector? But that could have been arranged earlier, perhaps with Nicolas de Romanis, whose attendance at the Curia was more constant than Hugolino's.[103] Did he fear liberal tendencies within the order? But it was too soon for that, and in any case he would not have tried to reverse them by appealing to a cardinal well known for his partiality to the Benedictine formulas.[104] Did he doubt that the French undertaking was wise? Hardly, although he may have begun to wonder whether he should supervise it in person. Such second thoughts were not sufficient to lead him to seek advice from anyone higher than the *seniores* under him; and besides the *vitae* do not show us a man easily dissuaded from a purpose once resolved upon. The fact that Hugolino managed to do exactly this does not at all prove that Francis came to him looking for a way out.

The one reasonable option left to us, if we are not content to regard the meeting as a mere courtesy call, is to affirm that the *poverello* sought to place the order in good hands during his absence. Twice before—in 1212 and 1213—this matter had presented no difficulty. At that time the order was still small; every friar knew Francis and shared his aspirations; Cardinal John kept open the lines to Rome. Now John was dead, and there was a new pope; the order was taking on a coherent administrative structure, and the hundreds who heard him preach at the Porziuncula included many who saw him there for the first time; hundreds and soon thousands more were professing his simple creed who never saw him at all.

101. *Vita prima*, p. 56; no mention is actually made of the bishop of Florence here, but the inference is not unreasonable. There is nothing at all said of this meeting in the *Vita secunda*, in Julian of Speier, or the *Legenda maiora* of Bonaventure.

102. Florence is not mentioned, and indeed the Leonine chronology is hopelessly tangled in the last part of the *Legenda*; the meeting as described on p. 103 of Faloci-Pulignani's edition, however, is basically convincing.

103. Between August 12, 1216, and June 6, 1217, for example, Nicolas subscribed eighteen bulls, Hugolino only ten (Potthast, *Regesta*, I, 678).

104. Zöllig, "Kardinal Hugolino," p. 7: "Was Hugolino in Camaldoli und Citeaux so hoch einschätzte, war ursprünglicher Benediktinergeist."

In 1219, before he left for the East, he appointed two vicars, Gregory of Naples and Matthew of Narni;[105] for 1217 we have no record of any such delegation of authority.[106] Probably he thought of it after the chapter had disbanded and it was too late to tell the friars that Leo (or Elias or Peter Catanei or someone else) had his confidence and should be obeyed as they obeyed him. The pope, whether at Anagni or Ferentino (where he was from July 19), was south of Assisi, and Francis was headed north. A guarantee from Guido that all would be well was no longer adequate. Only a cardinal, and a plenipotentiary legate at that,[107] could properly ensure that whatever Francis wanted done in and for the order in his absence would be faithfully carried out. The saint had never yet failed to approach the seat of power when he deemed it advantageous to do so. In the circumstances, Hugolino was the obvious recourse.

Nonetheless, the cardinal was in no position to accept a new charge that summer.[108] He sympathized with Francis's problem, he admired the little man's serene faith in the imminent spread of his brotherhood into the land of the Albigenses, but he just could not make room in his schedule for the kind of administrative chores already weighing on the founder's mind night and day. Instead he urged Francis to go back to Assisi and resume personal command of the Friars Minor; Pacifico and the others could continue on to Provence and points north.[109] Hugolino may have doubted their qualifications—their poor French caused them to be taken

105. Jordan of Giano, *Chronica*, (*AnalFranc* X), p. 4, adds interesting details: "Matthaeum vero instituit ad S. Maria de Portiuncula, ut ibi manens recipiendos ad Ordinem reciperat, Gregorius autem ut circumeundo Italiam fratres consolaretur."

106. Golubovich, *BB* I, 119–126, claims that Peter Catanei served as Francis's vicar about 1212–17, while R. Brooke, *Early Franciscan Government: From Elias to Bonaventure* (Cambridge, 1959), p. 82, believes that this appointment occurred in 1217. Nothing, however, appears to link this deed directly with the chapter-general of that year.

107. Cf. K. Ruess, *Die rechtliche Stellung der päpstlichen Legaten bis Bonifaz VIII.*, Görres-Gesellschaft: Sektion für Rechts- und Sozialwissenschaft, XIII (Paderborn, 1912); G. Paro, *The Right of Papal Legation*, *CUA Studies*, CCXI (1947); F. Claeys-Bouuaert, "Légat du Pape," *DDC*, VI (1957), cols. 371–377.

108. That Hugolino himself brought up the subject of the protectorate (Zöllig, "Kardinal Hugolino," p. 27, interpreting Thomas of Celano, *Vita prima*, p. 56; cf. Faloci-Pulignani, "Legenda Trium Sociorum," p. 103, where Hugolino is quoted as saying "offero me ipsum vobis, auxilium, consiliam, atque protectionem : . ."), may be true, but this bare fact is no proof that he desired to assume any more than the theoretical obligation of passing on word of the order's needs to Honorius once he had returned to the consistory.

109. The *Chronica XXIV Generalium*, *AnalFranc*, III, 10, quotes him as saying "Frater, ego nolo, quod a Curia elongeris, quia dominus Papa et domini Cardinales contra aemulos tuae Religionis melius ipsam forebunt et protegent forsitan, te praesente."

for heretics, and necessitated explicit papal protection in 1219[110]—but this was a point on which he might have been overborne by the sheer zeal and evident sound doctrine of Francis and his companions. Like John, he sensed that the church, hard pressed by vociferous rebels, could ill afford to lose the services of well-intentioned volunteers. And in large measure the Franciscans had already undergone their prescribed probation.

The rapport which grew from this first substantive conference was never broken in the next nine years, although it suffered strain several times. Until 1220 there are only occasional signs that the relationship was continuing, and none of these indicate any further personal contacts. Still, over those two and a half years a pattern was established and a habit confirmed, and when on his hasty return from Palestine early in 1220 Francis went before the pope to ask that Hugolino be assigned to the order as an official and permanent protector, an understanding had already been arrived at between the two men.

In this interim period the single most significant step taken by the cardinal to involve himself in the order's affairs was his move to become acquainted with Clare and her convent at San Damiano. His solicitude for the second order is already manifest in 1218, when Honorius addressed a rescript to him which empowered him to provide buildings for the habitation of the Clares in several dioceses, exempt from episcopal jurisdiction and tithes.[111] Two years later the cardinal sent Clare a most remarkable letter, exalting her saintly life and beseeching her blessing and favor.[112] Sometime between 1219 and 1227 he composed a rule for them along strict Benedictine lines—not surprising, in view of his leanings to that form of cenobitic life and of the obvious fact that as *moniales inclusae* they could hardly be sent out to roam the precincts of Mammon![113]

110. The tale of their near-catastrophic naïveté appears in Jordan of Giano, *Chronica*, p. 3. The bull alluded to is, of course, *Cum dilecti filii*, issued June 11, 1219 (*BF*, I, 2/2). The date is disputed; see my "Checklist" of bulls in *AFH*, LXIV (1971).

111. *Littere tue nobis*, August 27 (*BF*, I, 1 f./1).

112. *Ab illa hora*, 1220. Text in K. Esser, "Die Briefe Gregors IX. an die hl. Klara von Assisi," *FrzStud*, XXXV (1953), 227.

113. Zarncke, *Der Anteil des Kardinals Hugolino*, pp. 44–48. I would, with B. da Siena (*Il Cardinale protettore negli Istituti religiosi specialmente negli Ordini Francescane* [Florence, 1940], p. 26: cf. p. 130), put the date early rather than late. The whole topic of his relations with the Clares is treated comprehensively by Zarncke, *op. cit.*, pp. 26–77. Cf. René de Nantes, "Les origines de l'Ordre de Sainte Claire," *EtFranc*, XXVIII (1912), p. 122: Hugolino "donne à la discipline de l'ordre de Sainte Claire une organisation très précise et très sage, dont les points les plus importants se sont perpetués dans les règles successives et ont survécu a toutes les réformes." It is not likely that Clare resisted this *formula vitae*, as is alleged by Bergamino, "Francescanesimo, Chiesa e Impero," p. 564.

As for his relationship with the friars themselves, we know that on October 25, 1217,[114] two of them witnessed a transaction at Anagni between the cardinal and his two brothers. The fact that a "master Rainaldo, sub-deacon of the Lord Pope"—probably Hugolino's nephew[115] —also signed the document suggests that he and the friars constituted part of his retinue. They may simply, on the other hand, have belonged to the Anagni house, and happened to be available then for this occasion, though normally we would not expect to see them employed for the endorsement of purely secular contracts. Whatever the construction we put on this casual scrap of evidence, it is clear that Hugolino was already finding ways to use the Franciscans in his personal affairs. And of course he attended the famous "Chapter of Mats" on May 26, 1219,[116] and gave his benediction to the new ventures proposed for Germany, Spain, and the Holy Land.

These informal, albeit intimate, connections might have continued until Francis's death had it not been for two decisive factors: the saint's anxiety for the future of his order and the cardinal's own legalistic bias.

After the Florence encounter, and throughout the following year, nothing precise can be said of Francis's whereabouts.[117] The lack of reference in the *vitae* to any notable journeys in this period points to a continuing presence in Italy; perhaps a future critical-historical edition of the *Fioretti* and related literature will reveal that many of the tales there recounted originated then. Over the course of those months Francis became aware of the vital forces and spiritual energies that responded to

114. The date assigned by K. Federici, "I Francescani visti in Anagni in une donazione del 1219 [*sic*]," *L'Italia Francescana*, XL (1956), 448 f. It is impossible to determine from his subscription of bulls whether Hugolino was with the Curia at the Lateran on October 25, 1217, or at Viterbo on the same date in 1219 (Potthast, *Regesta*, I, 678).

115. Other clues tend to substantiate this hypothesis. In Hugolino's *Register* (1221) he appears frequently as a witness, once as a deputy, and constantly as the cardinal's chaplain and nuncio. (Levi, *Registri dei Cardinali*, pp. 20, 22 f., 34–38, 46–49, 94, 99. Cf. F. Tenckhoff, *Papst Alexander IV* [Paderborn, 1907], p. 2.) But on August 28, 1229, he addressed a letter to "R., subdiacono et capellano nostro," who may have been the same Rainaldo; his nephew was already a cardinal at that date. (Auvray, *Reg*, I, 206/335.) Yet "R." may have been someone else: he was not, however, Raymond of Peñaforte, who became a papal chaplain and penitentiary only in 1230. (R. Naz, "Raymund de Pennafort ou Penyafort ou Peñaforte," *DDC*, VII [1965], col. 461.)

116. Thomas of Celano, *Vita secunda* (*AnalFranc*, I, 1885), pp. 168 f.; *Chronica Anonyma Fratrum Minorum Germaniae* (*AnalFranc*, I), pp. 279 f. Cf. Brooke, *Early Franciscan Government*, pp. 287 f., on the traditional name of this chapter. Jordan of Giano, *Chronica*, p. 6, mentions that Cardinal Rainerio (i.e., Capocci) was at the 1221 assembly—obviously as Hugolino's stand-in while he was on legation.

117. H. Fischer, *Der heilige Franziskus von Assisi während der Jahre 1219–1221 ...*, Freiburger Historische Studien, IV (1907), 80.

his message; soon he would try to accommodate them through his third order, guided and shaped and protected in great part by Hugolino.[118] But in 1217 and 1218 he could only respond by urging men to live in peace and charity with one another, to honor the church, and for those not disadvantaged by marriage or infirmity, to join his order. His old companions and the new administrators elsewhere in Europe faced the same choice. During his absence in the East the order experienced a new kind of change brought about chiefly by the almost geometric multiplication of its membership, with all that that implied in relation to housing, administration, and the varying interpretations of Francis's example among the great majority of the new recruits who knew the founder only at second hand. When he came back in 1220 he expressed his alarm at the increasing indifference to property ownership and easy living by removing his vicars and taking up once more a personal command of the order.[119] And then, after dreaming of the little black hen that was himself, unable any longer to gather her burgeoning brood under her wings, he realized that it was not possible to keep the order faithful to his visions without help from Rome.[120]

The Curia was then at Viterbo,[121] and he appears to have gone there

118. Cf. Zarncke, *Der Anteil des Kardinals Ugolino,* pp. 78–102; F. d'Anvers, "Le Tiers-Ordre de Saint François d'Assise," *EtFranc,* XXXIII (1921), 360–382, 468–488; XXXIV (1922), 67–85, 195–210, 367–391, 538–560; "La diffusione e l'influenza politica del Terz'Ordine di S. Francesco nel secolo XIII. Esame critico di una frase attribuita a Pier della Vigna," *L'Italia Francescana,* I (1926), 56–67, 161–171; M. Bihl, "Elenchi Bononienses Fratrum de Poenitentia S. Francisci 1252–1288," *AFH,* VII (1914), 227–233; A. Fantozzi and B. Bughetti, "Il Terz'Ordine Francescano in Perugia dal sec. XIII al sec. XIX," *AFH,* XXXIII (1940), 55–113, etc.; T. A. Zaremba, *Franciscan Social Reform: A Study of the Third Order Secular of St. Francis as an Agency of Social Reform . . . , CUA Studies in Sociology,* XXVI (1947); G. G. Meersseman, "Disciplinati e penitenti nel Duecento," in *Il Movimento dei Disciplinati nel settimo centenario dal suo inizio . . . ,* (Perugia, 1962), pp. 43–72; P. Mandonnet, "Les règles et le gouvernement de l'Ordre de Poenitentia au XIIIe siècle," *Opuscules de Critique Historique,* I (1902), 143–250.

119. Our most explicit source is Jordan of Giano, *Chronica,* p. 5, who blames not Gregory or Matthew but Philip, Francis's choice to watch over Clare and her sisters, "qui . . . contra voluntatem beati Francisci . . . impetrant litteras a Sede Apostolica, quibus dominas defenderet et turbatores earum excommunicaret. Similiter et frater Iohannes de Conpello, collecta magna multitudine leprosorum et virorum et mulierum, Ordini se subtraxit et fundator novi Ordinis esse voluit. Regulam quandam conscripsi et pro ipsa confirmanda se cum suis Sedi Apostolicae praesentavit. Et praeter haec quaedam alia turbationem exordia in beati Francisci absentia, sicut illa veridica praedixerat, sunt exorta."

120. Thomas of Celano, *Vita secunda,* pp. 144 f. This vision he may have experienced earlier, but surely he recalled it and realized perhaps more fully its import now.

121. From December 20, 1219, to June 2, 1220. (Potthast, *Regesta,* I, 541–548.)

directly from Bologna.[122] There can be no question that his primary purpose was to formalize the position of Hugolino as cardinal-protector, so that he "might hear and deliberate upon [his] pleas and those of the Order."[123] Honorius consented to this (though it is well to note that once again no bull was issued to confirm the arrangement), and Hugolino's first official act was to revoke the letters of Philip and expel John of Compello from the papal court.[124] The two prime fautors of unwelcome change were thus disposed of for the moment, and Francis's appeal was thereby vindicated.[125]

The *Vita secunda* of Thomas of Celano[126] informs us that at some time Francis and Dominic met at the house of Cardinal Hugolino in Rome. (The story is rendered dramatically, if unhappily without a chronological setting.[127]) The question arose then whether Francis would approve of his friars' being elevated to bishoprics: he answered that they were called *minores* and should not presume to become *maiores*—one of the few indica-

122. Fischer, *Der heilige Franziskus*, p. 63, believes that the erection of the large convent there was what determined him to go to the pope. He puts the interview in February. See also D. Dallari, "S. Francesco d'Assisi 'scrittore,'" *L'Italia Francescana*, XXXIII (1958), 175 n.; K. Esser, *Das Testament des heiligen Franziskus von Assisi*, p. 161.

123. Jordan of Giano, *Chronica*, p. 5. Cf. Thomas of Celano, *Vita prima*, pp. 54 f.; *Vita secunda*, pp. 145 f. D. De Gubernatis, *Orbis Seraphicus* . . . , Vol. I (Rome, 1682), 500, puts a different construction on the event: "Quoniam vero ad Regulae praescriptum non fuit ab Apostolica Sede speciali deputatione Protector institutus, sed ex affectu proprio sponte oblatis"—possibly referring to his earlier offer at Florence.

124. Jordan of Giano, *loc. cit.*; cf. A. Quaglia, *L'Originalità della Regola Francescana*, 2nd ed. (Sassoferrato, 1959), pp. 21 f. We are never given more than the vaguest idea of what Philip's letters from the chancery contained. Hugolino himself on December 9, 1219, was instrumental in getting a privilege recognizing the holdings of the Monticello Clares! (*BF*, I, 3–5/3: *Sacrosancta Romana ecclesia*.) See note 119, *supra*.

125. Very few historians have doubted that his trip to Viterbo was necessitated by the reforms attempted while he was away. One who has minimized this factor is E. d'Ascoli, "Francescani e clero secolare," *L'Italia Francescana*, XXVIII (1953), 22. For the majority opinion, see Zöllig, "Kardinal Hugolino," pp. 28–30; Fischer, *Der heilige Franziskus*, p. 71; B. da Siena, *Il Cardinale protettore*, p. 21; Brooke, *Early Franciscan Government*, p. 65. In view of Jordan's and Thomas's clear statements, it is strange that Philip of Perugia ("Epistola de Cardinalibus Protectoribus," in *MGH. SS.* XXXII, p. 680) should say regarding his appointment by Honorius, "De isto quomodo datus vel petitus fuerit, nescio."

126. *AnalFranc*, X (1926), 215.

127. B. Altaner, "Die Beziehungen des hl. Dominikus zum hl. Franziskus von Assisi," *FrzStud*, IX (1922), 12, 22, opts for 1221; H. Fischer, *Der heilige Franziskus von Assisi*, pp. 83–102, makes out a fairly strong case for early 1220. But cf. Spätling, "Der Anteil der Franziskaner," p. 301, and Grundmann, *Religiöse Bewegungen*, p. 145; also the note on the dating problem in the *Vita secunda*, p. 215.

tions, but one both simple and clear, of his feeling on a subject that was to divide the order bitterly in the next decades.

At the chapter-general in May, 1220, Francis yielded the generalate of the order to Peter Catanei, who had gone with him to the East and was one of his closest companions. But Peter was also a lawyer.[128] Evidently a holy life was no longer enough, even in Francis's eyes, to bear the burden of government. And a year later we witness the touching spectacle of Francis sitting at the feet of Elias, tugging at that lawyer's garment when he wanted to communicate something to the brethren.[129] Then, however, physical affliction was setting in; the intestinal agony and blindness of the last years were not far away.

That same year saw the composition of a second rule for the Friars Minor.[130] Hugolino's hand is visible at several points—exactly which, as with the *Regula bullata* of 1223, remain moot—most probably in the novel distinction in chapters 17 and 21 between licensed preachers and mere exhorters of penance, a distinction which, however, exhibited the same traditionalism that had appeared in *Cum secundum consilium*, which imposed the year's novitiate.[131] Immersed as he was in the long development of church law, and versed as well in the recent history of penitential movements, Hugolino knew that one of the greatest dangers to doctrinal purity was the uninstructed zeal of novice preachers. Francis, familiar too with Patarine aberrancies, could not seriously have objected to the new distinctions. At no point do we see him rejecting these modifications of his simple "*propositum conversationis,*" though he must have deeply regretted their necessity. His was the position of a small-power statesman who has realistically admitted the value of alliance with a mighty neighbor, without fully understanding the sacrifices of autonomy that shall have to be made.

The *Regula non bullata* itself proved too diffuse, and lacked concreteness on several vital problems.[132] In particular, the office of cardinal-protector

128. "Iuris perito et Domino legum" (Jordan of Giano, *Chronica*, p. 4).

129. *Ibid.*, p. 6. Francis had, nevertheless, managed to address the friars a homily or two before giving way to Elias.

130. Before the chapter-general in May, at which Rainerio Capocci represented the protector, and probably before March, when his commission as legate began. For varying versions of the text, see Casutt, *Die älteste Franziskanische Lebensform*, pp. 135–168; Cuthbert, "La Règle Primitive," pp. 142–53; B. Zöllig, "Kardinal Hugolinos Anteil an der Regel des I. Ordens," *FrzStud*, XXI (1934), 37–46; Quaglia, *L'originalità della Regola*, pp. 24–29; L. Hardick *et al.*, *La Règle des Frères Mineurs: Étude historique et spirituelle* (Paris, 1961), pp. 32–39; K. Esser, "Zur Textgeschichte der Regula non bullata des hl. Franziskus von Assisi," *FrzStud*, XXXIII (1951), 219–237.

131. September 20, 1220 (*BF*, I, 6/5).

132. Yet its significance should not be discounted: "Con questa regola, l'ordine

stood in need of definition, along with those of the ministers and *custodes*. The kind of standards which a novice had to meet must be spelled out, and a high proportion of the scriptural rambling in the 1221 rule excised. The pressure on Francis from Hugolino and the *seniores* to rewrite the rule again was considerable, and Honorius himself must have been anxious to have an acceptable *formula vitae* to enroll among the rules of approved orders.[133] So the cardinal and the *poverello* conferred again, and produced the new rule for papal inspection late in 1223. Honorius nodded and passed it through the chancery, whence it emerged in *Solet annuere* on November 29.[134]

Hugolino, whose participation in writing the *Regula* of 1221, the rule for the tertiaries,[135] and Clare's institute prepared him for this last exercise in constitutional ingenuity, not only played a central role in the phrasing and acceptance of the *Regula bullata*, but also qualified himself thereby as its most authoritative commentator. The friars knew this when they picked several of their number in 1230 to ask him as pope for an explanation of several chapters. (The result, of course, was *Quo elongati*.[136]) Through the

---

prendava finalmente una fisionomia propria, marcando i contorni differenziali e codificando le basi della nuova spiritualità, affermava esplicitamente una disciplina ed acquistava una solida organizzazione, regolando le attività, le attribuzioni ed i rapporti reciproci dei superiori e dei sudditi" (Quaglia, *L'originalità della Regola*, p. 21).

133. Whether we can accept Kybal's version (*Die Ordensregeln*, p. 44) of how those two years passed is dubious; how can we know, for example, that the ministers added provisions then with which Francis disagreed? This story falls into the category of spiritual propaganda.

134. Hugolino's role is made clear in Faloci-Pulignani, *Legenda Trium Sociorum*, p. 103, where, after calling Francis to Rome with the new text, "fecit per eundem dominum Honorium cum bulla pendente solemniter confirmari." Cf. the *Chronica XXIV Generalium*, *AnalFranc*, III (1897), 29: "Cum dominus Hugolinus Cardinalis et Protector praefatus vellet, regulam per dominum Papam Honorium confirmari." *Solet annuere* appears in *BF*, I, 15–19/14, *et alibi*. For literature and a critical text, see L. Oliger, *Expositio Quatuor Magistrorum super Regulam Fratrum Minorum (1241–42) accedit eiusdem regulae textus cum fontibus et locis parallelis* (Rome, 1950), pp. 171–193. A very extensive interpretation of certain passages is found in A. M. Garra, *La Metà del Serafino*, 9 vols. (Ragusa, 1952); see also Quaglia, *L'originalità della Regola*, pp. 38–43; Hardick *et al.*, *La Règle des Frères Mineurs*, pp. 39–50.

135. Which it seems Honorius approved orally in 1221—whether at Francis's or Hugolino's urging we cannot tell. (F. d'Anvers, "Le Tiers-Ordre," p. 369.) See the text in Wadding, *AnnMin*, II, 10–17, and, most definitively, in P. Sabatier, "Regula antiqua fratrum et sororum de Paenitentia seu Tertii ordinis Sancti Francisci," *Opuscules de Critique Historique*, I (1901), 16–30.

136. *BF*, I, 68–70/56. Cf. H. Grundmann, "Die Bulle 'Quo elongati' Papst Gregors IX.," *AFH*, LIV (1961), 3–25, including a critical text.

cooperation with Francis and his ministers which all these labors entailed, he became identified as no other ecclesiastic before him with the daily rhythms of the order.

It is altogether natural, then, that where John and Nicolas receive scant mention in the order's anecdotal lore, several accounts of Hugolino's personal relations with Francis are scattered through the early sources. He wears the friars' garb, and eats with them on the dirt floors of their crude habitations. He washes their feet and ministers to them in fraternal love.[137] He visits them frequently in their convents, without disclosing his identity—even after becoming pope![138] He expresses surprise that Francis still goes out for alms even though they have found a secure lodging for the night, and the saint rebukes him gently: "I bear a royal dignity and the mark of nobility, I follow the Lord who though rich, was made a pauper for us."[139] He receives Francis at Rieti, where it happened the little man, old before his time, was seeking a doctor's ministration, and commends his fortitude and Christian example to the whole papal court.[140] Two summers after Francis's death he proclaims his dear friend's sainthood to the world, and commissions Thomas of Celano to write an edifying biography, in which Hugolino's own compassion and guidance figure prominently.

Yet when we insist upon a detailed record of his doings as protector, these pleasant vignettes are of little help. Only one letter is addressed to him by Honorius during the seven years of his protectorate which deals in any way with his concern for the order; one other mentions his mediation, and perhaps a half-dozen or so (addressed chiefly to Italian prelates, enjoining their solicitousness for new Minorite and Clare houses) reflect an indirect influence.[141] From his cardinalic register we learn that he approved a gift of twenty pounds to the convent at Bologna in 1221.[142]

137. Philip of Perugia, "Epistola de Cardinalibus Protectoribus," p. 680.

138. *Ibid.*, p. 681.

139. Thomas of Celano, *Vita secunda*, p. 175.

140. Thomas of Celano, *Vita prima*, p. 76; Julian of Speier, *Vita S. Francisci*, pp. 365 f. The Curia was at Rieti from June 23, 1225, to early February, 1226, hence this incident would have occurred after the infliction of the stigmata. (Potthast, *Regesta*, I, 640–645.) On the stigmata, see especially M. Bihl, "De Stigmatibus S. Francisci Assisiensis (occasione recentis cuiusdam Libri)," *AFH*, III (1910), 393–432; O. a Rieden, "De Sancti Francisci Assisiensis Stigmatum susceptione," *CollFr*, XXXIII (1963), 210–266, 392–422; XXXIV (1964), 5–62, 241–338.

141. At least thirty-four letters dealing with the order are known from Honorius's pontificate. See my "Checklist" in *AFH*, LXIV (1971).

142. October 28. Levi, *Registri dei Cardinali*, p. 108.

From several of his papal bulls we discover a prior involvement in establishing convents here and there,[143] some out of his own purse. These sources, when added to the biographical material just summarized, convey the impression that he regarded his functions as threefold: to foster the growth of the order (including Clares and tertiaries) by specific donative and constructive acts; to promote its structural development through the formulation of rules; and to intercede on the order's behalf with the pope whenever he thought it would hasten the granting of privileges and exemptions.

In short, he brought a degree of definition to the office of cardinal-protector which it had not had before, either in theory or in practice. The position took on during his tenure a form clearly circumscribed by legal tradition, yet capable of change as conditions arose for which no initial provision had been made. On this foundation his successors, first among them his nephew Rainaldo, continued to build. His active concern determined in large measure the course the order would follow after the death of its founder.[144]

RAINALDO DA SEGNI: CARDINAL AND PROTECTOR

The man who was to become Alexander IV was the son of Gregory's sister, and stemmed from the counts of Segni.[145] Information on his upbringing, schooling, and first steps in religion eludes us, as is so often the case with medieval churchmen. His uncle employed him in 1221 as his vicar in a few transactions on his Lombard legation.[146] He was in his own right a canon at Anagni, and bore the title *magister*.[147] When Hugolino

143. Cf., e.g., his grant of July 28, 1219, in the bull *Religiosam vitam eligentibus*, November 22, 1229 (*BF*, I, 54/41), to the Clares of Gattaiola, and one on the following day included in a bull of the same *initium* to the Camullia Clares, January 26, 1230 (*BF*, I, 57 f./45).

144. Cf. Salvatorelli, "Movimento francescano e gioachimismo. Francesco d'Assisi e il francescanesimo nel primo secolo dell'ordine," (*Relazione*, Vol. III: X Cong. Hist. Sciences, Florence, 1955), p. 437: "Il risultato specifico nella intese tra Francesco e Ugolino fu la fondazione dell'ordine francescano. Il risultato generico fu l'incanalamento del fiume maestoso della Chiesa romana dell'evangelismo francescano . . ."; and Mac-Donell, *Sons of Francis*, p. 21: "Had there been no Elias, no Cardinal Ugolino, there would have been no Franciscan Order; but a loose company of spiritual men in many lands would have looked to him as their father."

145. See note 83, *supra*.

146. Cf. note 115, *supra*.

147. Sibilia, *Alessandro IV*, p. 41. Cf. Salimbene de Adam, *Cronica*, ed. O. Holder-Egger, *MGH. SS.*, XXXII (1908–13), 453: "Litteratus homo fuit et studium theologie diligens . . . ."

became Gregory IX, he made his nephew chamberlain: he thus performed in the *camera apostolica* a role analogous to that of Sinibaldo Fieschi (the later Innocent IV) in the chancery at the same time.[148] Some evidence hints that he continued in that office as cardinal deacon of Sant'Eustachio, a position he attained in September, 1227, shortly after an identical ceremony in which Sinibaldo received the Church of San Lorenzo in Lucina.[149]

The summer of 1231 saw Rainaldo nominated *electus* of Ostia and Velletri, the bishopric Gregory had vacated upon becoming pope.[150] He was then engaged in a joint effort with the archbishop of Reggio Calabria to pacify the feuding factions of Anagni, his first such mission as cardinal.

Frederick, back in Gregory's good graces after the Treaty of Ceprano in 1230, got word in the fall that Rainaldo was on the way to his court, accompanied by Thomas, cardinal priest of Santa Sabina since 1216, to iron out a peace formula between Rome and Viterbo.[151] This was to be the first encounter between the two men. The emperor for his part found the mild-mannered and conciliatory young cardinal agreeably different from his fierce uncle, and was not backward in complaining to him of the pope's interference between him and the Lombard towns in 1233.[152] Rainaldo actually went north in 1236—again with Thomas—to patch up disintegrating relations with Frederick, and to calm an explosive Lombardy.[153] By 1240 the situation was even more critical, and again Rainaldo was a key figure in the negotiations, but to no avail.[154]

148. Sibilia, *Alessandro IV*, p. 55.

149. *Ibid.*, Tenckhoff, *Papst Alexander IV*, p. 3.

150. P. M. Baumgarten, "Miscellanea Diplomatica III," *RQ*, XXXII (1924), 44, assigns July as the month, based on the first reference to him as *electus Ostiensis*, in a papal letter of August 11, in which his letter of July 22 is given. (Auvray, *Reg*, I, 438/698.) He was finally consecrated in 1234: cf. Auvray, *Reg*, II, 153/2749; III, 57/4873; Ughelli and Coleti, *Italia Sacra*, I, cols. 67–69; Mann, *Lives of the Popes*, XV, 5.

151. Auvray, *Reg*, I, 554/924 (October 21). On Thomas, see Baumgarten, "Die Translationen der Kardinäle," p. 86.

152. Auvray, *Reg*, I, 226/1496 (July 12). Cf. J. Maubach, *Die Kardinäle und ihre Politik um die Mitte des XIII. Jahrhunderts* (Bonn, 1902), p. 3.

153. Auvray, *Reg*, II, 507/3384 f., 650 f./3667, 356–58/3675–86; Potthast, *Regesta*, I, 881/10378. Cf. Salimbene, *Cronica*, p. 383; D\ de Lequile, *Hierarchia Franciscana*, II (Rome, 1664), 65; Ciacconius and Oldoinus, *Vitae, et Res Gestae*, p. 81; Tenckhoff, *Papst Alexander IV*, p. 8; Von Westenholz, *Kardinal Rainer von Viterbo*, p. 49. While on this legation, Rainaldo and Thomas had time to look into some capitular irregularities at Padua: Auvray, *Reg*, II, 902/4188. The two of them smoothed over relations between the communal governments of Anagni and Ferentino as well: *ibid.*, III, 2 f./4794.

154. B. Sütterlin, *Die Politik Kaiser Friedrich II. und die römischen Kardinäle in den Jahren 1239–1250* (Heidelberg, 1929), p. 30. The last task Gregory entrusted to Rainaldo was the

Curiously enough, considering his earlier amity with Frederick, Rainaldo was one of three cardinals who voted in the first round at the Septizonium for the hawk Romano, cardinal bishop of Porto.[155] Because he stood well with Matteo Rosso Orsini, the senator and Franciscan tertiary who had forced the confinement of 1241 on the rump *collegium*, he chose to stay on at Rome after the demise of Celestine IV in November, and family interests strengthened his motivation to linger on while most of his colleagues migrated to Anagni.[156] When Sinibaldo finally mustered the unanimous backing of the other cardinals and assumed the papacy in June, 1243, he knew that Rainaldo had a close working familiarity with the Roman scene. For that reason Rainaldo continued to work at Rome during the arduous and frustrating overtures to Frederick until 1244,[157] and stayed behind, along with Stephen and Ricardo Annibaldi, as a vicar "without portfolio" of the Campagna and Marittima when Innocent sailed to Genoa.[158] Within that relatively confining ambit he addressed himself to squabbles that have, for the most part, successfully eluded the historian. On one occasion he reprimanded the citizens of Alatri for their untoward raid on Ferentino, and afterwards declared that the Senate owed the Ferentini £300 to rebuild their ruined wall.[159] We know he did not attend Lyon I, though Innocent had formally invited him.[160] In 1247 he and the other cardinals were told to redouble their efforts against Frederick in the Patrimony, and were commended for their performance to that time.[161] The *consiglio* and people of Terracina got off surprisingly leniently at Innocent's hands following the vicar's sharp response to their wanton

---

holding of some crusade-vow redemption fees collected by Friar William in France. (*BF*, I, 291/331, March 4, 1241.) Cf. Joelson, *Die Papstwahlen*, p. 47: "Besonders oft wurde er mit der Beilegung von Streitigkeiten betraut, einer Mission, die seiner gerechten, versöhnlichen Natur bestens entsprach."

155. K. Hampe, "Ein ungedruckter Bericht über das Konklave von 1241," *Sitzungsberichte der Heidelberger Akademie der Wissenschaften. Philosophisch-historische Klasse*, I (1913), 13.

156. *Ibid.*, p. 19. Cf. Joelson, *Die Papstwahlen*, p. 37.

157. G. von Puttkammer, *Papst Innocenz IV. Versuch einer Gesamtcharakteristik aus seiner Wirkung* (Münster, 1930), p. 13.

158. F. Pagnotti, "Niccolò da Calvi e la sua vita d'Innocenzo IV, con una breve introduzione sulla istoriografia pontificia nei secoli XIII e XIV," *ArchRSocRom*, XXI (1898), 88; C. Rodenberg, *Innocenz IV und das Königreich Sizilien* (Halle, 1892), p. 50; Tenckhoff, *Papst Alexander IV*, p. 17.

159. July 31, 1245, and July 18, 1246. (Potthast, *Regesta*, II, 1000/11765, 1035/12231; cf. Sibilia, *Alessandro IV*, p. 56.)

160. Potthast, *Regesta*, II, 978/10973 (January 31, 1245).

161. *Ibid.*, 1062/12592 (July 1).

destruction of a nobleman's dwelling.[162] At Rome in 1248, he dedicated an altar with the other cardinals;[163] then he and Stephen were rotated out, and Peter Capocci took over several of their operations.[164]

Several of Rainaldo's chaplains and relatives obtained benefices and episcopal sees at Innocent's direction, both before and after his return to Italy in 1251,[165] but the assignments Rainaldo received after 1249 were not of much importance.[166]

If his five years as apostolic vicar have left few traces, two other activities in which he engaged from the beginning of his cardinalate prepared him, in different ways, for the papacy. The first was his role as a kind of permanent roving papal mediator, sometimes called *auditor*; the other was his service to the order as its cardinal-protector.

Rainaldo first appears in the former guise in 1232, when Gregory supported his restrictions on building activities at Perugia, under penalty of a thousand marks.[167] Then in 1234 he arbitrated a divided election for a Rouen abbey, heard out the grievances of the bishop of Glasgow,[168] and smoothed the ruffled feelings of the abbess of Avellino, whose case is of considerable interest because her original petition has survived.[169] A wrangle between a Lateran prior and the patriarch of Constantinople over the church at Sillano dragged on for several years.[170] Ecclesiastical affairs at Sarmineto, Valva-Sulmona, Ascoli-Piceno, Pesaro, Cervia, Strasbourg, Monte Cassino, Frosinone, "Castrum Pregii," Orange, and Rome[171] occupied him until the end of Gregory's pontificate. Under Innocent, Rainaldo dealt with disputes at Assisi, Perugia, Parma, Ferentino, Naxos, and Gaeta.[172] It is thus patently wrong to believe that because he does not stand forth dramatically in the political conflicts of the time, and because

162. *Ibid.*, 1098/13060 (October 22, 1248).
163. Sibilia, *Alessandro IV*, p. 66.
164. Potthast, *Regesta*, II, 1115/*ad*13274 (April 7, 1249). Cf. Von Westenholz, *Kardinal Rainer von Viterbo*, 160.
165. Berger, *Reg*, II, 250/5365; III, 68/5780, 77 f./5815 f., 78/5821, 167/6280, 520/8084.
166. *Ibid.*, II, 196/5110; Potthast, *Regesta*, II, 1201/14566.
167. Auvray, *Reg*, I, 532 f./876, 534–36/880.
168. Tenckhoff, *Papst Alexander IV*, pp. 13 f.
169. Auvray, *Reg*, I, 1098–1100/12032 f.
170. *Ibid.*, II, 82 f./2627 f.
171. *Ibid.*, 105 f./2669, 116/2682, 343 f./3073, 606/3581, 1023 f./4356; III, 175/5048, 227/5145, 339/5333, 479 f./5987 f., 483–88/5990–95; Potthast, *Regesta*, I, 898/10606, 906/*post* 10702.
172. Berger, *Reg*, I, 14 f./55, 38/207; II, 156/4897; III. 295/6894; I. Affò, *Storia della citta di Parma*, Vol. III (Parma, 1793), 377 f.; Göller, *Die päpstliche Pönitentiarie*, p. 132; Fortini, *Nova Vita*, Vol. III, 166.

he stayed in Rome while the greater part of the Curia transferred to Lyon, he was a figurehead or a timeserver. Hitherto insufficient attention has been paid to his unspectacular but continuous immersion in the business of the papal court.

Above and beyond those quotidian chores, Rainaldo accepted the additional office of cardinal-protector of the Franciscan order. It proved to be his most important assignment, not only because of the concrete acts he undertook on behalf of the friars and the Clares, but also because of the way in which the job shaped his attitudes toward the religious life. His manner of dealing with *Etsi animarum*, Innocent IV's last-minute reversal of the friars' privileged status among the orders, and all the labyrinthine dilemmas to which it gave rise, is totally inexplicable without some knowledge of his previous connections with the mendicants.[173]

The early sources claim that Rainaldo became protector as soon as his uncle became pope and relinquished the office himself. (Strictly speaking, this could not have been the case, since Gregory took the oath in March, 1227, and Rainaldo did not become cardinal deacon of Sant'Eustachio until mid-September.) Salimbene claims that the Franciscans especially desired him for the post;[174] but Philip of Perugia, who got most of his information from Rainaldo's successor, John Gaetano Orsini, says: "I do not know whether he was singled out by name or chosen in some other fashion (. . . *nominatim vel aliter postulatus*)."[175] The two versions are not necessarily incompatible: one refers to the part of the friars in the process, the other to the constitutive act of Gregory himself.[176]

173. In reality very little has been done by scholars to produce a coherent narrative of his work in this area. For such attempts as have been made, see Van den Haute, *Breviarium Historicum Ordinis Minorum*, pp. 203 f.; Tenckhoff, *Papst Alexander IV*, pp. 20, 271 f.; Sibilia, *Alessandro IV*, pp. 68 f.; and, most recently, L. Pellegrini, *Alessandro IV e i Francescani (1254–1261)*, STF, XXXIV (Rome, 1966), 39–41, etc.

174. Salimbene, *Cronica*, p. 453.

175. "Epistola de Cardinalibus Protectoribus," p. 681. Cf. Tenckhoff, *Papst Alexander IV*, pp. 15, 313.

176. A later source asserts that he became protector only in the fifth year of Innocent's pontificate (1247–48), but this is demonstrably false. (Nunes, *Crónica da Ordem*, I, 84.) A modern student of the problem has suggested that not until 1248 did he formally receive the care of the Clares. (B. da Siena, *Il Cardinale protettore*, p. 27; cf. notes 186–189, *infra*.) Since in any case no document exists to prove the conferral of any office beyond that of cardinal deacon in 1227, the whole agreement was clearly pragmatic and *de facto* in character (though it did fulfill the requirements of chapter 12 of the rule). And since the Clares in 1227 were not yet either numerous or widespread, a tacit understanding concerning their welfare may well have been arrived at between Rainaldo and the then minister-general, John Parenti. A. Callebaut ("Le sermon historique d'Eudes de Château-

His first recorded act in this new capacity was to make himself known to two dozen Clare houses as the order's new protector, and to replace Fra Pacifico, Francis's choice to visit the sisters, with Filippo Longo, who may well have been the same Philip whose overanxious efforts to garner exemptions for the Clares in 1220 had prompted the formal installation of Hugolino![177] A few months before the premature demise of Anthony of Padua, Rainaldo asked the great thaumaturge to write down some of his celebrated sermons.[178]

Thereafter, absorbed as he was in the legations and heavy round of curial business of the 1230s, we hear very little of his doings as protector. Robert Grosseteste, in a letter probably written late in 1237,[179] urged the cardinal to watch over his beloved friars at Rome, and thanked him in advance in 1239 for his assistance to Simon, who bore letters to the Curia, but who was perhaps not a Friar Minor.[180] At Rainaldo's request, the abbot of Farfa conceded a church to the Clares at nearby Pireto.[181] Rainaldo passed on to Gregory news of the eremitical Augustinians in the March of Ancona, led by Giovanni Bono, who refused to wear habits which would distinguish them from the Franciscans, thus fomenting scandal.[182]

His relative obscurity from 1227 to 1241—if indeed what we have just noted is representative of those years—is not difficult to explain. Gregory kept up a lively personal interest in the order, and continued throughout his pontificate to feel a strong spiritual kinship with it. He thus intervened

---

roux à Paris le 18 mars 1229 autour de l'origine de la grève universitaire et de l'enseigne-ment des Mendiants," *AFH*, XXVIII [1935], 22 f.) accord with this view: Rainaldo, he says, was not limited by Gregory in his powers of office, and his primary purpose was "à procurer à l'Ordre la documentation canonique des privilèges."

177. August 12, 1228. (Wadding, *AnnMin*, II, 732.) Filippo Longo was Francis's seventh disciple, and died in France in 1259. (A. Zawart, "The History of Franciscan Preaching and of Franciscan Preachers [1209–1927]: A Bio-Bibliographical Study," [Report of the Ninth Annual Meeting of the Franciscan Educational Conference, Washington, D.C., 1927], p. 264.)

178. J. M. Pou y Marti, "De Fontibus Vitae S. Antonii Patavini," *Antonianum*, VI (1931), 227. Cf. Sixtus a Pisa, "Alexander IV," in *Lexicon Franciscanum Historicum*, fasc. 1: *Specimen Litterae A* (Rome, 1938), p. 92.

179. S. H. Thomson, *The Writings of Robert Grosseteste, Bishop of Lincoln 1235–1253* (Cambridge, 1940), p. 203/59.

180. H. R. Luard (ed.), *Roberti Grosseteste Epistolae Episcopi quondam Lincolniensis*, Rolls Series (1861), pp. 181 f., 198 f.

181. The letter of Abbot Matthew, dated January 15, 1239, appears in Innocent's confirmation of November 5, 1243, *Personas illas* (*BF*, I, 312–14/15).

182. *Dudum apparuit*, March 24, 1240 (*Ibid.*, 274 f./305).

directly in many important decisions affecting the order, and was in turn regarded by the friars as their natural ally.[183]

With the accession of Innocent IV, however, the situation changed appreciably. Though Innocent saw the importance of the mendicants—a perception which led him to preside over two of their chapters-general, and to use his Franciscan penitentiaries on major diplomatic missions—the chief preoccupation of the new pope was always political strategy. What related to the everyday running of the order concerned him scarcely at all, and that could be safely entrusted to Rainaldo and the ministers. Furthermore, he spent six and a half years of his pontificate outside Italy altogether, and since the order's natural center was in the peninsula, it seemed appropriate that he should delegate intermediate responsibilities to a man thoroughly secure in Italian surroundings—again, Rainaldo. Finally, since the cardinal was not in the inner circle of Innocent's advisers, but was at least the titular head of the *collegium* and had performed his duties creditably under Gregory, it was wise to give him a virtually free rein in the supervision of his Franciscan flock, so long as he did not run afoul of Innocent's own designs.

A general letter of August 21, 1244, which Innocent addressed to all the Clares from Genoa reflects very distinctly the degree to which the pope relied on Rainaldo for counsel on the proper handling of the sisters. Gregory, he said, had told his nephew that the Clares were bound by The Rule of St. Benedict only with regard to obedience, the relinquishing of private property, and perpetual chastity.[184] Rainaldo had in turn, it appears, communicated this oral confidence to Innocent before the latter's departure from Civitavecchia several weeks previously, and it now became a canonical pronouncement of major significance.

In that trying first winter in France, the dolorous plight of the friars at Limoges reached the pope's ears, thanks to Rainaldo's detailed dispatch. Driven off from land dearly bought from the citizens of the commune, but belonging in fact to a local abbot, the friars had appealed to the cardinal-protector for justice, and he had referred it as a matter beyond his immediate competence to Lyon. Innocent responded by instructing the bishop of Angoulême to look into the case and adjudicate it as he saw fit.[185]

183. See the section on Cardinal Hugolino *supra*, pp. 39–52.

184. *Cum universitati vestre* (*BF*, I, 350/67). The Clares at Bordeaux got a very similar reassurance, dated August 11, 1245: *Cum vobis sicut ceteris* (F.-M. Delorme, "En marge du Bullaire Franciscain," *FFDoc*, III [1938], 6 f./2).

185. *Dilecti filii . . . minister*, January 21, 1245 (Delorme, "Les Cordeliers dans le Limousin aux XIIIe–XVe siècles," *AFH*, XXXII [1939], 215 f.).

Three bulls in 1248 offer important, if somewhat contradictory, clues to his functions as protector of the Clares. On March 28, in connection with a petition from the sisters at Monticello, Innocent placed the matter in Rainaldo's hands, "since . . . the monasteries of the abovesaid order [i.e., of San Damiano] are known to be committed to your care."[186] On June 17 he entrusted the responsibility for all the Clares to Rainaldo alone; formerly, it seems, the provincial ministers had borne that onus, especially when it came to visitation: "and for that reason, as we have learned, you are unable to watch over them, or pursue the task of visitation in their monasteries as you were wont to do . . . ."[187] To prevent a decline in standards, therefore, he obtained complete freedom to visit, correct, and reform any convents he wished to inspect. Then, on October 28, a very similar set of instructions began to find its way from Lyon to Rome, the only difference being that the minister-general was indicated as the person having previously exercised over-all custody of the Clares.[188]

Rainaldo and the two other vicars in Rome got word in July, 1248, that they were expected to bend their energies to relocating the Friars Minor in the Eternal City; the editor of this letter infers that the Franciscans had been housed up to then in unsanitary districts.[189] The three cardinals moved slowly, however, and next summer had to be reminded again of the friars' needs; by that time the Benedictine abbey of Araceli, close by the ancient Forum, looked like the best site for their transplantation.[190] Yet it was not until November 28, 1250, that the switch was finally effected: we have the cardinals' letter of that date in Innocent's confirmation sometime afterwards.[191]

Returning again to the Clares, we find the pope granting on June 6, 1250, that Rainaldo might permit those houses that so desired to continue to follow the strict rule prepared for them by Cardinal Hugolino,[192] but that others could safely observe Innocent's own revised version of 1247.[193] A little interpolation leads us to the conclusion that the new rule had caused consternation in the older establishments, and it seems a sure bet that Rainaldo had communicated this unease to Lyon. Evidently this

186. *Dilecte in Christo* (*BF*, I, 511 f./272).

187. *Cum dilectis filiis* (A. De Latera, *Ad Bullarium Franciscanum . . . Supplementum* [Rome, 1780], 13 f./5).

188. *Cum dilecto filio* (*ibid.*, 19/7).

189. *Quanto dilecti filii*, July 23 (*BF*, I, 521 f./288: cf. Sbaralea's notes k, a, b).

190. *Dilecti filii fratres*, July 17, 1249 (*ibid.*, 530 f./304).

191. *Hiis que auctoritate*, July 5, 1252 (*ibid.*, 616–18/418: cf. 545/330).

192. On the date, see note 113, *supra*.

193. *Inter personas alias* (De Latera, *Supplementum*, 22–24/10).

double standard only created more doubt in the convents, and ultimately it was Rainaldo himself who came to the rescue by submitting a compromise *formula vitae* for Innocent's approval on September 16, 1252, with the full knowledge and consent of Clare at Assisi.[194] Although a few chapters, especially the first, contained quaint remnants, several others which mentioned the duties of the cardinal-protector were quite *au courant*, and deserve our close attention. He was to enjoy, to begin with, a great disciplinary latitude in the admission of novices and the extending of exceptional liberties to Clares whom he judged too delicate to live under the full rigor of the rule (chap. 2). Only the pope or the protector could give access to the inner sanctum of any convent (chap. 11). Franciscan *visitatores*, picked by the protector, had the power to reprimand abuses and impose corrective measures and to administer the sacraments in the convents whenever they deemed it needful. Over all stood the protector, to enforce the law:

> so that we [i.e. the Clares] might forever exemplify the poverty and humility of our Lord Jesus Christ and His most holy mother, always obedient and subject at the feet of his Holy Roman Church, and persevering in the Catholic faith. (Chap. 12)

Innocent's last word on the subject came on July 8, 1253,[195] when John of Parma and the friars were assured that their mandatory guardianship of the Clares was to be sharply reduced, to enhance the privacy of the sisters and to lighten their own load. Rainaldo would fill the vacuum now, and had in fact played a key part in convincing the pope of the justice of the friars' murmuring against the enactments of 1245.[196]

Surprisingly often in his last two years, Innocent confirmed by official means Rainaldo's disposition of cases involving the friars or the Clares, directed him to give the rule to new houses, or called his attention to creeping abuses.[197]

194. *Solet annuere*, August 9, 1253 (*BF*, I, 671–78/496). Cf. *Chronica XXIV Generalium*, p. 274; Tenckhoff, *Papst Alexander IV*, p. 20.

195. On the date, see the note in my "Checklist," *AFH*, LXIV (1971).

196. *Petitio vestra nobis* (*BF*, I, 619/419). As pope, Rainaldo confirmed *Petitio vestra* on August 18, 1255 (*BF*, II, 67/97).

197. *BF*, I, 591 f./385, 719/540 (Spoleto); 594/392, 600/399 (Fermo); 601/401 (Ascoli-Piceno); 604 f./403 (Lanciano); 626 f./432 (Novara); 629–31/437 f., 632–34/442 (Todi); 643 f./454 (San Germano); 648 f./462 (Zamora); 738/553 (Volterra); Z. Lazzeri, "Bulla Innocentii Papae IV an. 1253 'Privilegium Paupertatis' Monasterio Florentino iam concessum comprobans," *AFH*, VIII (1915), 311 f. (Florence); Eubel, *BFEp*, 69/706

Rainaldo's actual correspondence with the order must have been voluminous, just to judge from the number of cases he is known to have handled. Unfortunately, however, little of that correspondence survives.[198] Yet we do have a fairly complete file on one case, that of the Clares at Montpellier, and from that it is possible to glean something of his methods of operation. The abbess had communicated her trying circumstances to him, and he replied:

> ... not guided by deliberation, but rather led astray (*non ductae . . . sed seductae*) by letters patent from some of the Friars Minor at Montpellier, you have, without requesting or getting license from the same friars, gone on making promissory commitments, completely lacking Apostolic or other letters. We, wishing to apply a fit remedy to this problem, decree for your devotion by the tenor of these presents, strictly prescribing it for your obedience, that you do not in any wise have to fulfil the aforesaid commitment, or obligation, as far as it is now in force; we hereby declare the abovementioned letters, drafted for an obligation of this sort, to be of no force or legal value.[199]

The provincial minister of Provence, the man ultimately answerable for the conduct of the Montpellier friars, was admonished by Rainaldo on May 20, 1253, to keep a sharp eye on that community. Finally he appealed to the local *custos* and the guardian at Montpellier to rescue the Clares from the straits into which their own imprudent action had precipitated them.[200]

Throughout his cardinalate and in his papal years as well, Rainaldo da Segni nurtured a special affection for the two places most sanctified in the legend of Francis: Assisi and La Verna. It was he who pressed the

---

(Würzburg); Delorme, "Supplément au Bullaire Franciscain à propos du monastère de Sainte-Claire de Toulouse," *FrFranc*, III (1914), 129–131 (Toulouse). The cardinal had his own procurator, who apparently acted as a go-between in financial transactions involving the friars. Only one such case has come to light, however: the sale by the bishop of Perugia to the Franciscans of some land outside the city walls, an arrangement which passed through the hands of Rainaldo's procurator (*BF*, I, 680 f./499). On the little-known duties of the procurator-general of the order at the Curia, known to exist already in 1254, see Pellegrini, *Alessandro IV e i Francescani*, p. 74 n.

198. Cf. his mention in a later papal letter of written communication with the provincial minister at Strasbourg and the *diffinitores* at Essling (*BF*, II, 19 f./27).

199. December 13, 1252 (Agathange de Paris, "L'origine et la fondation des monastères de Clarisses en Aquitaine au XIIIe siècle," *CollFr*, XXV [1955], 40 f.). The letter is cited without indication of source in Le Bras, *Institutions ecclésiastiques*, p. 551 n.

200. April 20, 1254 (Agathange de Paris, "L'origine," p. 41).

dedication of the basilica in the founder's native city most assiduously upon Innocent while the latter was dwelling at the Sacro Convento. Because of those overtures Innocent extended an unusually generous indult of two years and eighty days' remission of temporal punishment to those who worshipfully visited the church within fifteen days after the anniversary of its dedication.[201] The Franciscan architect of the basilica, Philip of Compello, obtained the right to gather in offerings up to the amount he had expended on its construction, which Rainaldo or a subsequent protector of the order could dispose of as he wished.[202] Discoursing on the honored place the basilica should hold in the order and in Christendom, Innocent stipulated that it be replete with fine chalices, altar cloths, vestments, and bells[203]—a provision presumably added by the cardinal, who loved the trappings of divine service.[204]

Notwithstanding the fact that Innocent had himself taken the friars at La Verna under the apostolic wing,[205] Rainaldo informed the whole order that he intended to bestow his personal protection upon the house there.[206] He visited the site of the stigmatization while cardinal, and preached there as pope. In 1256 he allowed the friars at La Verna to beg in any of the order's sixteen Italian provinces, and to be exempt from travel taxes;[207] in 1260 he conceded them the rare privilege of wearing silken vestments during the celebration of the mass.[208]

Upon his accession as Alexander IV, Rainaldo kept the protectorate of the order in his own hands, and so notified the minister-general in

201. *Si populus israeliticus*, June 11, 1253 (*BF*, I, 662/482). Cf. Pagnotti, "Niccolò da Calvi," pp. 110 f.

202. *Decet et expedit*, July 10, 1253 (*BF*, I, 666/489).

203. *Dignum existimamus*, July 16 (*ibid.*, 666 f./490).

204. Salimbene, *Cronica*, p. 453: ". . . frequenter et libenter predicabat et celebrabat et ecclesias consecrabat."

205. *Licet cuncta Ordinis*, December 3, 1250 (De Latera, *Supplementum*, 25 f./16).

206. September 8, 1253 (S. Mencherini, *Codice Diplomatico della Verna e delle SS. Stimate di S. Francesco d'Assisi ne VII⁰ centenario del gran prodigio*, Documenta Francescani, III [Florence, 1924], 16 f./14).

207. *Romani est summi Pontificis*, May 3 (De Latera, *Supplementum*, 82–84/19). Cf. *Cum ad promendera*, July 25 (*ibid.*, 95 f./25); *Sanctorum meritis inclita*, September 1, 1257 (*BF*, II, 238/358).

208. *Cum olim adhuc*, August 28 (De Latera, *Supplementum*, 137 f./43; cf. Bonaventure, *Vita de S. Francisco*, *AnalFranc*, X [1926], 619). Alexander also reaffirmed in the strongest of language Gregory's insistence on the authenticity of the stigmata (April 5, 1237: *BF*, I, 214/223): *Grande et singulare*, July 10, 1255 (*BF*, II, 169/250: cf. Eubel, *BFEp*, 78/792a, and Mencherini, *Codice Diplomatico*, 20 f./16, on the date); *Benigne operatio divine*, October 19, 1255 (*BF*, II, 85–87/120); *Quia longum esset*, July 28, 1259 (*ibid.*, 358–60/502). See also Pellegrini, *Alessandro IV e i Francescani*, pp. 95–99.

1255[209] and again in 1260.[210] His performance in that dual role would prove of dubious value to the order and the church alike.

ALEXANDER IV AND THE STRUGGLE AT PARIS

In circumstances uncomfortably paralleling those of 1241, the depleted *collegium* convened at Naples under the podesta's critical vigilance, and speedily settled upon Rainaldo *per compromissum* on December 12, 1254.[211] The tale that he soon whispered to Ottaviano Ubaldini, cardinal deacon of Santa Maria in Via Lata, that he was not averse to bearing the papal dignity, but would leave the real powers of decision in political questions to him, must be labeled apocryphal,[212] though it does not basically run counter to what we know of Rainaldo's personal humility and general disinterest in political matters.

As to the more substantive problem of the reasons for his election, several have been offered by scholars: probably they all played a part in the final determination. Because Innocent had failed to clear up the extent of Manfred's legitimacy, considerable alienation from his Sicilian policy had surfaced in the *collegium*. Rainaldo, who preferred negotiating to fighting, would at least assure a breathing spell.[213] Because he was not notably aggressive, the other cardinals thought he would be more open

209. *Licet iniunctum nobis*, November 8 (F.-M. Delorme, "Alexandre IV et le protec-torat de l'ordre," *AFH*, XII [1919], 593–595; also in Wadding, *AnnMin*, III, 632 f.). Delorme's discovery of this letter only confirmed what was known long ago. Cf. Philip of Perugia, "Epistola de Cardinalibus Protectoribus," p. 681: "Hic, quamvis requisitus, nullum cardinalem dare voluit ordini, dicens, quod nolebat, quod fratres ipso vivente haberent alium cardinalem. Sed ordinem retinere voluit sibi ipsi, et ipse volebat eius immediatus esse protector . . . ." See also O. Holder-Egger, "Chronica Minor auctore Minorita Erphordiensi," *MGH. SS.*, XXIV, 201; *Chronica XXIV Generalium, AnalFranc*, III, p. 278.

It seems at least possible, nevertheless, that shortly after his election he thought of turning over the protectorate to Hugues de St.-Cher, the Dominican cardinal bishop of Frascati: the latter wrote Alexander, as intermediary, concerning the Strasbourg Clares on December 24 (*Solet annuere*, January 18, 1255 [*BF*, II, 8 f./9]).

210. *Licet iniunctum nobis*, August 9, 1260 (*ibid.*, 205/575).

211. Salimbene, *Cronica*, p. 453. Cf. Joelson, *Die Papstwahlen*, p. 52; Maubach, *Die Kardinäle und ihre Politik*, pp. 57 f.; Sibilia, *Alessandro IV*, pp. 31–36.

212. Salimbene, *Cronica*, p. 453, says only that Ottaviano was the arbitrator who chose Rainaldo; cf. Joelson, *Die Papstwahlen*, p. 54; J. Haller, *Das Papsttum: Idee und Wirklichkeit*, Vol. IV: *Die Krönung*, 2nd ed. (Darmstadt, 1962), 273.

213. Maubach, *Die Kardinäle und ihre Politik*, p. 56, puts the item at the head of the list: "ob die Politik der Kurie besonders in Bezug auf Sizilien im Sinne des verstorbenen Papstes weiter geführt werden oder nich?"

to advice or outright manipulation than had his Machiavellian precursor. And Alexander would be just the man to pacify the mendicants, up in arms because of *Etsi animarum*.[214] His piety was most welcome to the reform-minded segment of the *collegium*.[215] Thus, though he was not entirely ideal in anyone's eyes, he stood out as the one really logical choice. All sides chiefly expected him to buy time for the church to gird itself anew for the trials that lay ahead.[216]

Alexander's first concern after his consecration (December 21) was the suspension of *Etsi animarum*, which he deeply believed to have been an unwarranted assault on the privileges of the mendicants. The very next day he revoked it in *Nec insolitum*,[217] telling both the Franciscans and the Friars Preacher that, as he had smiled upon them in the past, so now "we shall hold you fast in our heart, and foster [your] order[s] in a paternal benevolence . . . ."[218] Effusive, comforting words, and as it turned out only Alexander's opening round in the papal counteroffensive against the French seculars and the masters at Paris who championed them.

The next significant development in the controversy was Alexander's promulgation of *Quasi lignum vitae*, April 14, 1255.[219] It illuminates the

214. November 21, 1254 (Eubel, *BF Supplementum*, 259–61/28). This bull essentially reduced the new mendicant orders to an equal canonical status with the older brotherhoods, and sought to redress several of the seculars' grievances against the friars—i.e., usurpation of parochial and diocesan rights. It was, in fact, the only significant reversal of papal favor toward the friars before Boniface's *Super Cathedram*.

215. Joelson, *Die Papstwahlen*, p. 53, says his election "muss als Sieg der kirchlichen Strömung über die politische gelten und wurde auch allerorten von den glaubenseifrigen Kreisen als solcher begrüsst."

216. Alexander's *Registers*, ed. C. Bourel de la Roncière (1902), J. de Loye and H. de Cenival (1907), and A. Coulon (1953), appear in the Bibliothèque de l'école d'Athènes et de Rome series. See also Potthast, *Regesta*, II, 1286–1472; L. Delisle, "Fragment du dernier registre d'Alexandre IV," *BiblEcCh*, XXXVIII (1877), 103–113; R. Fawtier, "Une bulle d'Alexandre IV pour l'Abbaye de Saint-Berthin," in *Historical Essays in Honour of James Tait* (Manchester, 1933), pp. 91–95; E. Pásztor, "Contributo alla storia dei registri pontifici del secolo XIII," *Bullettino dell'Archivo Paleografico Italiano*, 3rd ser., I (1962), 39–83; G. Battelli, "'Membra disiecta' di Registri pontifici dei secoli XIII e XIV," *Mélanges Eugène Tisserant*, Vol. IV, Studi e Testi, CCXXXIV (1964), 6 f.

217. *BF*, II, 3 f./2.

218. *Summa summi artificis* (*ibid.*, 1–3/1; cf. note d, p. 4).

219. *Ibid.*, 32–36/43. For general résumés of the battle under Alexander, see Tenckhoff, *Papst Alexander IV*, pp. 294–305; A. Koperska, *Die Stellung der religiösen Orden zu den Profanwissenschaften im 12. und 13. Jahrhundert* (Fribourg, 1914), pp. 135–177; Mann, *Lives of the Popes*, XV, 102–114; A. van den Wyngaert, "Querelles du clergé séculier et des Ordres Mendiants à l'Université de Paris au XIIIᵉ siècle," *FrFranc*, V (1922), 382–389; D. L. Douie, *The Conflict between the Seculars and the Mendicants at the University of Paris in the*

university crisis with great clarity, and discloses certain features of the contested seating of the two Dominican lectors, Elias and "Bonushomo," on which other sources are silent. The revelation that as late as August, 1254, Innocent was still inclined to take the mendicant side is of special interest, for that lingering partiality kicked up such a storm of protest at Paris that the pope was forced to reconsider, and to have the bishops of Senlis and Evreux summon both parties to further audiences at the Curia; but he died before the verdict was in. Alexander, acting from his *plenitudo potestatis*,[220] now decreed that some modification in the university statutes was imperative, chiefly in the matter of licensing masters: not only their competence as teachers, but also "the condition and necessity of the Church, and the spiritual health of the people" ought to be reckoned with. Though he reinstated Elias and Bonushomo, Alexander left intact the university's rights of examination and suspending lectures,[221] and to that extent at least *Quasi lignum vitae* was hardly the menacing juggernaut the masters soon made it out to be.

But so heated was the Paris atmosphere that even the reinstatement of the two Dominicans was intolerable. The masters, with their previous proctor at Anagni, William of St.-Amour, again at their head, wrote the pope on October 2 that the terms of *Quasi lignum vitae* were unacceptable in the extreme; that "the wood of life . . . is made for us the wood of death"; and that rather than treat the friars as equals, they were disbanding the university altogether.[222]

Three weeks later—perhaps just enough time for the masters' ultimatum to reach him at Anagni—Alexander denounced the *Introduction to the Everlasting Gospel*, the *libellus* which had provided the pretext for William's trip to the Curia in the summer of 1254.[223] On the basis of a negative report by three cardinals (including one Dominican, Hugues de St.-Cher, and Eudes de Châteauroux, who had strong ties to the university

---

Thirteenth Century, Aquinas Society, XXIII (London, 1949), 10–16; Sibilia, *Alessandro IV*, pp. 203–249; G. Leff, *Paris and Oxford Universities in the Thirteenth and Fourteenth Centuries* (New York, 1968), pp. 42–47; Pellegrini, *Alessandro IV e i Francescani*, p. 35 n. (good bibliography).

220. The phrase actually appears in a letter sent the same day to the bishops of Orléans and Autun: *Controversiam dudum* (De Latera, *Supplementum*, 52–54/3).

221. *Controversiam dudum*, to the theology masters, also on April 14 (*ibid.*, 54 f./4).

222. Denifle-Chatelain, *CUP* I, 292–97/256. Cf. Glorieux, *Répertoire des Maîtres en Théologie de Paris au XIII*ᵉ *siècle*, Vol. I (Paris, 1933), 14.

223. *Libellum quemdam*, October 23, and November 4, 1255 (De Latera, *Supplementum*, 69–72/12 f.). Stiffer measures against those who kept copies of the *Introduction* are enjoined in *Licet super quodam*, May 8, 1256 (*ibid.*, 85 f./21).

but was known also for his liking of the new orders[224]), submitted on July 8, the bishop of Paris was told to fix a terminal date for the abolition of the work in its entirety. By then, the author had been identified: he was a Friar Minor, Gerardo di Borgo San Donnino.[225] (Salimbene knew Gerardo, who had gone with John of Parma to Nymphaion in 1249; he also claimed to have read the *Introduction*, finding it a distasteful burlesque of Joachim's philosophy.[226]) Essentially the judgment of the commission, which had taken great pains to check the manuscript of the abbot's work against Gerardo's commentary and even to call in two learned Dominicans to testify, concurred with Salimbene's view that Gerardo "fabricates these novel and erroneous opinions, and it is owing to the greatest vainglory, that he exalts the Order in this manner, unbelievably and immoderately, above the others, nay even above the whole Church."[227]

This gesture, while it did not bear on the status of the mendicants at the university, sufficiently mollified the masters to lead them to accept the mediation of four ranking French prelates, and on March 1, 1256, a compromise solution was arrived at. The Dominicans could stay, but they could exercise only a limited role in university government.[228] Tragically unaware of this settlement, Alexander wrote most intemperately on March 3 that several of the masters "are amused at being called not peace-bringers, but sowers of scandal; not sons of the Lord, but of Satan." Reynaud, the harried bishop of Paris, was forthwith to excommunicate any masters who showed the least sign of persisting in their vendetta against the Dominicans.[229]

Before March 3, the situation at Paris was on the way to *détente*. After that date, an amicable agreement was no longer possible. The masters had no real option except to denounce the truce of March 1, seeing that the pope had cut the ground out from under the feet of his subordinates.

224. See the sermons cited in notes 23 and 176, *supra*.

225. William had taxed an anonymous Dominican with its authorship: A. van den Wyngaert, "Querelles du clergé séculier," p. 381.

226. Salimbene, *Cronica*, 454. What is known of Gerardo's career is given in I. Affò, *Memorie degli scrittori e letterati parmigiani*, Vol. I (Parma, 1789), 146–153.

227. H. Denifle, "Das Evangelium aeternum und die Commission zu Anagni," *ALKG*, I (1885), 115. The text of the protocol, edited from six manuscripts, takes up pp. 99–142. In all fairness it ought to be noted that the matter was somewhat prejudged by an earlier condemnation at Paris: the secular masters had found thirty-one "grave errors" in its doctrines in 1254 (text in Matthew Paris, *Chronica Majora*, VI, 335–339).

228. Denifle-Chatelain, *CUP* I, 304 f./268. One of the four archbishops was Eudes Rigaud, OM, of Rouen; the most-studied friar-prelate of the century. (The others were Philip, Bourges; Thomas, Reims; and Henry, Sens.)

229. *De quibusdam magistris* (De Latera, *Supplementum*, 74 f./16).

Henceforth, Alexander seemed incapable of moderation or detachment,[230] and cultivated a peculiar bitterness toward William of St.-Amour. He failed in his own mind to observe a distinction between the masters' grievances and the discomfiture of the secular clergy throughout France[231] —an analytical separation absolutely essential for the peaceful untangling of both issues.

Two papal letters which followed in the next six weeks amply demonstrated Alexander's unreasoning instinctual reactions. Because of clerical antagonism, he lamented, the Dominicans scarcely dared venture outside their cloisters, and Reynaud, who already had his hands full with the university mess, had perforce to quash this widespread hostility.[232] Because the well-being of the entire realm was endangered by the clerics' disgruntlement, Louis himself must now concert his energies with the bishop's to put it down.[233] The abbot of Saint-Maur-les-Fossées, who had no connection with the university at all, was commanded on May 5 to supervise the execution of his directives by Bishop Reynaud[234]—but how was that going to square with Louis?

The full measure of Alexander's spleen is painfully visible in *Cunctis processibus*, June 17, 1256.[235] William, he loftily declares, may no longer teach theology anywhere, and he, along with the other leaders of the masters' rebellion, must leave France at once. Gerardo, who had made a monumental fool of himself, cast opprobrium on his order, and gratuitously offended many leading intellectuals of the day, was simply and quietly incarcerated by his order[236]—and that only after the most

230. Cf. F. Bruys, *Histoire des Papes, depuis S. Pierre jusqu'à Benoît XIII* . . . , Vol. III (The Hague, 1733), 227: "C'étoit Alexandre IV qui causoit tous ces violens chagrins à l'Université par sa conduite tyrannique, & par la protection déraisonnable qu'il accordait aux Moines Mendians."

231. He had reason, if not justification, for begrudging them a fair hearing on their own account: besides their resistance to mendicant preaching, confessing, sepulture, and building, a number of abbots and other prelates were refusing to reveal the condition of their houses and chapters to visiting bishops (*Ad audientiam nostram*, March 26, 1256 [Bourel de la Roncière, *Reg*, I, 396/1324]). But this was an old problem; visitation difficulties had long existed in the provinces of Reims, Sens, and Rouen.

232. *Dilecti filii fratres*, March 30, 1256 (De Latera, *Supplementum*, 75 f./17).

233. *Dilecti filii fratres*, April 12 (*ibid.*, 77–81/18).

234. *Cum sicut venerabilis* (*ibid.*, 84 f./20). Cf. *Vehementi admiratione ducimur* (a telltale *initium*!), July 1, in which the Domicans are urged to enroll any students who come to their school—a further slap at the *consortium* (*ibid.*, 92 f./23).

235. *Ibid.*, 86–92/22.

236. On Gerardo's continuing truculence which led to his confinement, see Salimbene, *Cronica*, pp. 237 f.

strenuous efforts to salvage his ephemeral reputation. William, a man of real stature, was guilty only of an overbold desire to defend the ancient rights of the secular hierarchy, and for that he was summarily exiled, in the full light of day, to perpetual oblivion.

The trouble was, of course, that William did not content himself merely with a campaign against the very real incursions by the mendicants into the university and the diocesan and parochial preserves. He preached openly against the panhandling of the friars: for him it was far more respectable to belong to a convent with property in common, to work for a living, or to get a benefice. The tertiaries, he added, were a disgrace to their social origins, dressing like paupers and affronting civilized men[237] Because monks were by Gratian's definition "solitaries and quiet people and [ought to] dwell in their cloister[s] and keep silence," and because he could not imagine the friars as being anything other than aberrant monks, they had no business preaching to the masses, even with papal endorsement.[238] Before a sympathetic audience of seventeen French bishops, meeting at Paris on July 31, 1256,[239] he hinted that a general council might take up the matter,[240] but Alexander, naturally, could not entertain that explosive notion for an instant. He averred that popes could and did err[241]—and on the most elementary logic, either *Etsi animarum* or *Nec insolitum* was in error. But to inflate the latter observation into a general law, applicable to future as well as past pronouncements, was flirting with heresy. In short, William's polemical dagger struck too close

---

237. S. Clasen, "Die Kampfpredigten des Wilhelm von Saint-Amour gegen die Mendikantenorden," in *Kirchengeschichtliche Studien P. Michael Bihl OFM als Ehrengabe dargebracht*, ed. I.-M. Freudenreich (Colmar, 1941), pp. 82 f.

238. M. Peuchmaurd, "Mission canonique et prédication. Le prêtre ministre de la parole dans le quérelle entre Mendiants et séculiers au XIIIe siècle," *Recherches de Théologie ancienne et médiévale*, XXX (1963), 125–128.

239. A month and a half after Alexander had required that he leave France. He was thus already under a dark cloud; but the French prelates, who appreciated his yeoman service for their cause at Anagni, were very reluctant to aid in implementing the papal decree.

240. Y.-M. Congar, "Aspects ecclésiologiques de la quérelle entre Mendiants et séculiers dans la seconde moitié du XIIIe siècle et la début du XIVe," *Archives d'Histoire doctrinale et littéraire du moyen âge*, XXXVI (1961), 53 f. Cf. Glorieux, *Répertoire*, I, 343, on William's other hearings before French bishops; most are not recorded in J. D. Mansi, *Sacrorum conciliorum nova et amplissima collectio* . . . .

241. J. Ratzinger, "Der Einfluss des Bettelordensstreites auf die Entwicklung der Lehre vom päpstlichen Universalprimat, unter besonderer Berücksichtigung des heiligen Bonaventura," in *Theologie in Geschichte und Gegenwart: Michael Schmaus zum sechzigsten Geburtstag* (Munich, 1957), pp. 707 f.

to the heart of the problem. Other critics of papal favor toward the mendicants lived in those days, to be sure, and some, like Matthew Paris, Ruteboeuf, and Freidank, did not hesitate to put their acid pens to work in the name of local autonomy and the older traditions. But none offered such an easy mark as William.

The unkindest cut of all came on October 5, 1256, when William's *Short Treatise on the Perils of the Most Recent Times*[242] was condemned at Anagni.[243] Again a commission of cardinals had deliberated on its merits; this time, however, there was little attempt to encourage any strong arguments in favor of the work. Hugues de St.-Cher, John Gaetano Orsini (future cardinal-protector of the order), and Eudes de Châteauroux were all predisposed against William; only John of Toledo, cardinal priest of San Lorenzo, was plausibly neutral, and even he was a Cistercian. Albertus Magnus, Thomas Aquinas (who had already written a diatribe against William[244]), the Dominican master general, Humbert of Romans (who had faced William at the synod of July 31), and John of Parma all testified for the prosecution,[245] while William himself had only his own wit and ingenuity to sustain him.[246] That was not enough. Although he fingered a disturbing amount of distortion and misrepresentation of his work, repeating time and again that he had not said in his sermons or elsewhere what his detractors accused him of saying, it did his cause no good.[247] Anyone who refused by October 13 to surrender his copy of the *Treatise* to be burnt, or who dared in any way to represent the book favorably, was subject to immediate excommunication and the

242. William of St.-Amour, *Opera omnia* (Coutances, 1632), 17–72.

243. *Romanus Pontifex* (*BF*, II, 160–62/241). Cf. F. X. Seppelt, "Der Kampf der Bettelorden an der Universität Paris in der Mitte des 13. Jahrhunderts," *Kirchengeschichtliche Abhandlungen*, IV (1906), 127 f.

244. Glorieux, "Le 'Contra Impugnantes' de S. Thomas: ses sources—son plan," in *Mélanges Mandonnet : Etudes d'histoire littéraire et doctrinale du Moyen Âge*, Vol. I (Paris, 1930), 51–81.

245. Seppelt, *loc. cit.*

246. E. Faral, "Les 'Responsiones' de Guillaume de Saint-Amour," *Archives d'Histoire doctrinale et littéraire du Moyen Âge*, XXV–XXVI (1950–51), 337–394.

247. All the same, he must have scored minor hits with his pervasive reliance on Scripture, in much the same way that Wyclyf, Huso, and Luther would make their interrogators squirm in later centuries. Reporting a conversation with Louis, he said at Anagni: "dixi quod, cum non haberem mitram, nec anulum, nec auctoritatem, per quem mihi crederetur, idcirco attuleram libros Sacrae Scripturae ad probandam veritatem quam praedicaveram de periculis novissimorum temporum. Sed per Dei gratiam nullus mihi ibi se opposuit, nec libros oportuit aperiri" (*ibid.*, p. 354).

deprivation of Christian company, and "to be deemed . . . contumacious, disloyal and a rebel against the Roman Church."

The engine of repression accelerated now almost geometrically. First Louis, whose agents had initially apprised Alexander of the *Treatise*, and then Eudes Rigaud (the Minorite archbishop of Rouen and former regent-master in theology at the Franciscan school in Paris), Reynaud, and the archbishop of Tours, and finally all the prelates in France and dependent regions were advised of William's reprobate status and ordered to protect the mendicants from all abuse.[248]

Paris continued sullen for the remainder of Alexander's pontificate. No amount of papal badgering could entirely stamp out William's forbidden *Treatise*, or eradicate his sympathizers.[249] William himself, banished from Paris, but living quietly at his native town in the Franche-Comté, where he died in 1272,[250] did not stop writing against the friars. Louis, rarely harsh in cases of the faith, even asked the pope at one point if the brilliant master might not be permitted back: "since a veritable[251] multitude of Paris students are exiles on his account."[252]

Some idea of the impact of the *Treatise* on the Paris scene may be inferred from the long chain of hostile polemics and *pièces justificatives* it occasioned. Aquinas, Bonaventure, Thomas of York, and Gérard d'Abbeville—to name only those whose identity has been confirmed—sharpened their theological axes on each other's literary grindstones through the 1250s and 1260s.[253] The next generation of combatants included such

248. *Veri solis radius*, October 17; *Non sine multa*, October 19, 21; *Romanus Pontifex*, October 21 (*BF*, II, 163–66/243–46; De Latera, *Supplementum*, 97–100/26). Cf. *Quidam Scripture sacre* (the likely *initium*), March 30, 1257, to all patriarchs, archbishops, and bishops (*BF*, II, 211/321).

249. All the bulls, too numerous to identify in detail here, are in *BF*, II: 170–72/251, 209–11/319 f., 227 f./344, 233 f./341, 235 f./354, 237/357, 332 f./480, 352 f./497, 354–57/498–500, 410/585.

250. E. Aegerter, "L'affaire du *De Periculis novissimorum Temporum*," *Revue de l'Histoire des Religions*, CXII (1935), 270.

251. The text has *venerabilis*, clearly a mistake.

252. Denifle-Chatelain, *CUP* I, 405/357; they tentatively assign the letter to 1259. Cf. *Cum propter multiplices*, August 9, 1257, to William "in bonum dirigere gressus suos" (*BF*, II, 235/353). Cf. also C. Thouzellier, "La Place du *De Periculis* de Guillaume de Saint-Amour dans les polémiques universitaires du XIIIᵉ siècle," *Revue historique*, CLVI (1927), 83; M. Perrod, *Étude sur la vie et sur les oeuvres de Guillaume de Saint-Amour Docteur en théologie de l'Université de Paris Chanoine de Beauvais et de Mâcon (1202–1272)*, (Lons-le-Saunier, 1902), pp. 95–126.

253. J. H. Sbaralea and A. Nardecchia, *Supplementum . . . ad Scriptores*, 3 vols. (Rome, 1935), III, 126; S. Clasen, "Tractatus Gerardi de Abbatisvilla 'Contra Adversarium

diverse figures as John Pecham, Robert Kilwardby, Guillaume de Mâcon, and Henry of Ghent.[254] As late as 1633, upon the first publication of William's *Opera omnia*, reactionary monks managed to persuade the royal council at Paris to decree the death penalty for anyone caught selling the book![255]

The questions raised and the answers thrust forward during those crowded years constitute a fascinating and vital chapter in the history of ideas. Innocent, had he lived long enough, might have forestalled it all by a durable compromise growing out of his evenhanded *Etsi animarum*; Alexander, by taking sides and venting his personal feelings on a misunderstood opposition, rendered certain the prolongation of the dispute for decades after he had left the stage. To say, as does one of the authors of *Le Liber Pontificalis*, that "he squelched two pestiferous bits of special pleading"—meaning the *Introduction* and the *Treatise*—tells much less than half the story.[256]

---

perfectionis Christianae,'" *AFH*, XXXI (1938), 276–329; XXXII (1939), 89–200; *Der hl. Bonaventure und das Mendikantentum. Ein Beitrag zur Ideengeschichte des Pariser Mendikantenstreits (1252–72)*, Franziskanische Forschungen, VII (Werl-in-Westphalia, 1940); Glorieux, *Répertoire* I, 356–360; A. Teetaert, "Quatre questions inédites de Gérard d'Abbeville pour la défence de la superiorité du clergé séculier," *Archivio Italiano per la Storia della Pietà*, I (1951), 83–178; J. de Vinck (ed.), *The Works of Bonaventure, Cardinal, Seraphic Doctor and Saint*, Vol. IV: *Defense of the Mendicants* (Patterson, N.J., 1966); G. Leff, *Heresy in the Later Middle Ages: The Relation of Heterodoxy to Dissent c. 1250–c. 1450*, Vol. I (Manchester, 1967), 84–97; F. Hirschenauer, *Die Stellung des hl. Thomas von Aquin im Mendikanterstreit an der Universität Paris* (St. Ottilien, 1934). A useful diagram of the interrelationship of the various tracts appears in Van den Wyngaert, "Querelles du clergé séculier," p. 397; the only conspicuous error is the ascription of *Manus que contra Omnipotentem* to Bertrand de Bayonne rather than Thomas of York.

254. C. L. Kingsford, A. G. Little, and F. Tocco, *Fratris Johannis Pecham . . . Tractatus tres de Paupertate*, BSFS, II (Aberdeen, 1910). Van den Wyngaert, "Querelles du clergé séculier," p. 257 n., remarks that this edition omits chapters 1–6 and 13–14. See also Sbaralea and Nardecchia, *Supplementum . . . ad Scriptores*, II, 111–114; Little, "Measures Taken by the Prelates of France against the Friars (c. A.D. 1289–1290)," in *Miscellanea Francesco Ehrle . . .* , III, Studi e Testi, XXXIX (1924), 49–66. A lighter note was struck at the Synod of Orléans in 1287, when the friars were gently told that bishops and priests were "adequate for the pastoral care of the Christian lands, and . . . religious were better off preaching to the infidels" (Congar, "Aspects ecclésiologiques," p. 57). Many French diocesan synods of the two decades following Alexander's death in 1261, however, were quite bitter about the favors and dispensations that still flowed to the mendicants in a steady stream (Van den Wyngaert, "Querelles du clergé séculier," pp. 275 f.).

255. Aegerter, "L'affaire du *De Periculis*," p. 243.

256. L. Duchesne (ed.), *Le Liber Pontificalis: Texte, Introduction et Commentaire*, Vol. II (Paris, 1955), 455. Salimbene, *Cronica*, p. 454, uses a very similar phrase.

ALEXANDER'S PRIVILEGES TO THE ORDER

By December, 1254, if we ignore *Etsi animarum*, the Friars Minor had basked in the mild climate of apostolic favor for more than forty years. "Ask and it shall be given you, seek and ye shall find" had subtly superseded the ethic of humility and work fostered by Francis. For this state of affairs two factors were at bottom responsible: the ever-insistent immediate needs of a papacy simultaneously geared to tradition and to emergencies; and the natural tendency of an institutionalized revolution to lose first of all those elements which had made it revolutionary at the outset. To put the proposition in these impersonal terms is, of course, an oversimplification. Men with unique experiences, ideals, and ambitions animated the process and guided it through channels they had dug themselves. But the ground they excavated did not always yield to their will. All too often they struck sparks from the bedrock of the historical church itself, and had to devise other means of bringing their present experiments into the desired haven. The fact is that the mendicant orders, as they were designed and launched by Francis and Dominic, were too heavily freighted with privilege, and sooner or later had to run aground. To ballast the new craft, concession was piled on concession, exemption on exemption—not with the intention of obscuring the original simple virtues of the orders, but, the popes thought, to exhibit them more visibly to the world. We cannot linger now to unveil the deeper enigmas of purpose and motivation; suffice it to say that Alexander, because he so loved the friars, was even less capable of realizing the injury he was doing them by showering them with chancery largesse than were Gregory IX and Innocent IV before him.

We have just witnessed the vigorous tactics employed by Alexander in the complex quarrel focused at Paris. Undeniably the Dominicans figured more prominently in its beginnings, but the Friars Minor soon waded out just as far in the intellectual exchanges, and were lumped together with the sons of Dominic in the broadsides of the seculars. Alexander, once he had resolved to stick to his position in *De quibusdam magistris*, had therefore not only to shelter the Dominicans at the university with new privileges, but also the Franciscans. He chose to do so in a rather roundabout fashion. The brethren who had attained the rank of *lectores* in the order's convents, he decreed on March 28, 1257, might read and teach in any theological faculty without further license—except at the *studia generalia*, where a degree was mandatory.[257] Paris, of course, was a *studium generale*, and at first glance would not appear to be affected by this edict. Nor is there any allusion in the letter's text to the current battles. Yet the implication was obvious: if a *lector* had a degree, neither the *consortium* nor chancellor at Paris (i.e., of Notre Dame or Sainte-Geneviève) could rightfully bar him from teaching there. Bonaventure, just elected minister-general, was the prime recipient of *Exultante spiritu*, and was perfectly capable of drawing that conclusion himself.

The seraphic doctor, indeed, quickly built up an unprecedented rapport with Rome. True, Francis had maintained a strong tacit understanding with two popes and two (or three?) cardinal-protectors, but such intimate private arrangements were not feasible in the late 1250s. Bonaventure's accurate tuning to Alexander's wavelength led to his obtaining, on October 21, 1257, an extent of discretionary power over the order that went far beyond any previous commission, and stretched the language of the rule to its limits.[258] Briefly, these were the bull's terms: no friar could claim any privilege, indulgence, letter, mandate, or license from the Apostolic See without his consent; the pope confirmed in advance any punishment Bonaventure meted out to his underlings; any friar provided or elected to the episcopal dignity had to clear his new duties with the minister-general; he might excommunicate, suspend, or place under interdict persons with the same freedom as the papal penitentiaries. Each of these new rights, Alexander hoped, would broadcast the friars' good name: "so that the said Order under your governance may gloriously shine in its meritorious repute, we aim to apply every capacity and every effort that we can."

The formula *Nimis iniqua*, with which the popes commenced long lists of grievances suffered by the friars, was certainly not novel in Alexander's time. When he issued his version of this bull on April 3, 1258, however, it revealed both the new sharpness of the seculars' attacks on the order and his stubborn determination to defend it whatever the cost.[259] Detractors of the Franciscans had tried to force their burial in parochial cemeteries, to impose penance on individuals against the will of their superiors, to

257. *Exultante spiritu* (*BF*, II, 208/317). The provision concerning the *studia generalia* is perhaps a bit ambiguous, for the major schools of the order itself were sometimes so designated. (This privilege and many others are covered in Pellegrini, *Alessandro IV e i Francescani*, pp. 69–104; we will consequently review here only a few that are of central importance.)

258. *Ut ministerium tibi* (*BF*, II, 253 f./374).

259. De Latera, *Supplementum*, 114 f./33.

forbid them to celebrate mass in their own churches, to tax their movables, to intrude priests into their public ritual, and to collect for themselves the offerings at the friars' services. They had excommunicated lay benefactors of the order, and hounded the friars out of their own newly constructed convents. To these atrocities Alexander answered that he, like Innocent III, Honorius, Gregory, and Innocent IV, cherished the Friars Minor:

> . . . your religion, which is so exceedingly deserving, ought that much more to stand out by the prerogative of favor and special grace, and to be privileged and immune in all the aforesaid things, [which] we strictly abolish by the authority of these presents, lest further injuries be inflicted upon you in this wise by these prelates, or their subordinates . . . .

Once again Alexander's categorical refusal to admit that perhaps some of the friars had overstepped the bounds of propriety and could stand some remedial discipline does him no credit.

The most memorable privilege of Alexander's pontificate was *Virtute conspicuos*, August 2, 1258.[260] Who first called it a "great sea" we have no idea; it may even have been an enemy of the order. But by Salimbene's time the term was in common use.[261] It is an apt description: the most casual examination of the text will instantly expose its omnibus character. No less than thirty-three separate issues find here a definitive summary and solution. Everything from the hoary problems of the portable altar and the right to conduct mass in times of interdict to the more recent matters of caring for the Clares and the right to refuse *commissiones causae* passes in review, and virtually without exception Alexander's rulings incorporate and synthesize earlier legislation.[262] The only really new provision concerns the service of friars to prelates or legates: anyone so employed, including crusade preachers, might now freely be recalled or substituted for by the ministers, and the minister-general could prescribe ecclesiastical censure for those friars who bucked their command. *Virtute conspicuos* was not, like *Quo elongati* or *Ordinem vestrum*,[263] a commentary on the rule; it was rather more like *Nimis iniqua*, in that it stressed the sheltered autonomy of the order from secular imposition, and lauded the

260. *BF*, II, 298–303/436.

261. Salimbene, *Cronica*, p. 453: "Ordini fratrum Minorum privilegium, quod Mare magnum appellatur, dedit."

262. The exact references appear in Sbaralea's notes, *BF*, II, 298–303.

263. November 14, 1245 (*BF*, I, 400–402/114).

great virtues of the new institute. It would remain for many years the high-water mark of papal preference and is one of the reasons for identifying the end of Alexander's pontificate as a convenient terminus for the present study.

CONCLUSION

From the preceding survey we may establish several facts about the first three (or four?) cardinal-protectors of the Franciscan order; much still remains in suspense. All were drawn to the job by a deep sympathy with what they took to be the special virtues of the order. Nevertheless there were vital differences among them in the approaches they took to their work with the order.

John of St. Paul was unobtrusive but available as an informal middleman, and he may have sensed better than any of his successors Francis's reluctance to institutionalize the order. Yet in fairness to them it must be said that by 1217, when Francis met Hugolino at Florence, the inner dynamic of the movement had impelled the friars to organize and structure their enterprise to a far greater degree than the founder could have foreseen in 1210. Hugolino, after that encounter, would apply to the new brotherhood a mind accustomed to the old categories of religious life; as Gregory IX he continued, for example in *Quo elongati* and *Nimis iniqua*, to shape it more and more along conventional lines. We cannot indeed at any point ignore the guiding hand of the papacy as a separate factor in the equation; only with Alexander IV do the purposes of the cardinal-protector and the Apostolic See coincide in the same person. Rainaldo da Segni, initially guided by his uncle in the discharge of his duties to the order and the Clares, gradually grew into the office, and under Innocent IV he was involved in a range of responsibilities as protector that widened as his other ecclesiastical functions diminished. His harsh dealings with the secular masters at Paris and with hostility to the friars in other quarters grew from his one sure belief: that privilege and favor to the order was the only way to preserve it from the ills of the day. Bonaventure, whose generalate overlapped four years of Alexander's pontificate, certainly shared this conviction. John of Parma before him had not, and this may explain to some degree both the moderation of *Etsi animarum*—John was an intimate acquaintance of Innocent IV, and may well have urged him to see matters somewhat as William of St.-Amour pictured them—and the unceremonious ousting of John in 1257 by the lax party.

Finally, the evolution of the office of cardinal-protector was largely determined in its direction by the challenge offered lay society and the church alike by Franciscan poverty and zeal for a renewal of life in Christ. That challenge was almost immediately turned by the Curia to its own ends, and thereby transformed almost beyond recognition. Its primary instrument in effecting this transformation was, in the broadest sense, government; and although the most conspicuous source of government in the church and over the order was the papacy, the papacy found the cardinal-protector to be an essential subordinate in sifting through the great mass of the order's business and passing on for Roman adjudication only the gravest or most puzzling dilemmas of Assisi. But Francis did not govern, he exemplified—and therein lay his revolutionary uniqueness. Few minister-generals and no cardinal-protectors—who did govern— exemplified the living priorities of Francis. No cardinal-protector in our period was a member of the order; all had, however, previously associated themselves with other observances—John had been an abbot; Hugolino a great supporter of Joachimites, Benedictines, and Cistercians; and Rainaldo a secular canon. All three had risen high in the Curia and wielded authority as an integral part of their spiritual and political functions. But Francis, despite his deference to monks, priests, and all churchly authority, still wrote a *regula primitiva* unlike any other, and claimed to act authoritatively only through the mediation of Christian example. For Francis the power to move men might lie in the heaping of ashes on one's head, or in dancing from an excess of inspiration in the piazza of Bologna; always the greatest power lay in the transformation of self. For the church and its administrators, including pre-eminently the cardinal-protectors, and soon enough too for the chief officials of the order itself, power was none of these things, and yet remained the single *sine qua non* of survival.

APPENDIX
INTERPRETATIONS OF THE OFFICE

John of St. Paul was informally designated by Innocent III to serve as the protector of the new order's interests in the Curia. Historians have thus far found no previous analogue to this designation, although from time to time Cistercians or Cluniacs who attained the cardinalitial dignity may have interceded on their order's behalf in curial litigation, and Leo Brancaleone seems to have enjoyed a comparable position as *gubernator* of the Poor Catholics a few years later.[1] Yet John was still the first, and it is on this account rather surprising to find that so few attempts have been made to analyze the exact nature of the cardinal-protector's office and duties.[2] Some justification for this neglect lies in the nature of our sources. Without exception the early biographers speak only in the most general terms of the work done by John, Hugolino, and Rainaldo, who between them filled the post for just over half a century. Only with the advent of

1. C. Thouzellier, *Une Somme Anti-Cathare. Le Liber Contra Manicheos de Durand de Huesca*, Spicilegium Sacrum Lovaniense, XXXII (Louvain, 1964), 36–38.

2. The first such study was written by Philip of Perugia in the form of a letter to Gonsalvo, minister-general of the order from 1304 to 1313. It is edited as Appendix III to Holder-Egger's edition of Salimbene's *Cronica*, *MGH. SS.*, XXXII, 678–684. Oddly enough Philip makes no mention of Cardinal John. (For his other works and a thumbnail *vita*, see Sbaralea and Nardecchia, *Supplementum . . . ad Scriptores*, II, 382 f.) The essay by D. de Gubernatis a Sospitello, "De eminentissimo Cardinali Ordinis Protectore" (in his *Orbis Seraphicus*, I, 490–508), is still important and has not in some respects been superseded. The brief essay in G. Piatti and G. Tria, *De Cardinalis Dignitate, et Officio*: (Rome, 1746), 423–429, is markedly unhistorical.

Among the more recent examinations of this vital link between Rome and Assisi, we should single out B. Melata, *De Cardinali Protectore*, Ex Bibliotheca Romane ephemerides Analecta ecclesiastica, XVII (1902); Gratien, *Histoire de la Fondation*, pp. 532–536; L.-R. Misserez, "Cardinal-Protecteur," *DDC*, II (1937), cols. 1339–1344; B. da Siena, *Il Cardinale protettore*, bibliographical note 9, and rundown on the protectors of other orders, 1229–89, pp. 36 f.; S. L. Forte, *The Cardinal-Protector of the Dominican Order*, *DissHistIHFP*, XV (Rome, 1965). I have not seen the unpublished Paris dissertation (1938) by J. G. d'Eysden, "Les cardinaux Protecteurs des Instituts religieux (des origines à Grégoire XI—1373)," cited in L. Pellegrini, *Alessandro IV e i Francescani*, p. 39 n. The long study by F. Roth, "Cardinal Richard Annibaldi, First Protector of the Augustinian Order, 1243–1276," *Augustinianum* 2 (1952), 26–60, 108–149, 230–247; 3 (1953), 21–34, 183–313; 4 (1954), 5–24, has little bearing on the present study, save that Cardinal Richard's duties, as explained to him by Pope Alexander, were to be similar to those of the Protector of the Franciscans—Alexander himself.

John Gaetano Orsini between 1261 and 1263 [3] is it possible to reconstruct a detailed record of the activities of the protectorate. Neither in the rule of the order [4] nor in the statutes of the church [5] were his obligations spelled out in any but the broadest of categories.

In many ways the growth of the office paralleled the growth of the order itself. Pragmatism and flexibility were its most salient features. When the demands of the order on the cardinal-protector multiplied, he responded by systematizing the indulgences and privileges which he issued, and in turn the petitions sent to him took on a more standard appearance. [6]

3. *Beata Clara*, October 18, 1263 (*BF*, II, 509–21/98), mentions that he was already the order's protector, and would now be given charge of the Clares as well.

4. Chapter 12 (*BF*, I, 14/18): "Ad hec per obedientiam iniungo ministris, ut petant a domino Papa unum de Sancte Romane Ecclesia cardinalibus, qui sit *gubernator, protector et corrector* istius fraternitatis, ut semper subditi et subiecti pedibus eiusdem sancte Ecclesie, stabiles in fide catholica, paupertatem et humilitatem et sanctum evangelium domini nostri Iesu Christi, quod firmiter promissimus, obseremus" (italics mine).

Kybal, *Die Ordensregeln*, p. 81, remarks that this entire section had no precedent in the *Regula non bullata* of 1221. It was thus a late provision, but hardly an afterthought, as there was undoubtedly a real need by this time to define the constitutional relationship of the protector to the order. Of some interest is the fact that the "Four Masters," in their *Expositio super Regulam Fratrum Minorum*, ed. L. Oliger (Rome, 1950), p. 168, saw no reason to gloss this chapter at all, despite its diffuseness. They end their account with the words: "Super hiis igitur et quae omissa restant, vestra discretione [i.e., Haymo of Faversham's] provident qualiter ad conscientiarum securitatem et utilitatem ordinis per sedem apostolicam disponatur. Valete in Domino." (Another old, unidentified commentary, which did touch "gubernator, protector et corrector," appears in Melata, *De Cardinali Protectore*, p. 9 n. See also Bonaventure, "Expositio super Regulam Fratrum Minorum," in *Opera Omnia*, VIII [Quaracchi, 1898], 436.)

5. Innocent IV, in *Ordinem Vestrum*, November 14, 1245 (*BF*, I, 400–402/114), saw no compelling need to go beyond what the rule stated explicitly in chapter 12, though he commented ten other chapters, and did allude very briefly to the cardinal-protector in his exposition of chapter 7. De Gubernatis, *Orbis Seraphicus*, I, 490, indicated that even in the late seventeenth century canon law still had not taken cognizance of the office: ". . . nulli iure tacendum esse, mihi videtur." In practice, however, definite limits to his jurisdiction had been set since the late fourteenth century, by which time almost every order had a highly placed advocate at the Curia. (Cf. *Cunctos Christifideles*, May 27, 1373: text in *BF*, VI, 504–508/1268, and B. da Siena, *Il Cardinale protettore*, pp. 162–164.) See also Misserez, "Cardinal-Protecteur," col. 1340; Forte, *The Cardinal-Protector of the Dominican Order*, p. 10. For his position today, see P. F. Schreiber, *Canonical Precedence*, *CUA Studies*, CDVIII (1961), 123.

6. Cf. de Luca, "Un formulario della cancelleria francescana, e altri formulari tra il XIII e XIV secolo," *Archivio italiano per la Storia della Pietà*, I (1951), p. 250 (I, 61): the formula for a Clare abbess in asking his help "pro aliquo enormi casu, qui in suo monasterio contigit"; *ibid.*, p. 251 (I, 62): how to ask a cardinal, "amico ordinis" (not necessarily the protector!), to speed the case of a patron of the order through the Curia; *ibid.*,

What do the authors who have dealt with this question have to say about the functions of the cardinal-protector? Philip of Perugia lists three reasons why Francis besought the pope (Honorius, in 1220) to give him Hugolino:

> The first I have heard from the old fathers. It is that when for some reason the friars should need to have recourse to the Apostolic See, and the status and smallness of the brotherhood should prevent them from having easy access to the pope, he wished that one cardinal might be assigned to the Order, whom the friars might approach on occasion, almost as a vicar of the pope. Another reason, which I heard from Lord John Gaetani, before he became pope, and when he had the care of the Order, was this: We ought to speak instead of the poverty of the Order, which saves the friars from all ownership and the right over temporal things. Then he said: "The blessed Francis acted most wisely in desiring that the Order should have a leader outside its membership (*unum caput extra se*), who would have power over temporals, and whose proper function it would be to supervise the use of things by the Order (*quo quasi mediante usus rerum ordini conveniret*)." And this assertion is confirmed by that chapter of the Rule's explication: "Because indeed the ownership of books . . ." and so on, where the institution of a procurator by the Cardinal is discussed. The third reason is that which appears in the Rule: "That always obedient and subject . . . ," and so forth.[7]

D. De Gubernatis, in a brief commentary on chapter 12 of the *Regula bullata*, has this to say:

> In these three instances, that is as Apostolic Deputy, Vicar-Delegate, and *locumtenens* of the pope they could legally correct the Order, and intervene in its government, from the very beginning of their office:

---

p. 254 (I, 80): on the proper style of address for a *visitator* of the Clares requesting the protector's approval of someone seeking entrance into a particular convent.

7. Philip of Perugia, "Epistola de Cardinalibus Protectoribus," p. 680. The reference to the "Rule's explication," Holder-Egger tells us, is really to the *Liber Sextus*; it was part of a decretal of Nicolas III, formerly Cardinal John Gaetani, Philip's chief source. Again it must be stressed that his analysis was written a century after the first cardinal-protector was appointed, and though it depends on an earlier oral tradition, it is still not free of anachronisms. The emphasis on supervision of material goods could hardly have applied to John or even to the early years of Hugolino's protectorate. Francis's own views of the office, which must be largely inferred, are set forth in B. da Siena, *Il Cardinale protettore*, pp. 41–43.

there is no indication of further authority which they were competent to exercise . . . .[8]

In reference to the office as it appeared later in the century, J. B. Sägmüller writes:

> It was now a matter of course, that in all of the more important cases the General of the Order and the heads of individual houses reported to the protector; he, however, passed on adjudication of the most difficult cases to the pope.[9]

And A. Quaglia, thoroughgoing in his discussion of other parts of the rule, says with regard to the cardinal-protector only that he had two functions: to stand in the pope's stead, and to serve as his legate for the affairs of the order.[10]

8. *Orbis Seraphicus* I, 494 f.
9. *Die Thätigkeit und Stellung der Kardinäle*, p. 113.
10. *L'originalità della Regola*, p. 145.

PLAN AND REALITY IN A MEDIEVAL MONASTIC ECONOMY: THE CISTERCIANS

Richard Roehl

University of California, Berkeley

PLAN AND REALITY IN A MEDIEVAL
MONASTIC ECONOMY: THE CISTERCIANS*

I. INTRODUCTION

Monks were the original historians of Europe's middle ages and, consistent with this tradition, medievalists have always devoted much of their attention to monks and monasticism. More than just the force of custom was operating, of course, for the written sources from this period—the historian's raw material—as often as not were produced by monks and deal with the affairs of the monastery. This situation has on occasion led to some distortion or overemphasis of the role assigned monasticism in medieval history; yet it is still correct to view western monasticism as having been intimately involved with the development of European civilization.

Not least with respect to economic matters is the history of medieval monasticism of importance. One need hardly be an economic determinist to recognize the influence which monasticism had upon the medieval economy, and vice versa.[1] It might appear rather perverse to accord much attention to the economic aspects of medieval monasticism, for the monks, professing a vow of poverty and withdrawing from traffic with other men, ought to have had little concern for economic activities. But even monks, for so long as they remained in this world, had to make some provision at least for their basic physical needs. And the pursuit of just this minimal goal could result in a significant impact on the European economy.[2]

The economic bases for the support of monastic life did not necessarily need to differ at all from those employed in lay society. In general, the operation of the monastic economy was indistinguishable from that of

1. As appears to be the view of one student of the subject, B. D. Hill, *English Cistercian Monasteries and their Patrons in the Twelfth Century* (Urbana, 1968), p. 9.

2. See J. A. Raftis, "Western Monasticism and Economic Organization," *Comparative Studies in Society and History*, III, No. 4 (July, 1961).

* This article was derived from the author's Ph.D. dissertation, Department of Economics, University of California, Berkeley, 1968. In addition to reaffirming the acknowledgments made there, I would like to express my gratitude for the detailed and very valuable comments from an anonymous referee for the *Studies*.

the secular estates.[3] The monasteries of the Cistercian order, however, are usually regarded as having constituted the singular major exception to this generalization. The present essay accepts the conventional assumption that the Cistercian interpretation of St. Benedict's rule implied a departure from the economic practices of contemporary monasticism; indeed, the position adopted here is somewhat stronger, i.e., that the Cistercian program embodied an identifiable economic plan.[4] The following section discusses the origins, specification, and economic implications of this plan. The question is then raised as to the extent to which the plan was actually realized in practice. Finally, some speculations and tentative conclusions are offered.

II. THE PLAN

The Cistercian order had its genesis in a movement of religious reform. The history of the order's beginnings has been often and well told, and requires no recitation here.[5] It is necessary, however, to establish the legitimacy of employing the characterization of "Cistercian economic plan," to differentiate in a meaningful way the Cistercian economy from other contemporary economic practices.

First, the reformers at Molesme and, subsequently, Cîteaux certainly did not conceive of themselves—initially at least—as the founders of a new monastic order, but rather as the upholders of the letter and the spirit of true Benedictine monasticism.[6] They argued that contemporary practice in monastic life had fallen away from the original purity of the rule, and they aimed simply to effect a restoration. In this sense the impulse was

3. *Ibid.*, p. 458.

4. The application of this concept to the study of medieval economic history was originated by C. M. Cipolla. See his note, "Questioni aperte sul sistema economico dell'alto medio evo," *Rivista Storica Italiana*, LXIII, No. 1 (1951). Also, cf. G. Murphy, "Buddhist Monastic Economy: The Jisa Mechanism," *Comparative Studies in Society and History*, III, No. 4 (July, 1961).

5. The standard reference is J.-B. Mahn, *L'Ordre Cistercien et son Gouvernement*, Bibliothèque des Écoles françaises d'Athènes et de Rome, CLXI (Paris, 1943).

6. E. Hoffmann, "Die Entwicklung der Wirtschaftsprinzipen im Cisterzienser Orden," *Historisches Jahrbuch*, XXXI (1910), 702; and W. A. Parker-Mason, "The Beginnings of the Cistercian Order," *Transactions of the Royal Historical Society*, N.S. XIX (1905), especially 201–202. This position is well stated in Book I, chap. 1 of Caesarius of Heisterbach, *Dialogue on Miracles*.

Giles Constable has warned against too easily identifying the Cistercian perception of pristine Benedictinism with the reality of the original form.

conservative, not revolutionary. But the execution of this intention implied revolution, for the first Cistercians located the root cause of the unsatisfactory state of monasticism in the economic forms upon which it rested. To recapture the pristine essence of St. Benedict's program it would be necessary to break cleanly and completely with these forms and to base monastic existence on an altogether different socioeconomic system. Monasticism had become too worldly and it had done so, in their view, precisely because its economic base was in the world, thus involving the monks themselves inexorably and inextricably with the world. In order to pursue the monastic vocation according to Benedict's ideal, absolute separation from secular society was essential, and this in turn meant that the economy of the monastery must be completely innocent of all mundane relationships. The point is that the Cistercian program of reform had intrinsic in it certain basic economic implications, and involved integrally a definable economic program.[7]

The Cistercian founders were very clear and unambiguous on this issue. While making no imputations as to the purity of other monks' faith, they nevertheless insisted that improper economic forms of necessity corrupted the practice; in their view, one of the most important causes of the fallen state in which monasticism then found itself was economic. It followed inevitably that correction of the situation required the establishment of other, different economic arrangements, and the founders at Cîteaux did not shrink from this conclusion. It is because of this explicit recognition that the documents from the period of the order's origin permit the delineation of a comprehensive and consistent economic program or plan.[8]

Until quite late in the medieval period, all monks in western Europe were essentially Benedictines, in that they took as the basic rule for their communities that which had been drawn up by Benedict of Aniane. Saint Benedict had prescribed that the monk not live "by the sweat of other men," but rather by the work of his own hands. Such a prescription,

---

7. See, e.g., A. Gerards, "Wirtschaftliche Hintergründe zur Zeit der Gründung des Cistercienserordens," *Cistercienser-Chronik*, LVIII, N.S. 16/17 (December, 1951); G. Uhlhorn, "Der Einfluss der wirtschaftlichen Verhältnisse auf die Entwickelung des Mönchtums im Mittelalter," *Zeitschrift für Kirchengeschichte*, XIV, No. 3 (1893).

8. On the dating of these documents, see D. Knowles, "The Primitive Cistercian Documents," in his *Great Historical Enterprises. Problems in Monastic History* (London, n.d.). See also Jean A. Lefèvre, "Que savons-nous du Cîteaux primitif?" *Revue D'Histoire Ecclésiastique*, LI, No. 1 (1956), and the works cited in his first two notes, p. 5; and Ch. Dereine, "La Fondation de Cîteaux d'apres l'Exordium Cistercii et l'Exordium Parvum," *Cîteaux*, X, No. 2 (April, 1959).

however, was discordant with what had become, by the end of the eleventh century, the normal economic system for monastic support. The *Grundherrschaft* of the Cluniacs and others was a *rentier* economy in which the landlord (in this case the monastery) disposed over revenues in money, kind, and services, which were due from those who worked the land held from him. In the eyes of the Cistercians this was a flagrant and direct violation of the letter and the spirit of Benedict's policy. The reformers argued that the very processes of collecting and administering such revenues, and the litigations and other disputes which so often arose from those dealings and relationships, could not possibly contribute to the cloistered security requisite to the fulfillment of a religious vocation. Therefore the Cistercians condemned that economic system and unconditionally renounced and rejected all revenues from churches, altars, advowsons, tithes of other men, burial services and grounds, dependent farms or villages, dependent peasants or villagers, ground rents, and fees from ovens and mills.[9]

The essence of Benedict's rule for the ordering of the monk's life was the division of his time between physical labor and the duties of the Divine Office. Within Benedictinism, however, there had almost always been a tendency to substitute cerebral or other similar activity for manual work; but now the Cistercians asserted that anything other than work with one's own hands was at variance with Benedict's intention. The Cistercian was to live exclusively by the fruit of his own labor (which could be interpreted to include the collective labor of the community). However, the recognition shortly became unavoidable that there was an inherent contradiction involved, for exclusive reliance upon the labor of the monks for the community's physical sustenance was so demanding that little or no time remained for reading, prayer, and other devotional activities.[10]

The difficulty posed by the determination to renounce all revenues and to live by their own labor was resolved by the adoption of an institution

9. As expressed in chap. xv of the *Exordium Cistercienses Coenobii* (*Exordium Parvum*), composed by the third abbot of Cîteaux, (St.) Stephen Harding (died 1134): "Et quia nec in Regula, nec in Vita sancti Benedicti eumden doctorem legebant possedisse ecclesias, vel altaria, seu oblationes aut sepulturas, vel decimas aliorum hominum, sue furnos, vel molendina, aut villas, vel rusticos, nec etiam feminas monasterium ejus intrasse, nec mortuos ibidem excepta sorore sua sepelisse: ideo haec omnia abdicaverunt . . . ." The *Exordium* is published in a number of places, including P. Guignard (ed.), *Les Monuments primitifs de la Règle Cistercienne publies d'apres les manuscrits de l'abbaye Cîteaux*, Analecta Divionensia . . . , VI (Dijon, 1878).

10. See A. Hauck, *Kirchengeschichte Deutschlands*, Vol. IV, 5th ed. (Leipzig, 1925), 349; and D. Knowles, *The Monastic Order in England* (Cambridge, 1940), p. 348.

which, though hitherto not entirely unknown within branches of Benedict-inism, was to be developed by the Cistercians to a degree never before attained. This was the institution of the *conversi*, or lay brothers.[11] Origin-ally at Cîteaux there had been no provision for such individuals; but very early (1100–1101) the decision was taken to admit lay brothers. Prompted, as it appears, by the need for more labor power, the Cistercians resorted to the device of admitting a class of "half-monks." These—in the apt phrase—"villeins in monastic dress"[12] were bound by the same vows as were the monks, but were strictly distinguished from the latter in several respects. The *conversi* were theoretically reckoned equal members of the community in both life and death, but their role was nonetheless to be first and foremost that of workers. This fact emerges fairly clearly from the documents. The *Usus conversorum*, composed toward the end of the twelfth century as a codification of the rights and duties of the *conversi*, deals primarily with spiritual and behaviorial matters. In a few places, however, the basic purpose of the institution emerges more explicitly, as for example in the stipulation of fewer days of rest, and in the provision of larger rations of victuals and fewer fasting days for the lay brothers than for the monks. The *conversi* constituted a labor force and were to be supported in an appropriate manner.[13]

It might at first appear surprising that there were men who chose to enter the ranks of the *conversi*. The fare was simple, material comforts few, and the *conversus* was required to foreswear the normal object of the peasantry—the acquisition of land and the establishment of a family upon it. In spite of all this one can observe that the Cistercians did not lack for aspirants to the rank of the *conversi*, at least for some considerable period of time.[14] The reasons for this state of affairs really are not difficult to ascertain. Although the original theory was that *conversi* might come from all classes of secular society, it seems that it rapidly became customary for them to be drawn primarily from the lower levels.[15] This was only rational,

11. See J. S. Donnelly, *The Decline of the Medieval Cistercian Lay Brotherhood*, Fordham University Studies, History Series, III (New York, 1949), especially 4–19; and E. Hoff-mann, *Das Konverseninstitut des Cisterzienserordens in seinem Ursprung und seiner Organisation*, Freiburger Historische Studien, I (Freiburg [S], 1905); and Uhlhorn, *op. cit.*, p. 370.

12. The term is H. M. Colvin's; see his "Deserted Villages and the Archaeologist," *Archaeological News Letter*, IV, No. 9 (June/July, 1952).

13. See chaps. iii, xiii, and xv of the *Usus*, in Guignard, *op. cit.*

14. H. Svoboda, *Dis Klosterwirtschaft der Cisterciensen im Ostdeutschland*, Nürnberger Beiträge zu den Wirtschaftswissenschaften, 19/20 (Nuremberg, 1930), p. 62.

15. Donnelly, *op. cit.*, pp. 20–21; Hoffmann, *Konverseninstitut*, pp. 5, 49; Svoboda, *loc. cit.*; F. Winter, *Die Cistercienser des nordöstlichen Deutschlands*, Vol. I(Gotha, 1868) p. 103.

in view of their intended occupations. Some of these recruits came from one or another of the various categories of dependent peasants; others, though technically enjoying personal freedom, were burdened with the inevitable and manifold obligations customarily borne by the medieval peasant. In any case, it was almost always true that the entrant improved his legal and social position and favorably altered his life circumstances, by becoming a *conversus*.[16] On another level we must recognize that this was an age with concerns in many respects fundamentally different from those of our own. Medieval man can be properly understood only when due appreciation is given to his strong transcendental preoccupations. In this context, the appeal of the Cistercians is obvious: they were renowned among contemporaries for their piety and sanctity. Pursuit of the ascetic mode of life, which may sometimes appear rather excessive to us, was then regarded as the highest of virtues, and association in such a life was thought to bring with it inestimable benefits and rewards. Nonmaterial considerations and motivations could play a large part, perhaps even the largest part, in the decision of a peasant to become a *conversus* in the Cistercian order.[17]

Whatever the nature of the motivations involved, the Cistercian plan assumed that aspirants to the lay brotherhood would be forthcoming in adequate numbers. While there were other, supplemental elements of the monastery's labor force—the *familiares*, and day-wage laborers on occasions of peak demand—the *conversi* together with the monks themselves were intended to meet the normal and regular labor requirements of the community.[18] This institution of the lay brotherhood drew upon a segment of medieval society which had been ignored by monasticism

---

There is not, however, total agreement on this matter; compare K. Halliger, "Woher kommen die Laienbrüder?" *Analecta Sacri Ordinis Cisterciensis*, XII, Nos. 1/2 (January/June, 1956), with E. Werner, "Bemerkungen zu einer neuen These über die Herkunft der Laienbrüder," *Zeitschrift für Geschichtswissenschaft*, VI, No. 2 (1958).

16. See Hoffmann, *Konverseninstitut*, pp. 67–68, and "Entwicklung," pp. 720–721; Svoboda, *loc. cit.*; and Winter, *loc. cit.*

17. E.g., see Hoffmann (*Konverseninstitut*, p. 68), who well expresses the superiority supposedly resulting from the allegedly nonpecuniary motivation of these workers: "Zufrieden mit kärglicher Kost arbeiten sie so jahraus jahrein für den Unterhalt ihrer Brüder und für die Wohlfahrt des Klosters mit einer Treue und Uneigennützigkeit, wie sie sich von Frohnarbeiter oder Tagelöhnern nicht erwarten lässt." See also L. Dolberg, "Cistercienser-Mönche und Conversen als Landwirthe und Arbeiter," *Studien und Mittheilungen aus dem Benedictiner- und Cistercienser-Orden*, XIII, Nos. 2, 3, and 4 (1892); and Uhlhorn, *op. cit.*, p. 372.

18. See the *Exordium*, chap. xv.

for centuries, and the initial response was "immediate and wide-spread."[19]

The Cistercian adaptation of the lay brotherhood institution solved the problem of securing the monastery's labor supply without dependence on or involvement with members of the outside world. Land, the other major input to agricultural production, was also subjected to an organizational form which, in Cistercian hands and articulation, became a truly novel administrative arrangement. As is well known, the Cistercians took quite literally the injunction to isolate themselves from "the world," and they sought, in the words of the *Exordium*, to establish themselves "in sites remote from the habitations of men."[20] In the period of the order's foundation the major mechanism by which the monks acquired lands was that of gifts and pious donations by landowners. Such a device, dependent as it is upon the vagaries of donors, does not lend itself readily to a rational pattern of landholdings. But presumably the monks could accept offered properties or not, as they chose; and, on occasion, much could also be achieved through the employment of an enlightened policy of exchange of scattered land parcels. Insofar as they might exercise selectivity, the monasteries of the Cistercian order were directed to prefer those properties situated in unpopulated and uncultivated regions, in the wilderness, so to

19. The description is Knowles's *Monastic Order*, p. 251.
One would naturally like to know something about the magnitude of numbers involved. Regrettably, but hardly surprisingly, little is known about such matters. Architectural remains can provide some impressionistic indications. In the monasteries, *conversi* normally were housed in the cellarer's building, on the west side of the cloister, and one may usefully study the plans and photographs in F. van der Meer, *Atlas de l'orde cistercien* (Amsterdam and Brussels, 1965), and in D. Knowles and J. K. S. St. Joseph, *Monastic Sites from the Air* (Cambridge, 1952). J. S. Donnelly publishes some figures for *conversi* in Welsh and English Cistercian abbeys, but few of them relate to the period here under consideration ("Changes in the Grange Economy of English and Welsh Cistercian Abbeys, 1300–1450," *Traditio*, X [1954], 452–454). Hallinger offers some further numbers (*op. cit.*, pp. 52–54) for the twelfth through fifteenth centuries. Finally, L. J. Lekai presents a few more (*Geschichte und Wirken der Weissen Mönche. Der Orden der Cistercienser* [Cologne, 1958], pp. 60–61). The materials in Donnelly and Lekai are potentially the most useful, for they list the numbers both of monks and of *conversi* in a specific house in a given year and it is the proportions between the two which are most interesting. But all the available figures are extremely spotty and discontinuous; one gains from them the impression that the ratio of *conversi* to monks in general might vary between 3:2 and 3:1; but even this fuzzy range lacks virtually all precision, and must not be regarded with much confidence. Cf. Hoffmann, *Konverseninstitut*, p. 71.

20. "Suscepturos quoque terras ab habitatione hominum remotas, et vineas et prata et silvas, aquasque ad faciendos molendinos, ad proprios tamen usus et ad piscationem, et pecoraque, diversaque necessitati hominum utilia" (*Exordium*, chap. xv).

speak. The land of the abbey was to be worked essentially by the monks and their *conversi*. However, some of the lands might well be located at such a distance from the monastery that travel to them and back would leave insufficient time in the day for useful work to be done upon them. So, as the monks were strictly forbidden to pass the night beyond the cloister walls,[21] the *Exordium* prescribed that work on lands so situated be done exclusively by the lay brothers, who were to reside in the neighborhood. Thus was evolved the institution of the grange.[22]

Stated most simply, the grange was a farm, or more precisely perhaps, the outfarm of a main farm. A *conversus* was to be appointed "master" of each individual grange, while all the granges of a given monastery stood under the administration of the cellarer,[23] who was accountable to the abbot.[24] Very early, regulations were promulgated concerning the position-

21. *Instituta*, chap. vi; see also chaps. xvi, xvii, and xxi; in Guignard, *op. cit.*

22. *Exordium*, chap. xv: "Et dum alicubi curtes ad agriculturas exercendas instituissent, decreverunt ut praedicti conversi domos illas regerent, non monachi, quia habitatio monachorum secundum Regulam debet esse in claustro ipsorum. Quia etiam beatum Benedictum non in civitatibus, nec in castellis aut in villis, sed in locis a frequentia populi semotis coenobia construxisse sancti viri illi sciebant, idem se aemulari promittebant." See also the *Instituta*, chaps. i, viii, and lxxii.

23. The abbot was prohibited from turning over the administration of a grange—or of any other property—to anyone other than the cellarer; *Instituta*, chap. lxvii.

24. *Instituta*, chap. lxxvii. See also Winter, *op. cit.*, p. 14. But, cf. H. Wiswe, "Grangien niedersächsischer Zisterzienserklöster. Entstehung und Bewirtschaftung spätmittelalterlichfrühneuzeitlicher landwirtschaftlicher Grossbetriebe," *Braunschweigisches Jahrbuch*, XXXIV (1953), especially 81 and 88.

Here again, as in the case of the *conversi*, one wishes for some quantitative specifications. T. A. M. Bishop ("Monastic Granges in Yorkshire," *English Historical Review*, LI, No. 2 [April, 1936]) indicates in one place (p. 199) that they were generally two to three hundred acres in extent, though sometimes they might reach over one thousand acres; however, a little further on (p. 209) he states: "The average area of a Cistercian grange was, perhaps, between three and four hundred acres." This presumably refers to arable acres, which would then be in fair agreement with the observations of R. A. Donkin ("The Cistercian Order in Medieval England: Some Conclusions," *Institute of British Geographers: Transactions and Papers*, XXXIII [December, 1963], 187). It is possible that Bishop intends the former figures to apply to English monastic granges in general, while limiting the latter to Cistercian granges in Yorkshire, but this is not entirely clear. (Though cf. p. 203: "The granges which belonged to the houses of canons regular were not so large as those of some Cistercian monasteries. . . . The average size of an Augustinian or Gilbertine grange was perhaps two hundred acres.") Hoffmann (*Konverseninstitut*, p. 87) asserts that, on the average, a grange possessed fifteen to twenty *Hufen*, i.e., was in area four hundred and fifty to six hundred morgen, thus falling in the category of a "middle-sized" estate. See also Uhlhorn, *op. cit.*, p. 372; and R. A. Donkin, "The Cistercian Grange in England in the 12th and 13th Centuries, with Special Reference to Yorkshire," *Studia Monastica*, VI, No. 1

ing of granges; in addition to the stipulation of a maximum distance between the monastery and its grange, a minimal separation between the granges of two abbeys (as also was the case for the abbeys themselves) was required.[25]

From this emerges the outline of a theory for the development or expansion of the Cistercian order. The original impetus is the acquisition of some land, presumably as a gift, suitably located in some remote, uncultivated site. A small band of monks and lay brothers begins to work the land, and construct the church and other basic structures which comprise the monastery. As the abbey accumulates more properties the complement of monks and *conversi* expands, and the more remote (though still within some more or less specific radius) lands are organized and worked in subdivisions called granges. From time to time the abbey may find itself with the opportunity to establish a new community; acquiring sufficient land which is too remote from the abbey to allow incorporation into its operation, a group of monks and *conversi* go off to repeat the process of founding a monastery. The lands of each monastery of the order are worked by that community's manpower of monks and lay brothers, and each is basically self-sufficient in its operation.[26]

The Cistercian economic plan thus would fall under the classification of firm rather than national planning, to employ modern and violently anachronistic terminology. The ideal is an agrarian unit producing almost exclusively for its members' needs, but producing by the members' labor almost everything necessary to satisfy their legitimate needs. In reality, of course, autarchy could only have been approximate. What is of importance here, however, is that economic self-sufficiency was sought, not as an end in itself, but as a means; the economy was of interest to the Cistercians only as a mechanism enabling maximum devotion to the intensive preparation for the next world which they wished to pursue in undisturbed seclusion from the rest of the present world.[27] The economic program they

---

(1964). The state of our knowledge on this important subject remains unsatisfactory; we need many more monographs similar in focus and quality to C. Higounet's *La Grange de Vaulerent. Structure et exploitation d'un terrior cistercien de la plaine de France, XIIIe–XVe siècle*, École pratique des hautes études—VIe section. Centre de recherches historiques: Les hommes et la terra, X (Paris, 1965); and C. Platt, *The Monastic Grange in Medieval England. A Reassessment* (New York, 1969).

25. Respectively, *Instituta*, chaps. v and xxxii; and Statute No. 6 of the General Chapter for 1134; as presented in J.-M. Canivez (ed.), *Statuta Capitulorum Generalium Cisterciensis ab anno 1116 ad annum 1786*, Bibliothèque de la Revue d'Histoire Ecclésiastique, 9-14B, Vol. I (Louvain, 1933), 32–33.

26. *Instituta*, chap. v.

27. And the institutions of the lay brotherhood and the grange were the structural

developed to this purpose applied to a single unit, the monastery; but it could be indefinitely reiterated in as many separate units as was desired.[28]

It is appropriate here to draw some implications and make some comparisons as to the relative efficiency of this Cistercian economic program, on the theoretical level. The discussion can be separated into three parts— cost functions, technology, and organizational forms. A plausible argument can be made that the Cistercian reform program implies for the economy a basic cost structure which seems to be advantageous as compared with the costs borne by other estate operators. Specifically, the austere, even puritanical, consumption regime ordained by the founders at Cîteaux meant that expenditures on fabric and ornamentation would have been but a fraction of those usual in monasteries of non-Cistercian persuasion.[29] Thus, assuming identical levels of gross revenue or product, deduction of expenses under this head would leave the Cistercian abbey with greater net disposable assets than a community of, say, black monks; and the same argument would typically apply a fortiori to the household of a secular landlord of comparable rank.[30]

---

supports to which the Cistercians resorted to implement their unique economic program, which was prerequisite to the realization of their program of religious reform.

28. Wiswe seems to hint that there is something peculiar in the circumstance that, as a Cistercian house became wealthy through gifts of land, it chose to expand not via the foundation of a daughter house, but by the erection of a grange (op. cit., p. 34). I think, however, that such uneasiness is unwarranted in view of the exposition concerning location and manpower considerations, in the text above. Moreover, Winter asserts that an abbey was not permitted to found a daughter unless it had a strength of at least sixty monks (op. cit., p. 8), a caution for which there appears to have been some grounds; see R. Lehmann, Die ältere Geschichte des Cisterzienser-Klosters Dobrilugk in der Lausitz (Heidelberg, 1917), pp. 66–68. The rate of proliferation of Cistercian houses also would argue against Wiswe's implication.

Nor does the statement in the text contradict that of Gerards (op. cit., p. 66): "...jedoch muss vom Standpunkt des Wirtschaftshistorikers aus im Auge behalter werden, dass das Wirtschaftprinzip der Gründer von Cîteaux keineswegs auf einen Orden zugeschnitten war, der sich über ganz Europa ausbreiten sollte." It is not necessary to believe that the founders at Cîteaux foresaw the subsequent great expansion of an order, but only that the economic system which they devised and instituted was capable of such reproduction. It might also be noted that practices among all abbeys of the order were to be uniform (Instituta, chap. ii).

29. This austerity was eloquently expressed in their buildings; F. Bucher, "Cistercian Architectural Purism," Comparative Studies in Society and History, IV, No. 1 (October, 1960).

30. See, for example, the comments of A. Thiele, Echternach und Himmerod. Beispiele benediktinischer und zistersiensischer Wirtschaftsführung im 12. und 13. Jahrhundert, Forschungen zur Sozial- und Wirtschaftsgeschichte, VII (Stuttgart, 1964), 47; Uhlhorn, op. cit., p. 376;

A second advantage involves the variable costs associated with the maintenance of a labor force. The regime prescribed for the Cistercian monk was considered austere even by contemporary standards. As for the lay brothers, their circumstances as to clothing and similar necessities were much the same as those of the monks, while their diet, though somewhat hardier than the monks', was probably not greatly distinguishable from that of the peasant. This suggests that the physical level of existence of the Cistercian labor force (monks and *conversi* together) was on average somewhat below that of the members of non-Cistercian economic units. Thus, the variable charges for the subsistence of the labor force which supported the non-Cistercian monasteries and secular landlords would have exceeded those costs for a community of white monks, and the difference in net disposable income would again have been in favor of the Cistercians.[31]

A further advantage enjoyed by the Cistercians concerns the ratio of economically productive to economically nonproductive individuals supported by the estate. Cistercian monks were intended to be active participants in the work of production; and the (able-bodied) *conversi*, of course, were exclusively positive contributors to production. Thus the proportion of economically active in the total population was unusually high—higher than under the alternative arrangement of a lordship supported by the contributions of a dependent peasantry. The latter would have had a far larger fraction of economic "parasites," i.e., children too young to contribute to production, women distracted by child rearing and other secondary activities, and the ailing, infirm, and aged. Monasteries would also have their share of the old and ill, of course; but they would not have to provide for those in other categories. In addition, this meant that the support of an individual until he reached an economically productive age was provided from some source external to the monastery, and then the monastic community reaped all the returns from this outside investment. Also, in so far as the average productivity of women was lower than that of men, the Cistercians, with their exclusively male labor force, enjoyed an additional margin over peasant-based economies.

Another consideration, relating to the comparative productivities of the Cistercian and non-Cistercian labor forces, is what many writers have referred to as the exceptionally high degree of commitment the *conversus*

---

and M. L. Ryder, "The Animal Remains found at Kirkstall Abbey," *Agricultural History Review*, VII, No. 1 (1959).

31. See, e.g., the comments of M. W. Heffter, *Die Geschichte des Klosters Lehnin* (Brandenburg, 1851), pp. 77–78; Hoffmann, *Konverseninstitut*, p. 96; and Thiele, *op. cit.*, p. 146.

had to his vocation. The economic content of this ascription of strong motivation in the work force is a higher average level of productivity. Such assumptions about incentive systems are debatable and probably irresolvable; but, to the extent that this bit of traditional wisdom is grounded in fact, it provides an a priori presumption of higher productivity for the Cistercian economy.[32]

The question of technology has also been the subject of some debate. The argument that the meetings of the General Chapter provided the Cistercians with a clearinghouse for the exchange of technical information and knowledge implies that each Cistercian monastery had prompt access to technical improvements and discoveries made anywhere in Europe, and could employ the most efficient technology appropriate to its specific situation.[33] This may indeed have been so, though in view of the fact that not one single surviving title from any convocation of the General Chapter deals with any technical matter, such exchange must have been completely informal. In fact, there seems to be virtually no firm evidence that the Cistercians employed any technology which was not also available to and practiced by their contemporaries.[34]

The final area in which the Cistercians may have enjoyed a real economic advantage vis-à-vis other landlords is in the realm of organization. Disposing over large landed areas and having a strongly centralized administration, the Cistercian monastery could specialize agrarian production to take advantage of variations in physical geography to a degree far beyond that attainable in the atomized production of the *rentier* landlord. In this sense, it would be quite plausible to argue that the Cistercians may have benefited from significant organizational economies of scale.[35]

32. See above, note 17.

33. Thus R. Ohle, *Die Bedeutung der Zisterzienser für die Besiedelung der Mark Brandenburg,* Mitteilungen des Uckermärkischen Museums- und Geschichtsvereins, zu Prenzlau, VII, No. 2 (Prenzlau, 1921), 27; Uhlhorn, *op. cit.,* p. 366.

34. See B. H. Slicher van Bath, *The Agrarian History of Western Europe, A.D. 500–1850,* trans. O. Ordish (London, 1963), p. 154; and Wiswe, *op. cit.,* pp. 75–76, 79.

35. Slicher van Bath, *loc. cit.;* Donkin, "Some Conclusions," p. 186; Uhlhorn, *op. cit.,* p. 374; and Wiswe, *op. cit.,* pp. 78–79. D. C. North has speculated that "improved economic organisation was as important as technological change in the development of the Western world between 1500 and 1830" ("The State of Economic History," *American Economic Review,* LV, No. 2 [May, 1965], 87–88). Perhaps his earlier boundary deserves to be extended further into the past.

Knowles writes of "the successful and superior methods of the Cistercians, whose domestic organization gave to their enterprises many of the advantages possessed in the modern world by the multiple-branch concern of vertically controlled group-industry over the small manufacturer and trader" (*op. cit.,* p. 352).

III. The Reality

Historians have traditionally assumed that the picture just described of the Cistercian economy was also conformed to in reality: the positive operations were presumed to have corresponded to the normative statements. The purpose of this essay is to question the extent to which that assumption is correct. And that is an empirical question.

At the outset we have to face certain problems inherent in the nature of the empirical evidence, some of which are general to the study of medieval history, while others are more specific to this particular investigation. Most of what is known to us about the history of medieval Europe is derived from written sources. There are of course a number of important and useful auxiliaries which can be employed to supplement the basic written sources—aerial photography, analysis of physical remains, art history, etc.—but in the end they remain just that, supplementary. The documents are fundamental.

Regrettably, not all of the documents which were generated in the period survived to the modern era. Worse still, it is not even safe to assume that the incidence of loss was roughly uniform or "neutral" among the various classes of documents: some categories would have been preserved with far greater care than others. This means that even the simplest quantitative device—the ratio of one type of document to another—is normally quite unreliable.

During the period with which we are here concerned, the custom of recording economic—and that means above all agricultural—relationships in written instruments became generalized. Yet even when one has a document in hand, he cannot always be certain that what it says is true. Forgery, often undertaken for other than nefarious reasons, was not uncommon, and it raises more problems for the historian. All this is well known, but nonetheless deserves emphasis here. Chartularies are collections of records concerning matters of landholding and using, and as such they are prime suspects for the work of a forger's hand.[36] Chartularies are

36. See Wiswe, *op. cit.*, p. 36; see also G. Duby, *L'économie rurale et la vie des campagnes dans l'Occident médiéval* (Paris, 1962), pp. 133–134, 383. One of the most common cases of misrepresentation involves the disguising of a purchase as a gift. In so far as this occurs among the documents upon which this study is based—and that frequency of incidence is unknown—it would bias the evidence against the conclusions I have drawn. I have accepted the dating and content of the documents as given by their editors, a procedure which surely results in some appreciable error, but to which there was no alternative at the time.

For the single instance known to the present writer of a proven forgery among the relevant documents, see A. Kunkel, "Die Stiftungbriefe für das meklenburg-pommersche

also the single most important source of empirical evidence from the Cistercian monasteries studied here.

Chartularies possess yet another specific liability. While providing abundant evidence concerning proprietary relationships, and thus revealing much about the operation of a *rentier* economy, they are essentially silent in the case of an economy run according to the Cistercian economic plan.[37] What records are we likely to encounter which will bear witness to the degree in which the monastery was operating self-sufficiently? The acquisition of land will be recorded; but if it should then be retained in hand by the landlord, centrally administered, and worked by the labor force of the community itself, no subsequent records will be generated. This leads to the conclusion that the evidence for the "successful" functioning of the Cistercian economy (i.e., operation consistent with the plan) is of a negative nature: in the case of a Cistercian abbey known to have been active but for which there survives no evidence of *rentier* operation, we presume that its economy actually accorded with the plan.

These, and other inadequacies of the source materials are not negligible, and they do not make the historian's task any easier. But neither do they prevent him altogether from arriving at some informed assessments and judgments. As Giles Constable has affirmed, "in spite of the difficulties of authenticity, interpretation, and evaluation, it still seems possible to discover from the charters and other sources certain broad tendencies in the position of monks and the nature of monastic economy."[38]

The present study has as its empirical core the records of six Cistercian monasteries located in eastern Germany. This was a geographical area in which the order was especially active, and in which it achieved great fame.[39] It was a colonial area, a frontier, and as such it should have presented the monks with a relatively large degree of freedom to develop along the lines they desired to follow. Comparatively unpopulated, these

---

Cistercienserkloster Dargun," *Archiv für Urkundenforschung*, III, No. 1 (1911). There certainly must be others.

37. As noted by G. Duby, *Receuil des pancartes de l'Abbaye de la Ferté-sur-Grosne: 1113–1178*, Publications des Annales de la Faculté des Lettres d'Aix-en-Provence, N.S. II (Gap, 1953), 19. See also the remarks of Donnelly, "Changes," p. 404; Thiele, *op. cit.*, p. 148; and Wiswe, *op. cit.*, p. 68.

38. In Constable, *Monastic Tithes: From their Origin to the Twelfth Century*, Cambridge Studies in Medieval Life and Thought, N.S. X (Cambridge, 1964), 7–8.

39. The literature on this subject is vast. Some citations to it can be found in the bibliography to Appendix II in my Ph.D. dissertation—to which important additions are F. Mager, *Geschichte des Bauerntums und der Bodenkultur im Lande Mecklenburg*, Deutsche Akademie der Wissenschaften zu Berlin, Veröffertlichungen der Historischen Kommis-

territories were what we would today term economically underdeveloped; thus there was little in the way of a pre-existing economic milieu to impose itself and infringe upon the economy of the monasteries.[40]

On the other hand, the six monasteries were established over a period of about one century. It is obvious that one cannot make the conventional and convenient assumption of *ceteris paribus* over such a span of time, and we will return later to take explicit account of the impact on the Cistercian economy of the changes which took place both externally and internally. For the moment let us proceed by briefly summarizing the six foundations.

Dobrilugk. This abbey seems to have been founded about 1165, by Theodorich III, margrave of Meissen, and his brothers Otto and Theodo. The surrounding area was evidently one of forest and swamp,[41] though one authority claims that the name derives from the Slavic *dobra-lucha*, meaning *gute Wiese*, "good meadow."[42] There may have been some German (i.e., Thuringian and Frankish) population in the region before the arrival of the monks.[43]

Zinna. This house was founded in southwestern Brandenburg by Archbishop Wichmann of Magdeburg, in 1170 or 1171. The site seems to have been the typically remote one of swamp and forest,[44] though it is again asserted that the Cistercians did not antedate German colonists in the region.[45]

Doberan. This monastery originally was founded by Pribislaw, chief of the Abodrites in this region, in 1171.[46] Located near a Wendish village from which it took the name, it was apparently established on ground

sion, I (Berlin, 1953); and S. Epperlein, "Gründungsmythos deutscher Zisterziens-erklöster westlich und östlich der Elbe im hohen Mittelalter und der Bericht des Leubuser Mönches im 14. Jahrhundert," *Jahrbuch für Wirtschaftsgeschichte* (1967).

40. See, for example, the comments of Wiswe, *op. cit.*, p. 42; and W. Wittich, "Der religiöse Gehalt der Kolonisation des ostelbischen Deutschlands," *Jahrbücher für National-ökonomie und Statistik*, CXLIV (1936), 656.

41. Lehmann, *op. cit.*, p. 61.

42. Svoboda, *op. cit.*, p. 29.

43. Ohle, *op. cit.*, p. 39.

44. W. Hoppe, *Kloster Zinna. Ein Beitrag zur Geschichte des ostdeutschen Koloniallandes und des Cistercienserordens*, Veröffentlichen des Vereins für Geschichte der Mark Brandenburg (Munich and Leipzig, 1914), p. 135; Svoboda, *op. cit.*, pp. 29–30, 32, 36.

45. Ohle, *loc. cit.*

46. E. Michael, *Geschichte des deutschen Volks, seit dem dreizehnten Jahrhundert bis zum Ausang des Mittelalters*, Vol. I, Culturzustände des deutschen Volkes, während des drei-zehnten Jahrhunderts (Freiburg [i.B], 1897), p. 92; F. L. Röper, *Geschichte und Anekdoten von Dobberan in Mecklenburg*, 2nd ed. (Doberan, 1808), p. 78.

sacred to the Slavs as a place of worship; and, following Pribislaw's death in 1178, it was destroyed in the Slavic uprising of 1179,[47] and seventy-eight monks were killed. It was subsequently refounded by Pribislaw's son, Henry Borwin, in 1186, not in exactly the same place, but still in a customarily desolate and swampy one.[48]

Dargun. Located on the Pomeranian border, this abbey was originally founded out of the Cistercians' Danish house of Esrom, in 1172. The founders were the brothers Chotimar, Miregrav, and Monic, rich nobles of the Schwerin region. During the Danish wars, however, the brothers quit this establishment and moved further east into Pomerania, eventually forming the new monastery of Eldena. In 1209, the house at Dargun was re-established by monks from Doberan. The site was once again the usual remote one.[49]

Lehnin. This monastery was founded by Albert the Bear's son, Margrave Otto I, in 1181, and the Ascanians remained closely associated with the abbey. The site was damp, swampy, and forested;[50] however, at least one scholar believes there were German settlers already present at the time of foundation.[51] One of the daughter houses founded out of Lehnin was Chorin.

Chorin. The site of this monastery had been granted to the Cistercians by 1260, and perhaps even in 1258.[52] The Premonstratensians may previously have located an abbey there, perhaps as early as 1231,[53] but it is not clear that they ever made use of the permission they had to construct there.[54] The original site appears not to have been very happily situated, which could account for the Premonstratensians' lack of enthusiasm or

47. Svoboda claims that Dobrilugk and Zinna were also destroyed during this uprising (*op. cit.*, p. 36).

48. F. Compart, *Geschichte des Klosters Doberan bis zum Jahre 1300*, Beiträge zur Geschichte Mecklenburgs vornehmlich im dreizhnten Jahrhundert, I, No. 5 (Rostock, 1872), 10–11; Michael, *loc. cit.*; Röper, *op. cit.*, pp. 78–81; Svoboda, *op. cit.*, pp. 29–30, 32.

49. Michael, *op. cit.*, pp. 93–94; A. Wiswe, *Die Cistercienser in Dargun von 1172–1300. Ein Beitrag zur meklenburg—pommerschen Colonisationsgeschichte* (Rostock, 1888), p. 17; Svoboda, *op. cit.*, pp. 29–30, 32.

50. Heffter, *op. cit.*, p. 36; W. Nussbeck, *Beiträge zur Besitzgeschichte des Klosters Lehnin* (Greifswald, 1912), pp. 9, 14 f., 18, 20, 30; B. Schulze, "Der Anteil der Zisterzienser an der osteutschen Kolonisation, besonders in Brandenburg," *Jahrbuch für brandenburgische Landesgeschichte*, II (1951), 24; G. Sello, *Lehnin, Beitrag zur Geschichte von Kloster und Amt* (Berlin, 1888), p. 16.

51. Ohle, *loc. cit.* Sello states that the area was completely uninhabited by Wends, at the time of the Cistercians' arrival there (*op. cit.*, p. 13).

52. G. Abb, *Geschichte des Klosters Chorin* (Berlin, 1911), p. 63; H. Berghaus, *Landbuch der Mark Brandenburg . . .* , Vol. II (Brandenburg, 1855), 300–301.

53. Berghaus, *op. cit.*, pp. 299–300.

54. Ohle, *op. cit.*, p. 59.

success, however it may have been. In any case, the Cistercians chose to remove themselves to a more appealing location, which they did in 1273. Chorin was founded by the margraves Johann I and Otto III, and it remained under the patronage of the Johannian branch of the Ascanian dynasty until the effective extinction of that line, in 1319.[55]

These six accounts suggest the close associations which often developed between a particular Cistercian house and the person and family from whom it received the original donations of land. The benefactors were inspired by a mixture of motives involving, *inter alia*, what were essentially political considerations,[56] and a desire to gain merit in the eyes of God. The latter could be enhanced by services and honors emanating from the monastic community. The *Instituta* had prohibited the burial of laymen within the monastery walls,[57] and this prohibition was reiterated, with special reference to royalty, at the General Chapter meeting of 1152.[58] But in 1157 an exception was formally made for the case of lay founders of abbeys; and by 1322 the official policy was to confer the spiritual benefits of association with the house upon any and all who contributed to its construction.[59] The high esteem in which the Cistercians frequently were held by their contemporaries regularly found tangible expression in such gifts to new and young houses, and what impresses one in examining the chartularies of Cistercian abbeys is the sheer volume of these donations, which cover the full range of sizes.[60]

Of course there is little precision in the descriptions of these properties, and the terminology of land units hardly permits any meaningful aggregation. Nevertheless the orders of magnitude involved emerge fairly unambiguously. For instance, when an enumeration—which is surely incomplete—of the donations which the abbey of Lehnin (founded in 1181) had received by the middle of the thirteenth century, comprises well over one hundred hides of land,[61] it is clearly justifiable to regard the house as

55. Abb, *op. cit.*, pp. 14–15, 21 f.; Berghaus, *op. cit.*, p. 302; Schulze, *op. cit.*, pp. 29–30.

56. Well exemplified in the case of Lehnin; see Ohle, *op. cit.*, pp. 40, 65.

57. Chap. xxvii.

58. *Statuta*, 1152, No. 10, in Canivez, *op. cit.*, Vol. I, p. 47; hereafter references to the *Statuta* will cite the year and the number of the statute followed by the volume and page numbers in Canivez.

59. 1157, No. 63, and 1322, No. 3, in I, 68, and III, 358, respectively.

60. Instances can be seen as follows (putative dates are given in parentheses). For Dargun, in G. C. F. Lisch (ed.), "Unkunden des Klosters Dargun," *Meklenburgische Urkunden*, Vol. I (Schwerin, 1837), No. 2 (1173?), No. 5 (1216), and see also pp. 212–214; No. 6 (1216), No. 10 (1226). For Doberan, in E. J. Westphalen (ed.), *Monumenta inedita rerum Germanicarum et Megapolensium . . .* , Vol. III (Leipzig, 1743), Part 1, No. 12 (1237), No. 15 (1242), No. 24 (1249).

61. See A. F. Riedel (ed.), *Codex diplomaticus Brandenburgensis*, Part 1, Vol. X (Berlin,

generously endowed. And when we find that within half a century of their establishment the Cistercians at Chorin had been endowed with a minimum of one hundred and sixty hides and at least six vills,[62] we may legitimately conclude that this monastery was a landlord of important rank.

During the first phase of their existence, it appears that for most Cistercian monasteries the pious gift was the major mechanism by which landed property was accumulated. In order for the resulting pattern of landholding to have been compatible with the normative economy of the Cistercians, the donations would have had to exhibit two characteristics: they had to be made in "pure alms," completely unfettered by feudal relationships or obligations; and the lands transferred must be large and compact enough to allow them to be worked efficiently, independent of all other contiguous lands.

All the donations to Chorin and Lehnin referred to above, in so far as may be judged from the language of the documents embodying them, were transmissions in pure alms. Whether or not they also conformed to the latter condition cannot be determined directly, although the putative scale of many of the individual donations leads one to suspect that a good portion of them did so. But the result is not assured. And, in general, the conclusion is unavoidable that the pattern of a monastery's landed possessions produced by donation could have conformed to the special requirements of the Cistercian economic program only by coincidence; for such conformance to have resulted regularly, for many abbeys, can only be considered highly improbable. It is not surprising, therefore, to find that other means of acquiring lands were employed by the Cistercians. They occur in the records almost from the beginning of a given monastery's history, and their incidence is an increasing function of the passage of time. Gradually, they displace the pious gifts as the most important mechanism of territorial aggrandizement.[63]

1856), pp. 186 (1197), 192 (1212), 195 (1221), 204 (1248); see also pp. 202, 210–211, 213, 216, 220–221, 238.

62. See P. W. Gercken (ed.), "Diplomatarium monasterii Chorin," *Codex diplomaticus Brandenburgensis*, Vol. II (Salzwedel, 1770), No. 216 (1233), No. 222 (1268), Nos. 230 and 231 (1277 and 1281), No. 234 (1287), No. 242 (1299), No. 245 (1305); see also Nos. 252 and 254; Riedel (ed.), *op. cit.*, Part 1, Vol. XIII (Berlin, 1857), No. 44 (1308); see also No. 50, pp. 237–238 and No. 71, p. 251. See also Abb, *op. cit.*, pp. 2 and 74; he also presents a good pictorial representation of the original nucleus, in the map following p. 150. See also Berghaus, *op. cit.*, II, 301.

63. This will be developed in the text below. Also see the comments of Higounet, *op. cit.*, p. 20; Thiele, *op. cit.*, p. 159; and Uhlhorn, *op. cit.*, pp. 350 and 373.

Before discussing these alternative acquisitive techniques, some reasons may be offered to account for the declining role which donation in pure alms played in the expansion of the Cistercian estates. Basically three considerations seem germane; but they are not mutually exclusive, and it is likely that all were operative and contributory. First, potential donors may have become less inclined to bestow portions of their properties upon the Cistercians as the latter, for various reasons, lost approbation in the eyes of their contemporaries. Second, potential donors may have become less able to make such gifts; the general monetization of the economy added to the constraints, while the supply of uncultivated lands and frontier areas was diminishing, at least until the middle of the fourteenth century. Third, the Cistercians themselves may have resorted to alternative acquisition policies that would be more appropriate to their needs and goals.

One alternative mechanism which the Cistercians did employ is that of purchase. Resort to purchase might be a consequence of each of the three circumstances mentioned. The argument for the reluctance as opposed to the inability of potential donors to continue making sizable gifts of land is given some force by the observation that numerous purchases involved large units of land, one or more vills; for example, Chorin begins to do so as early as 1275, Dargun at least as early as 1216, Zinna from the early thirteenth century, and so on.[64] However, at least equally significant is the large body of evidence relating to purchases of considerably smaller parcels—a field, a few hides, a meadow, some pasture, etc.[65]

64. For Chorin, see Gercken, *op. cit.*, No. 227 (1275); No. 257 (1320); Riedel, *op. cit.*, Part 1, Vol. XIII, No. 59 (1327). For Dargun, Lisch, *op. cit.*, No. 4 (1216), Nos. 11–13 (1226–27); No. 28 (1241); No. 41 (1251); No. 75 (1282); No. 98 (1297). For Doberan, see Westphalen, *op. cit.*, Part 1, No. 28 (1253); No. 36 (1257); No. 57 (1278); Nos. 58 and 59 (1280); No. 63 (1281); No. 66 (1282); No. 68 (1285); No. 83 (1293); No. 96 (1297); Part 2, No. 6 (1302); No. 26 (1306); No. 28 (1306); No. 36 (1307); No. 48 (1310). For Dobrilugk, see J. P. Ludewig (ed.), *Reliquiae Manuscriptorum ommis aevi Diplomatarium ac Monumentorum, ineditorum adhuc,* Vol. I (Frankfurt and Leipzig, 1720), No. 22 (1226); No. 35 (1240); No. 48 (1252); No. 75 (1267); No. 88 (1279); No. 101 (1285); No. 118 (1296); No. 124 (1297); No. 129 (1297); Nos. 153 and 154 (1300); No. 166 (1305); No. 170 (1307); No. 183 (1313); No. 222 (1329); No. 234 (1335). For Lehnin, Riedel, *op. cit.*, Part 1, Vol. X, pp. 198–199 (1233–41); 201–203 (1244), 207–208 (1252), 214–215 (1275), 217 (1287–88), 221 (1295), 226–227 (1305), 230 (1313–15), 237 (1321), 243 (1339); see also Heffter, *op. cit.*, pp. 62–63; and Nussbeck, *op. cit.*, pp. 17, 31. For Zinna, see Riedel, *op. cit.*, Part 4, Vol. I (Berlin, 1862), pp. 296–297 (1218, 1222, 1268, 1285, 1307); see also the comments in Hoppe, *op. cit.*, p. 133, and document No. 2, pp. 206–207.

65. E.g., for Chorin, see Riedel, *op. cit.*, Part 1, Vol. XIII, No. 46 (1308) and No. 47 (1309). For Dargun, see Lisch, *op. cit.*, No. 79 (1283), No. 81 (1287), No. 99 (1298). For Doberan, see Westphalen, *op. cit.*, Part 1, No. 8 (1232), No. 39 (1262), No. 42 (1264),

Purchases of this nature might well be indicative of a policy of consolidation. Rather than refusing outright or otherwise disposing of a piece of land too small to be worked economically, or perhaps hemmed in by or intermingled with lands belonging to others, the abbey could attempt to buy up enough contiguous parcels to make a workable and autonomous holding. The evidence of smaller purchases, if not providing conclusive proof of the pursuit of a policy of consolidation, is at least consistent with it. The fact that these smaller purchases evidently do not begin occurring until the monastery is several decades old, lends some confidence to the inference.

An even more striking manifestation of such a policy would seem to be the very large body of evidence relating to the exchange of one parcel of land for another.[66] Transactions of this type are precisely what one would expect to encounter if an abbey were pursuing a policy of consolidation and rounding out of holdings; and their appearance seems to coincide approximately with the commencement of purchasing activities involving smaller parcels. The only other rationale which might be suggested is that a monastery obviously would have been happy to exchange some small or unproductive plot of land, in return for a larger or more fertile one. But it is difficult to imagine that partners for such trades could have been very numerous. The possibility of course exists that in such deals the monastery made a compensating payment which was not mentioned, for some reason, in the document recording the exchange. But the fact of the matter is that this is not suggested by the specifications of the units exchanged. Furthermore, in a not inconsiderable number of instances, the monastery's objective of consolidation or filling out of holdings emerges rather clearly.[67]

No. 43 (1265), No. 56 (1278); Part 2, No. 21 (1305), No. 84 (1345); see also the remarks of Compart, *op. cit.*, pp. 60–61. For Dobrilugk, see Ludewig, *op. cit.*, No. 53 (1255), No. 54 (1255), No. 56 (1256), No. 62 (1266), No. 78 (1271), No. 87 (1276), No. 106 (1286), No. 134 (1298), No. 136 (1298), No. 141 (1298), No. 158 (1300), No. 160 (1301), No. 165 (1302), No. 179 (1311), No. 183 (1313). For Lehnin, Riedel, *op. cit.*, Part 1, Vol. X, pp. 195 (1221), 207 (1251), 229–230 (1308–13), 232–235 (1317–18).

66. Instances are, for Chorin, Riedel, *op. cit.*, Part 1, Vol. XIII, No. 24 (1276), No. 41 (1305), No. 70 (1338); for Dargun, Lisch, *op. cit.*, No. 10 (1226), No. 14 (1228), No. 16 (1229), No. 32 (1244), No. 44 (1252); for Doberan, Westphalen, *op. cit.*, Part 2, No. 1 (1301), No. 29 (1306), Nos. 63 and 64 (1319); for Dobrilugk, Ludewig, *op. cit.*, No. 136 (1298), Nos. 222 and 224 (1329); for Lehnin, P. W. Gercken (ed.), "Registum diplomatum monasterii Lehninensis," in *op. cit.*, Vol. VII (Stendal, 1782), pp. 328 (1258), 332 (1299); and for Zinna, Riedel, *op. cit.*, Part 4, Vol. I, p. 296 (1204).

67. As for Chorin, Riedel, *op. cit.*, Part 1, Vol. XIII, No. 20 (1274–75), No. 54 (1319), No. 55 (1320), No. 59 (1327), No. 70 (1338), No. 84 (1350); for Doberan,

Up to this point a survey of the evidence would incline us toward the conclusion that there was a high degree of correspondence between the theoretical conception of Cistercian economic life and the reality of that life. Cistercian monasteries, beneficiaries of the popular religious enthusiasm, were endowed with extensive landed properties. Quite early, while they were still continuing to enjoy free gifts of land, they began to enter into the land market, first by purchasing, and then more and more by exchanging. These latter policies enabled the abbeys to give some direction to the expansion of their estates. The net impact of all this is that the Cistercians would have been able to acquire the landed basis essential to their special economic program: these are the policies that could have led to the formation of those large, consolidated, autonomous estates which the theoretical propositions of the order required for their fulfillment.

But this is far from being the whole story which the documents have to tell. As mentioned above, many of the donations, and the purchases as well, involved a vill or vills. Sometimes they are explicitly noted to have been abandoned or to have gone to waste; and where this was so, they presented no problem with respect to the Cistercian economic program. But this cannot always have been the case; and some, perhaps even most, of the vills which the Cistercians acquired in fact were already inhabited by peasant cultivators. In many of the charters they are specifically mentioned: the abbey receives such and such a vill and "the men of that place."[68] Here arose a very real problem, for the dictates of the order enjoined the monks from holding dependent peasants and receiving rents. What, then, were they to do about the peasants who sat on land which the monastery acquired?

On occasion, the Cistercians solved the problem strictly in accordance with the letter of their economic program: the peasants involved simply were removed from the land, and the vill was often subsequently converted to a grange.[69] In fact, this seems to have become a rather common practice

---

Westphalen, *op. cit.*, Part 2, No. 76 (1328), Nos. 77 and 78 (1334); for Dobrilugk, Ludewig, *op. cit.*, No. 75 (1267), No. 92 (1285), No. 136 (1298), Nos. 153 and 154 (1300), No. 165 (1302), No. 179 (1311), and also the comments of Lehmann, *op. cit.*, p. 69; for Lehnin, see Nussbeck, *op. cit.*, p. 18.

68. *Inter alia*, for Chorin, Abb, *op. cit.*, p. 99; Dobrilugk, Ludewig, *op. cit.*, No. 166 (1305), and Lehmann, *op. cit.*, p. 69; and for Lehnin, Nussbeck, *op. cit.*, p. 18.

69. E.g., Chorin, Riedel, *op. cit.*, Part 1, Vol. XIII, No. 18 (1274), and also Abb, *op. cit.*, p. 99; Dargun, Lisch, *op. cit.*, No. 70 (1274), No. 77 (1282), and also A. Wiswe, *Die Cistercienser*, p. 61; Dobrilugk, Ludewig, *op. cit.*, No. 124 (1297), and Lehmann, *op. cit.*, pp. 62–64; for Lehnin, see Nussbeck, *op. cit.*, p. 10, and Sello, *op. cit.*, p. 65; and

among the Cistercians, and as a result they acquired a quite unenviable reputation as the destroyers of vills and the dispossessors of peasants.[70]

However, there is also a considerable body of evidence which establishes that this was neither their invariable nor constant policy. Indeed, one finds that the Cistercians did begin to retain lands on which peasant cultivators resided, and on which they remained. What value did the monks derive from lands so circumstanced? The answer to that question is very straightforward: the payments which the peasants returned for the use of the land were now received by the abbey. The monastery became a rent-receiving landlord.[71]

This development, of course, was in direct violation of the whole letter and spirit of the Cistercian reform; but this consideration appears to have exercised little or no deterrent effect. In defense, it might be argued that the monks were only passive agents, that is, that they unfortunately might be the recipients of gifts—over which they had no control—which might be badly out of harmony with the needs of their special economic program. The response to this argument is that they could always have declined such ill-conceived gifts; and, while it is not possible to prove that the monks did not always make strenuous efforts to remove rent-paying tenants from donated lands, it is also impossible to prove the affirmative proposition. But the most serious difficulty in making a defense for the purity of the monks' intentions is that they acquired rent-returning lands not only at the possibly misguided insistence of donors, but also in substantial

---

Zinna, Berghaus, *op. cit.*, Vol. I (Brandenburg, 1854), 516 (1311). See also the comments of M. W. Barley, "Cistercian Land Clearances in Nottinghamshire: Three Deserted Villages," *Nottingham Medieval Studies*, I (1957); H. Muggenthaler, *Kolonisatorische und wirtschaftliche Tätigkeit eines deutschen Zisterzienserklosters im XII. und XIII. Jahrhundert*, Doberl-Leidinger Deutsche Geschichtsbücherei, II (Munich and Leipzig, 1924), 35 and 105; and A. Wiswe, *op. cit.*, p. 54.

70. See Walter Map's *De Nugis Curialium*, especially I, chap. xxv; and W. Meyer (ed.), 'Zwei Gedichte zur Geschichte des Cistercienser Ordens," *Nachrichten der Königlichen Gessellschaft der Wissenschaften zu Göttingen: Philolgisch-Historische Klasse* (Berlin, 1908), especially 1:100, p. 404.

71. Examples are Chorin, Gercken, *op. cit.*, Vol. II, No. 218 (1258), No. 221 (1267), No. 272 (1346), and Riedel, *op. cit.*, Part 1, Vol. XIII, No. 81 (1347), No. 82 (1348), No. 86 (1350); Dargun, Lisch, *op. cit.*, No. 67 (1271); Doberan, Westphalen, *op. cit.*, Part 2, No. 10 (1303), No. 20 (1305), No. 58 (1314), No. 59 (1316), No. 60 (1316), No. 69 (1320), No. 72 (1324), No. 73 (1324), No. 80 (1337), and G. C. F. Lisch (ed.), "Urkunden zur Geschichte der Kirche zu Doberan," *Jahrbücher des Vereins für mecklenburgische Geschichte und Alterthumskunde*, IX (1844), No. 30 (1302); Lehnin, Gercken, *op. cit.*, Vol. VII, p. 332 (1299).

measure by their own voluntary acts of purchase.[72] And precisely what had been feared from such involvements—the disputes and litigation to which these worldly entanglements so often led—in the sequel came to pass. In the course of time the Cistercians became reputed as skilled combatants in the legal arena, a pursuit which could easily involve heavy expenditures.[73]

The reality is that the Cistercians gradually became very deeply immersed in the land rental market, and this is a development of basic importance. It has long been generally accepted that what was distinctive about the Cistercians was that the economy of their monasteries belonged to the *Gutsherrshaft* variety, virtually all the abbey's land being held in demesne and worked by a non-rent-paying labor force. While the evidence presented here is not sufficient to assert that the Cistercians completely abandoned this system and reverted to a purely *Grundherrschaft* basis, it does indicate that the economies of Cistercian monasteries could quite often become characterized by a very strong element of the *rentier* land-lordship. The point is worth emphasizing, for the textbook description of the Cistercian economy often seems to accept uncritically the normative for the positive version.

This result came about by essentially three main processes. First, the Cistercians began to acquire lands which yielded rent payments. Second, the individual monasteries began to let out at rent various parcels of their land, large and small, which had hitherto been farmed in demesne.[74] Finally, the monasteries seem to have insured their material support more and more by securing revenues not only from real estate, but from a wide variety of sources. Depending upon local circumstances these included salt pans, mills, patronage over churches, and rights to proceeds deriving from

72. E.g., Chorin, Gercken, *op. cit.*, Vol. II, No. 238 (1295), and Riedel, *op. cit.*, Part 1, Vol. XIII, No. 85 (1350); Doberan, Westphalen, *op. cit.*, Part 2, No. 68 (1319); Lehnin, Riedel, *op. cit.*, Part 1, Vol. X, pp. 208 (1252), 217 (1287), 221–222 (1297). See also the comments of Donnelly, "Changes," pp. 415 and 449.

73. See, for example, Chorin, Riedel, *op. cit.*, Part 1, Vol. XIII, No. 59 (1327), No. 77 (1344), No. 82 (1348); Dargun, Lisch, *Urkunden*, No. 64 (1269), No. 82 (1287), No. 87 (1288–89), No. 94 (1294–97), No. 99 (1298); Doberan, Westphalen, *op. cit.*, Part 1, No. 32 (1256), No. 76 (1288), No. 90 (1296), Part 2, No. 68 (1319); Dobrilugk, Ludewig, *op. cit.*, No. 27 (1231), Nos. 107 and 109 (1287–89); Lehnin, Gercken, *op. cit.*, Vol. VII, p. 337 (1248); and Riedel, *op. cit.*, Part 1, Vol. VIII (Berlin, 1847), No. 88 (1258), and Part 1, Vol. X, pp. 219–220 (1294); see also Heffter, *op. cit.*, p. 63.

74. See Chorin, Abb, *op. cit.*, p. 101; Dargun, Lisch, *Urkunden*, No. 55 (1262), No. 68 (1271); Doberan, Westphalen, *op. cit.*, Part 1, No. 109 (1299), Part 2, No. 82 (1345); Dobrilugk, Lehmann, *op. cit.*, pp. 65, 76; and Zinna, Berghaus, *op. cit.*, I, p. 512, and Hoppe, *op. cit.*, document No. 3.

authority of jurisdiction.[75] They might also have begun to extensively market certain products, and thus they developed great concern for the formal acquisition of freedom or exemption from the payment of tolls and fees on transportation routes to markets and in the market places themselves.[76]

If these developments were as fundamental as I am suggesting, it is unlikely that they could have taken place without attracting some official notice within the order; and, indeed, the Cistercians possessed, in the annual meetings of the General Chapter, the perfect device for dealing with infractions of policy. The legislation enacted by the General Chapter recorded all formal modifications in the original constitution and program. This is not to say that one should expect to observe the General Chapter initiating basic policy changes; but rather we ought to see here a reflection of the reality, as *de facto* changes became, with some time lag, *de jure*.

The category which bears most directly upon the subject of interest here is that of those enactments which dealt with tenurial relationships and arrangements. The original Cistercian program had proscribed the receipt of all types of revenues; land was only to be held and worked directly by the community. The meeting of the General Chapter in 1208, however, saw an explicit departure from these doctrines; an ordinance of that session stated:[77]

75. E.g., Chorin, Gercken, *op. cit.*, II, No. 236 (1288), No. 237 (1292); Riedel, *op. cit.*, Part 1, Vol. XIII, No. 9 (1261), No. 11 (1267), No. 31 (1288), No. 33 (1292), No. 47 (1309), No. 61 (1330), No. 72 (1339), and also Abb, *op. cit.*, pp. 97–98. Dargun, Lisch, *Urkunden*, No. 18 (1232), No. 20 (1238), No. 30 (1241), No. 34 (1248), No. 46 (1252), No. 51 (1257), No. 54 (1261), No. 57 (1264), No. 88 (1289), and also A. Wiswe, *op. cit.*, pp. 69–70, 96. Doberan, Westphalen, *op. cit.*, Part 1, No. 2 (1190), No. 39 (1262), No. 43 (1265), No. 56 (1278), No. 57 (1278), No. 58 (1280), No. 77 (1289), No. 81 (1292), No. 103 (1298); Part 2, No. 4 (1302), No. 27 (1306), No. 47 (1310), No. 65 (1319), No. 79 (1336), No. 82 (1345), No. 83 (1345). Dobrilugk, Ludewig, *op. cit.*, No. 29 (1234), No. 45 (1248), No. 87 (1276), No. 154 (1300), No. 214 (1324), No. 245 (1339). Lehnin, Riedel, *op. cit.*, Part 1, Vol. X, pp. 186 (1197), 189 (1205), 202 (1244), 220 (1294), 229 (1308), 231 (1317).

76. Examples are, for Chorin, Gercken, *op. cit.*, Vol. II, No. 240 (1296), No. 265 (1335), and Riedel, *op. cit.*, Part 1, Vol. XIII, No. 58 (1324), Nos. 66 and 67 (1335), No. 68 (1336); Dargun, Lisch, *Urkunden*, No. 31 (1242), No. 61 (1265), No. 78 (1283), No. 92 (1294), and also A. Wiswe, *op. cit.*, p. 60; Doberan, Westphalen, *op. cit.*, Part 1, No. 2 (1190), and also Compart, *op. cit.*, p. 82; Lehnin, Sello, *op. cit.*, p. 78; and for Zinna, Hopper, *op. cit.*, pp. 160–161. See also the comments of Gerards, *op. cit.*, p. 77; and J. W. Thompson, "The Cistercian Order and Colonisation in Medieval Germany," *American Journal of Theology*, XXIV (January, 1920), 92.

77. 1208, No. 5, in I, 346.

De terris qui minus utiles fuerint aut sic remotae quod utiliter excoli non possint, sic dispensat Capitulum generale, ut liceat iis qui tales habuerint dare ad medietatem vel aliter prout poterunt competenter.

In 1220, this relaxation was extended and the leasing of entire granges and other properties over fixed periods of time was permitted, subject to the requirement of obtaining prior consent and approval.[78] Four years later this dispensation was freed from its earlier restriction to those "less useful or more remote" properties, and became generally applicable "where expedient."[79] Efforts were made to keep acts of commendation within the constraints of the framework as it had evolved through successive general chapters;[80] but the fact that abbeys were beginning to receive rents on some of their properties is clearly attested.[81] It appears that these concessions led not infrequently to the—inadvertent or otherwise—ultimately complete alienation of some of the monasteries' lands. By 1312, evidently in recognition of such dangers, the General Chapter moved to tighten up the regulations concerning commendation; the next year this attempt was renewed and extended to sales.[82] In 1314, the General Chapter affirmed that the permission to dispose of properties had associated with it the concomitant duty of attempting to replace these with more useful ones, and was not to be taken as a general license for any and all commendations. Yet immediately in the following year more or less uncircumscribed freedom to commend lands and possessions to seculars, for life or in perpetuity, was instituted.[83] This was qualified by provision for a certain degree of control, to be exercised by the annual visitations; and further hedgings of this concession were subsequently enacted.[84] But the conclusion seems unavoidable that the process initiated in 1208 had proven to be both irreversible and accelerating.

By the year 1335, the general condition of Cistercian life and practice had become such that Pope Benedict II was moved to essay a thoroughgoing reformation of the order. Portions of his constitution of reform which have economic implications are far from minor. In the context of the present discussion, it required that acts of commendation or sale of possessions, rents, rights, etc., be authorized by visitor, General Chapter,

78. 1220, No. 5, in I, 517.
79. 1224, No. 10, in II, 31.
80. 1230, No. 34, in II, 91.
81. 1261, No. 10, in II, 477.
82. 1293, No. 2, 1312, No. 9, 1313, No. 1, in III, 261, 326, and 327, respectively.
83. 1314, No. 5, 1315, No. 4, in III, 329–330.
84. E.g., 1318, Nos. 6 and 18, 1322, No. 14, 1334, No. 11, in III, 339, 343, 361, and 409, respectively.

or even the pope himself.[85] The not inconsiderable number of petitions seeking such leave addressed to the General Chapter during the ensuing years perhaps testifies more to the continued activity of such dealings than to the real effectiveness of Benedict's reform.[86] It must be further observed that the pope endeavored not so much to return the Cistercians to their original economic principles as to oblige compliance with the changes which had been instituted in the interim.

A final important area in which similar changes in official policy took place concerns market transactions. The original theory implied that such activities be kept to an unavoidable minimum.[87] Of course, total abstention from the market was rarely, if ever, achieved; in particular, the monastery must always have engaged in the sale of occasional surplus production. But this minor incidence was capable of transformation into a major preoccupation. By 1157, for example, the General Chapter felt it appropriate to pronounce:[88]

> Multa de mercatoribus nostris querela est, multa confusio. Quia tamen ad nundinas nominates interdum mittere fratres nostros coemendarum mercium quibus utimur necessitas persuadet; hoc saltem consentiamus, ut nihil omnino vendamus in eis; sed cum vendimus res nostras ubi ubi, caveamus inhonestas commutationes, quas iterum venumdare debeamus, nec accipiamus in precio nisi aurum, argentum, aut nummos, vel tales merces quibus in ordine ordinate utimur. Constituimus etiam ne quoquo modo res nostras venales transmare convehamus.

In 1194, the assembled abbots decreed that those whom they termed the "merchants of our Order" should not negotiate sales at long-term contract in order to sell more dearly.[89] In fact it appears that by the end of the twelfth century the only prohibition which retained force was that against buying for the purpose of reselling, with a view toward profit.

If one focuses upon what may be considered the basic features of the Cistercian economic plan—exclusive self-cultivation of lands, rejection of all the standard feudal revenues, refusal to live "by the sweat of others"—

85. In Canivez, *op. cit.*, Vol. III, pp. 410–436, especially pp. 411–418.

86. A few examples from years immediately following are: 1341, No. 5, 1344, Nos. 30–32, 34–36, 38, 40–48, 53, 57, 58, 1345, No. 4, and 1347, No. 9, in III, 467–468, 485–493, 503–504, and 507, respectively.

87. *Instituta*, chap. li.

88. 1157, No. 35, in I, 64. See also Uhlhorn, *op. cit.*, pp. 374–375.

89. 1194, No. 3, in I, 171.

then the preceding analysis strongly suggests that a judgment must be passed against their faithful adherence to that program. Due to the inherently negative quality of the evidence which would indicate that the normative policies were being executed, the strongest assertion permitted is that the economy of the Cistercian monasteries studied here was a mixed one, exhibiting significant ingredients of the *rentier* type. The normative purity was, at a minimum, greatly diluted.

IV. Conclusion

It would be unsatisfactory merely to report what seems often to have been a growing dichotomization between plan and reality in the Cistercian economy. In conclusion, therefore, I offer some speculations as to the causes underlying the sequence.

As indicated previously, the successful functioning of the Cistercian economy may be expected on theoretical grounds to have resulted fairly regularly in the generation of some economic surplus.[90] The evidence points to the employment of much of this surplus toward the acquisition of more land for the abbey. But this could not have been a one-step operation. The Cistercian economy was essentially an agrarian economy; surplus production was in the form of agricultural produce. It was necessary to transform this into a more liquid asset, if the monks were to enter into the land market. They must, then, have had recourse to the sale of their surplus in the markets for agricultural products. On the scale on which we find the monasteries buying up lands, their engagement in the market place must indeed have been extensive.

Reference was made earlier to the argument which holds that the Cistercians became entangled in the secular milieu more or less willy-nilly —land acquisitions, through donation or otherwise, were not always in strict harmony with their normative posture. It was also suggested that gifts of land may have begun to come less often because of developments in the general economic environment. These are all aspects of a broader interpretation which maintains that the times were changing, that the European economy was becoming more and more "monetized," that the two centuries or so following the order's creation witnessed the transformation from a basically natural economy to a market economy. The Cistercian order, so this argument goes, was conceived at the end of the old era and wedded to the economic structure of a vanishing age; as time passed,

90. See above, pp. 92–94.

the Cistercian economic program was simply more and more out of step with the new age.[91] Ultimately, it had to give in.

This version of European economic history has been the subject of substantial debate and polemic; however, if one thinks in terms of a change in degree, emphasis, style, then the rendition may be acceptable.[92] As to the necessary impact of this evolution upon the Cistercian economy, I find the argument rather dubious. There is of course—what I consider to be—the fact of the abandonment of the original plan. But to observe this fact and then point to the general transformation of the European economy is to fall victim to the *post hoc ergo propter hoc* fallacy of logical argumentation. It can be conceded that such a change in the economic environment might well have made the attainment within it of the Cistercian economic ideal considerably more difficult—but not necessarily impossible. I think we are required to look a little further for an explanation of the deviance between theory and reality.

Some writers claim to discover in the history of the *conversi* class, the explanatory variable in the evolution of the Cistercian economy. The Cistercian labor force, in this theory, began to dry up as the supply of

91. E.g., Hoffmann, *Konverseninstitut*, p. 99; *idem.*, "Entwicklung," p. 726; Muggenthaler, *op. cit.*, p. 158; R. A. L. Smith, *Canterbury Cathedral Priory: A Study in Monastic Administration*, Cambridge Studies in Economic History (Cambridge, 1943), p. 126; Uhlhorn, *op. cit.*, pp. 347, 378–379; and Wiswe, *op. cit.*, p. 72.

Some authors delineate a sequence in acquisitive policies employed by the monasteries, starting with donation, moving to exchange, and culminating in purchase. Sometimes an explicit argument is made that exchange was a transitional stage, necessary while the abbeys were growing but before the economic environment had become sufficiently "monetized" to allow for the vigorous, active pursuit of expansion via purchase. See, e.g., C. Higounet, *op. cit.*, p. 47; and cf. Duby, *L'économie rurale*, pp. 384–386.

Such an argument, it seems to me, fails to draw an adequate distinction between rationalization of real estate holdings and territorial aggrandizement per se. As argued above, p. 102, the mechanism of exchange could not normally have resulted in any significant expansion of total holdings.

With regard to purchase, it is useful to note that secular trends over the period would imply that landowners on fixed incomes (*rentiers*) were being disadvantaged as a consequence of the general rise of prices, while the Cistercians, acquiring and working more and more lands, benefited by the contemporary appreciation in land values. See W. Abel, *Agrarkrisen und Agrarkonjunktur. Eine Geschichte der Land- und Ernährungswirtschaft Mitteleuropas seit dem hohen Mittelalter*, 2nd ed. (Hamburg and Berlin, 1966), pp. 27–40.

92. Consult M. Bloch, "Économie-nature ou économie-argent: un pseudo dilemme," *Annales d'Histoire sociale*, I (1939); A. Dopsch, "Gab es im Hochmittelalter einen Strukturwandel der Wirtschaft?" in the collection of his papers entitled, *Herrschaft und Bauer in der deutschen Kaiserzeit . . .*, Quellen und Forschungen zur Agrargeschichte, X, 2nd ed. (Stuttgart, 1964; first published 1939); and M. M. Postan, "The Rise of a Money Economy," *Economic History Review*, XIV, No. 2 (1944).

suitable aspirants to the status of lay brother declined. The decline was both quantitative and qualitative.[93] Without labor adequate to the needs of working their lands, the monasteries were compelled to accept rents and other revenues, and more especially to let out their properties at farm.[94] This is a reasonable and logical argument, and it is consistent with a considerable amount of (sometimes quite indirect) evidence. The records of the General Chapter, for instance, contain episodic but recurrent indications of very serious disciplinary as well as other problems caused by the *conversi* in many monasteries. The malaise appears to have been general.[95]

It then becomes necessary to understand why both the quality and the quantity of entrants into the Cistercian lay brotherhood should have been

93. See Donnelly, *Decline*, pp. 40–41, but cf. p. 66; Duby, *L'économie rurale*, pp. 507–508; Gerards, *op. cit.*, p. 78; Hoffmann, *Konverseninstitut*, pp. 98, 100–101; Uhlhorn, *op. cit.*, p. 377, and note 2; H. Wiswe, *op. cit.*, pp. 72–73; and Muggenthaler, *op. cit.*, p. 113.

94. Donelly, *Decline*, pp. 58–59; Gerards, *loc. cit.*, Abb, *op. cit.*, p. 101; H. Wiswe, *op. cit.*, p. 61; Wittich, *op. cit.*, p. 655; and Muggenthaler, *op. cit.*, pp. 153–154, 168.

The argument can run in both directions. Decline in the quality of *conversi* was an incentive to the monasteries to let out lands so as to minimize the problems caused by *conversi*, by minimizing the number of lay brothers required by the community; and the contraction in the supply of *conversi* forced the abbeys to let out their lands, because the labor force was inadequate to the working of the demesne. See, e.g., Donnelly, "Changes," p. 458; and *Decline*, p. 52. But also cf. Bishop, *op. cit.*, p. 211; Donkin, "Some Conclusions," p. 188; and H. Wiswe, *op. cit.*, pp. 70, 72, 98.

95. E.g., see these General Chapter *statuta*: 1192, Nos. 16 and 19; 1195, No. 20; 1196, Nos. 44 and 52; 1199, No. 39; 1206, No. 23; 1226, Nos. 4 and 23; 1228, No. 14; 1232, No. 10; 1236, No. 32; 1237, Nos. 3 and 32; 1261, Nos. 7 and 32; 1274, No. 12; 1275, No. 13; 1279, No. 64; 1338, No. 13; in, respectively, I, 149; I, 185; I, 205 and 207; I, 240; I, 324; II, 48 and 52–53; II, 67–68; II, 102; II, 159; II, 169 and 174; II, 476–477 and 482; III, 128–129; III, 141; III, 192; III, 453.

One problem which recurs in the records concerns the propensity of *conversi*—and indeed even monks—to absent themselves from the abbey over long periods of time, in the employ of various secular magnates. Such employment had always been prohibited (see the *statuta* of 1157, No. 47, in I, 66; 1175, No. 33, in I, 84); but violations were numerous (e.g., 1212, Nos. 29, 45, and 48, in I, 395–396, 399–400; 1218, No. 31, in I, 491; 1219, No. 30, in I, 509; 1221, No. 18, in II, 4). By 1232, the General Chapter, subject to its special approval, was permitting such arrangements for *conversi* (1232, No. 10, in II, 102); in 1233, the provision was repeated (1233, No. 3, in II, 108). Over the following years petitions to the General Chapter seeking this permission were frequent (e.g., 1238, Nos. 17, 18, 20, and 25, in II, 180; 1242, Nos. 43 and 45, in II, 260; 1246, Nos. 21 and 22, in II, 305; 1250, Nos. 7 and 8, in II, 347); and by 1274 the practice was common (1274, No. 12, in III, 128–129).

Donnelly (*Decline*, pp. 71–80) lists one hundred and twenty-three revolts of *conversi* over the period 1168–1308. The General Chapter appears to have approved the introduction of a prison for unruly lay brothers about 1200; see Winter, *op. cit.*, p. 26. As

deteriorating. In part, it may again be a question of the Cistercian order gradually having been left behind, having gotten out of step with an emerging new age, here specifically in respect of the religious character of the times. In the twelfth century, in particular, it had been the reformed monastic orders which captured the imagination and religious fervor of the society. As has been mentioned, this in part accounts for the extremely rapid growth of the Cistercian order, after Bernard's conversion, as well as for the flood of donations to new and young Cistercian abbeys. But the thirteenth and fourteenth centuries witnessed a virtually unprecedented phenomenon in western Europe, the appearance of uncloistered monks whose vocation was as much in this world as it was directed toward the next. To judge by the popular response accorded the mendicants, their development was very much in answer to a felt need in the society, a need which conventional monasticism had been increasingly unable to satisfy. It is often suggested that the changing nature of society and in particular its growing urbanization explains the relative appeal of the mendicants, whose favorite sphere of activity was the city, as compared with the cenobites, who withdrew to rural isolation. Be that as it may, it does seem clear that the mendicant orders presented a very real challenge to the Cistercians. The former became the new objects of popular favor; and, more importantly perhaps, they competed with the latter for recruits. It is useful to observe that the mendicants' strongest appeal seems to have been to members of those lower classes which hitherto had supplied the Cistercian order with its *conversi*.[96]

In summary, it might be suggested that the basic cause of the Cistercian failure lay in its initial success. The founders at Cîteaux succeeded in reforming their monastic practice. This resulted in popular enthusiasm for the order, which was manifested in part by sizable endowments for its abbeys. The introduction and successful operation of the economic plan resulted in the generation of some economic surplus. This in turn afforded the opportunity for further physical expansion, which widened even more the monastery's economic base. The ultimate result was the creation of the

---

H. Wiswe points out, the evidence here again is not unbiased, for it is the disturbances which are always reported, while satisfactory and unexceptional conditions do not merit recording (*op. cit.*, pp. 96–97).

The malaise may in fact have been quite general, rather than just limited to the Cistercians; see, e.g., D. Knowles, "The Revolt of the Lay Brothers of Sempringham," *English Historical Review*, I, No. 199 (July, 1935).

96. See H. Wiswe, *op. cit.*, p. 73; and F. Schevill, "San Galgane: A Cistercian Abbey in the Middle Ages," *American Historical Review*, XIV, No. 1 (October, 1908), p. 31.

possibility—and the temptation—to modify the original austerity of the monks' regimen. The modifications in life style and in the economy reinforced one another in a symbiotic manner, and there was little resistance to the changes. The consequence was the transformation of the religious quality of the monks' life and of the economy upon which that life was based. A program of religious reform had been associated with a normative economic program: deviation from the ideal in one respect implied deviation in the other.[97] The Cistercian reform failed and the failure was total; with respect both to religion and to economic organization, the order rejoined the mainstream of western monasticism.

The tentative conclusions arrived at in this study, on the basis of acquaintance with the records of a very small number of abbeys, are lent strength by the work of the present author and of others on monasteries in parts of Europe beyond Germany; preliminary indications are that the facts of the evolution in the Cistercian economy are much the same, at least for England and France.[98] Of course, much detailed investigation remains to be accomplished before broad generalizations may be offered confidently.

97. Gerards, *op. cit.*, p. 66; Hoffmann, "Entwicklung," p. 727; Thiele, *op. cit.*, p. 149; and Uhlhorn, *op. cit.*, pp. 378, 401–402.

98. G. T. Beech, *A Rural Society in Medieval France: The Gâtine of Poitou in the Eleventh and Twelfth Centuries*, Johns Hopkins University Studies in Historical and Policial Science, LXXXII, No. 1 (Baltimore, 1964); H. Dubled, "Aspects de l'économie Cistercienne en Alsace au XIIᵉ siècle," *Revue d'Histoire Ecclésiastique*, LIV, No. 4 (1959); Duby, *L'économie rurale*, p. 418; R. Fossier, "Les Granges de Clairvaux et la règle cistercienne," *Cîteaux in de Nederlanden*, VI, No. 1 (1955), p. 266; but cf. O. Martin-Lorber, "L'Exploitation d'une grange cistercienne à la fin des XIVᵉ siècle et an début du XVᵉ siècle," *Annales de Bourgogne*, III (July/September, 1957); and Hill, *op. cit.*

FLORENCE, BY THE GRACE OF THE LORD POPE...

Richard C. Trexler

University of Illinois at Urbana-Champaign

ACKNOWLEDGMENTS

For their help in clarifying the material in this paper, I thank Domenico Maffei, John Najemy, Julius Kirshner, John Stevens, and Randolph Starn. My special thanks are due Gene Brucker and Frederic Jaher for reading and criticizing it. The views and errors are my own. The research was completed while I was a Fellow at the Harvard University Center for Italian Renaissance Studies (Villa I Tatti).

FLORENCE, BY THE GRACE OF THE
LORD POPE...

> Faith, useful above other things, the great sustainer
> of the needs of the Republic.
>
> Matteo Villani[1]

Trecento Florence was not a sovereign state. But it desired to be. The legal concept of communal sovereignty was being worked out by Bartolus, and the commune worked toward this clearly understood goal. Its attitude toward the church, says one author, was not much different from that of the modern state: It attempted to limit privilege and break down judicial immunities.[2]

These statements are fairly representative of modern thinking on the dynamics of the Italian commune.[3] According to this view, the greatest hindrance to sovereignty in domestic affairs was the existence of a local clergy whose lord was in Rome. Cautious historians have not minimized the task lying before the commune, but there has been little question that weakening clerical immunities was a long-range goal of an emerging secular state.[4] These same historians have also harbored no illusions concerning the power of the papacy to limit the foreign policy initiatives of

1. *Croniche di Giovanni, Matteo e Filippo Villani* (Trieste, 1858), Matteo: III, 106. All subsequent references to the Villani are to book and chapter.

2. G. A. Brucker, *Florentine Politics and Society, 1343–1378* (Princeton, 1962), pp. 57, 96 f.

3. See for example L. Martines, *Lawyers and Statecraft in Renaissance Florence* (Princeton, 1968), chap. 10. For bibliography, see *ibid.*, pp. 448 ff.

4. For Marvin Becker this process was practically complete by the 1380s; see most recently "The Florentine Territorial State and Civic Humanism in the Early Renaissance," in N. Rubinstein (ed.), *Florentine Studies* (London, 1968), pp. 110 f. For the period under consideration in this paper, see the same author's "Church and State in Florence on the Eve of the Renaissance (1343–1382)," *Speculum*, XXXVII (1962), pp. 509–527. The most recent article on this period is by P. Partner, "Florence and the Papacy, 1300–1375," in J. Hale *et al.* (eds.), *Europe in the Late Middle Ages* (London, 1965), pp. 76–121. Lauro Martines has made an important discovery showing the decline of communal judicial sovereignty in the second half of the quattrocento (*op. cit.*, pp. 281 ff.).

the commune. The pope, because of his support of the Italian international merchant, because of his ability to cause damage to a city's merchandizing through excommunication and interdiction,[5] and because of his use of local clergy and favored families in his own interest, definitely impinged on the diplomatic maneuverability of the city.

This view of the papacy is not much different from the modern concept of the limitation of sovereignty by neighboring states. Lebanon, for example, may act freely to the extent that its divided population and the relationship of forces in the Middle East permit it to.

For all the caution of post-*Risorgimento* historians, however, the analysis of the Italian commune continues to suffer from the old bias of the anti-clerical nationalists, who automatically equated independence with the limitation of the clergy. Historians often continue to write as if there existed in Italy in the Late Middle Ages a number of independent states. Every North Italian schoolboy grows up to study the history of his "free, independent, and glorious" city. "At the beginning of the second half of the fourteenth century," writes Alberto Tenenti in a recent book, "Florence is one of the numerous independent communes of the Italian peninsula. The magistrates of the city do not derive their authority from abroad, and they can treat with foreign princes as equals."[6] In keeping with this operating principle, the historical problems of each town are generally examined from within. Writing is divided between domestic and foreign politics, the papacy being considered one of the many foreign stumbling blocks affecting political action.

Overdrawn as this portrayal may be, it allows me to locate the central problem of this paper, that of Matteo Villani's "faith." Historical writing on Italian republics would not in the least lead us to suspect that the vaunted *libertas* of these communes might *not* include the means and authority to draft, enforce, and revise their own laws. One would naturally assume that the hindrances to drafting and passing laws affecting the management of the commune were strictly internal, enforcing them the existence of privilege, revising them the presence of internal opposition. That a commune like Florence might not have been able to institute or

5. R. C. Trexler, *Economic, Political, and Religious Effects of the Papal Interdict on Florence, 1376–1378* (Frankfurt am Main, 1964).

6. A. Tenenti, *Firenze dal Comune a Lorenzo il Magnifico, 1350–1494* (Milan, 1970), p. 11. G. Salvemini took over this Risorgimento point of view and passed it on to modern critical historiography. For him communes were like modern states; they of necessity "constituted themselves in perfectly autonomous organisms and assured themselves the unlimited exercise of sovereignty" ("Le Lotte fra Stato e Chiesa nei comuni italiani durante il secolo XIII," in his *Studi Storici* [Florence, 1901], pp. 40 ff.).

revise legislation without the special permission of another power—to wit, the papacy—conflicts with our most basic assumptions about the nature of the Italian "state system" of the Late Middle Ages. And yet, this was precisely the case in Florence in midtrecento. Despite characterizations of the period from 1343 to 1379 as the most democratic in the republic's history, when a government heavily influenced by newcomers sought the goal of a "territorial state," in part by ruthlessly regimenting the Florentine church to its local will, Florence was much less independent during this period than has generally been realized.[7]

It is the argument of this paper that the regime which ruled Florence from 1345 to 1375 survived because the papacy was willing to permit its continuance. The limits of its sovereignty were not only diplomatic, they were institutionalized; they were structural. Historians have pictured the clash with the Inquisitor in 1346 as symptomatic of the new regime, marked from the outset by anticlericalism and the rude assertion of communal autonomy.[8] This misses the forest for the trees. In fact, the regime was first stabilized by the cession of significant segments of its judicial autonomy to the papacy, and could hope to continue for long only through its cession of those rights. Historians have seen the solution of the financial crisis of the 1340s in decisive communal action to defend its wealth from attacks from abroad.[9] In fact, it will be argued, more basic to preventing communal bankruptcy in that decade was the credibility of the commune to its own citizens. And the only way to create financial confidence in the commune was to consciously bind the hands of the government and send the key to the Roman Curia. The following essay will present the evidence for this view of church-state interdependence.

The amortization of an irredeemable public debt on February 22, 1345, was a turning point in the history of the commune. It represented a financial revolution in that private investments in the new debt (the *Monte Comune*) were secured not by the wealth or coercive power of the

7. It has been argued that the old merchant oligarchs were rich, close to the papacy, and took little interest in their business dealings with Rome. The new men, still close in many cases to a money lending, usurious past, chaffed under the official usury conscience of Rome, resented their social superiors' monopolistic access to ecclesiastical offices, etc. In part from these feelings came the desire and the energy to assert the sovereignty of the commune (Brucker, *Politics*, pp. 135 ff.; M. Becker, *Florence in Transition*, 2 vols. [Baltimore, 1967–68], I, 206).

8. A. Panella, "La Politica Ecclesiastica del Comune di Firenze dopo la Cacciata del Duca d'Atene," *Archivio Storico Italiano*, LXXI, No. 2 (1913), 271–327.

9. A. Sapori, *La Crisi delle Compagnie Mercantili dei Bardi e dei Peruzzi* (Florence, 1926).

commonweal, but by the papacy.[10] Given this startling fact, it behooves us to start by examining the elements of citizen faith before this date, and then describe the new financial structure.

In two recent volumes on Florence covering the first three quarters of the century, Marvin Becker has put forward the view that communal coercion was "gentle" in the period before the 1340s, and "stern" thereafter. The term gentle *paideia* is used by Becker to characterize a laissez-faire attitude of the coercive authority in the earlier period. Laws were more frequently suspended to allow for the exercise of influence before the 1340s than they were subsequently.[11] In this view, then, the state—an objective thing with its own *ragione*—was present from the beginning. Whatever the means to educate its citizens, they were *its* means.

A glance at the coercive practices of the earlier period do verify one aspect of this theory; indeed, the coercive mechanisms of the commune were its own. They were internal. Most directly, this means that communal law had financial penalties payable to the commune, and corporal penalties carried out by its officials.

This ability of the commune to enforce its own laws extended from that group of laws which regulated the behavior of private citizens up through the body of law which spelled out the operation of the commune itself: those governing the distribution and rights of office, taxing and repayment of communal loans, communal defense of commercial interests, etc., in short, the pillars of faith of the political class.

Of the two categories of law above, the stability of the communal regulative laws was clearly paramount in the minds of contemporaries. For a spicer to use false weights was despicable; for the priors to break the laws of office-holding (*divieti*) was to endanger the republic itself. Thus this latter group of laws was treated with greater solemnity. Once passed, they were encased in a legal form which aimed at insuring their relative perpetuity.

When a particularly crucial law of this type was passed, one which required a long-term guarantee, it was given *precise* form. A rider or *clausula penalis* was attached to it which made the attempt to modify such a law a punishable offense.[12] In certain cases, modification in any form

10. Until recently, only R. Davidsohn seems to have noticed this. And with his unerring sense for detecting moral hypocrisy, he immediately put his finger on one of its most significant implications: the conflict between questionable interest and papal approval of that interest (*Storia di Firenze*, 8 vols., [Florence, 1956–68], V, 235 f.).

11. Becker, *Transition*, I, 203, 209.

12. A. Bozzi, "Penale, Clausola," in *Enciclopedia Giuridica Italiana*, Vol. XIII (Milan, 1911), especially pp. 210–227.

or at any time was forbidden. This was particularly the case with communal loans, where any modification was an intolerable breach of communal faith. We shall call these precise laws *perpetual*. In other cases, modification was possible, but only after a solemn procedure in which varying high majorities of the thirty-seven-man executive (the *tre maggiori*) had to recommend the change before the bill could go to the legislative councils. Depending on the faith required, twenty-eight, thirty-three, or a unanimity of the executive might be necessary. These precise laws are called *solemn* in what follows.

The security clause in its pre-1345 form may be perused in the statutes of the *capitano del popolo* of 1322–1325.[13] According to the two rubrics involved, the clause was used first of all to secure laws ordaining the procedure for the election, entry, residence, and final syndication of the principal foreign officials of the commune. All the varied *divieti* attached to these offices were covered by this clause. Secondly, laws regulating the disposition of the estates of *cessantes et fugientes* (bankrupt merchants who had fled the commune) were not to be modified, and were secured by this clause. *Rappresaglia* laws, certain laws governing the scribes of the *Signoria*, the modification of the statutes of the *capitano* or of the *podestà*—all were secured by this rider. Finally, there were laws of a temporary nature, such as those authorizing state loans, which were secured in this fashion, although they were not taken into the body of the fundamental statutes.[14]

Examining the clause itself will give us an idea of the penal force necesssary to perpetuate these laws. It aimed at preventing modification by specifically naming each step in the legislative process at which an intention to modify such a law might be furthered.[15] The priors were forbidden to ordain that it would be useful to call a private or public meeting to consider modification. Attendance at such a meeting was prohibited. Such a recommendation at this illicit meeting was out of order. Speaking specifically of the *divieti* laws affecting *capitano* and *podestà*, the rubric prohibits these officials from calling their respective legislative councils to consider such modifications.[16] Under threat of heavy fines, councilors were held to report such felonies.

The penalties attached to each prohibition were first of all financial,

13. R. Caggese (ed.), *Statuti della Repubblica Fiorentina*, Vol. I (Florence, 1910) (*Statuto del Capitano del Popolo degli Anni 1322–1325*), II, 6–7 (pp. 92–97).

14. *Ibid.*, pp. 92 f.

15. *Ibid.*, pp. 93 f., 96 f. The single steps are those in the later document printed in the Appendix (see below, pp. 213–15).

16. Caggese (ed.), *Statuti*, p. 97. See also below, p. 132.

then removal from office and, for the councilors guilty of transgression, banishment from the Dominion. The fine for government officials was generally L1,000, approximately 335 florins (ca. 1325). Councilors were fined L500 for infringement. Removal from office and/or banning were additionally stipulated for priors, councilors, *podestà*, *capitano*, and notaries involved in the irregularities.[17]

In addition to these penalties, a system of bonding was used for certain officials. This insured the payment of fines when they were incurred. When the priors and *gonfaloniere della giustizia* took their oath of office, each had to post a bond of L1,000 through communally approved bondsmen and swear to uphold specified laws, for example, the *divieti* laws on the *capitano* and *podestà*.[18] This oath was taken before a notary who acted as a repository of the rights of the commune "and anyone else who has or could have an interest."[19] This meant that the damaged party, he who under certain circumstances could recoup monies from this bond, was the commune, or it and unknowns who had been damaged by the attempt to modify the law or by its (illegal) modification. Finally, the *esecutore della giustizia* was given the perpetual right to prosecute violators of this clause. Thus there was no statute of limitations for this type of malfeasance in office.

These penalties may be characterized as stringent, but not massive enough to discourage a determined and moderately rich legislator from attempting a modification. Most important, the penalizing and the imbursing agent of the penalties was the commune. The city was defending its own laws with its own means. This meant that the laws might be modified through personal influence, exercised from within the commune itself.

The *divieti* laws governing the foreign officials served the purpose of insuring that outsiders brought in to adjudicate would not then subvert communal liberty.[20] They limited the term of office, forbade re-elections, regulated the recurrence of families in such offices, and so forth. It does not have to be stressed how important it was to tie the hands of the Florentine political class in this matter. It was just as important to stabilize the body of laws governing the disposition of bankrupt persons' estates.[21] These laws sought to insure that the estates would be available

17. *Ibid.*, pp. 94, 96 f.

18. *Ibid.*, p. 96.

19. "Stipulando vice et nomine Communis Florentie et omnium quorum interesset vel interesse posset . . ." (*ibid.*).

20. For this typical theme, see the suspicions regarding an *esecutore della giustizia* in Brucker, *Politics*, p. 63.

21. On the process of receivership, see Davidsohn, *Storia*, V, 556–569.

to the commune for clearing the bankrupts' debts. At the same time, titles or usufruct rights over real property given by the commune to creditors in recompense for a debt had to be impeccable. A penal clause was the means chosen to guarantee title over immobile property. Since the debts of these merchants often involved foreign parties, this surety was necessary for safeguarding of the wider merchant community. Without it, the danger of *rappresaglie* against Florentine merchant colonies was much greater.

The faith of the commune was, however, most crucially in question when it borrowed. Here the penal clauses were of course insufficient in themselves. The lenders, and especially those lending voluntarily at high interest, could not count on "the security of the state" with which modern Europeans are acquainted. The commune needed collateral as did any other borrower. The debts of the commune were considered redeemable before 1345, and the lender sought the best guarantees for the return of interest and capital which the commune could offer. The most common of these was the binding assignment or stipulation of certain future revenues to pay the interest and capital on the loans.[22] These revenues were usually the communal gabelles. In addition, it was common to oblige the revenues which the commune had at its disposition from the sale or usufruct of lands of banished citizens. Titles or rights on these lands had to be predictable in order to be effective collateral. If lenders too often saw a banished individual being readmitted and reclaiming his patrimony and the past usufruct of that estate, they would reject this type of security. A modification of this security was to actually sell or farm gabelles to individual citizens, who therewith had in their own hands the means to recoup their investment.

In the briefest form, these are the various legislative and practical means through which the pre-1345 commune created the faith in its institutions necessary to claim the support of the political class.

Surely, however, the coercive force of these securities in the best of times was made possible by certain structural symbioses binding Florentines to forces beyond the commune. There were two external, structural securities which are important to an understanding of the subsequent crisis.

The first is the triangular relations between the capital-producing commercial *compagnie* of Florence, the papacy, and the commune. Until the financial catastrophe of the 1340s, the great companies had on the one side a virtual monopoly of the collection business of the Roman see, as

22. B. Barbadoro, *Le Finanze della Repubblica Fiorentina* (Florence, 1929), pp. 526, 583–587.

well as substantial incomes from the English crown.[23] The predictability of their incomes from the transferral of the papal collections and from their steady investments in the papacy and other monarchies had a decisive effect on the security of Florentine legislation. For, on the other side, until the crisis of the forties these companies' interests were in large measure identical to those of the commune itself. This was expressed in their controlling voice in the halls of government in Florence.[24] Consequently, a very essential part of the security on a communal loan before the bankruptcies was the flow of capital from the Roman see and from England. Given the capital dependence of lesser Florentine firms on the three giant banks of the Bardi, Acciaiuoli, and Peruzzi, it may be said that in a sense, the citizens of Florence were loaning to themselves. As long as this continued, the security of Florentine institutions would remain relatively high. If the banks collapsed, or the homogeneity of interests between great banks and government was sullied, the strength of communal institutions would be severely tested.

The second external security concerns the judicial status of Florentines abroad. There were three cases in which these merchants were not, in fact, subject in first line to the city courts, but to foreign ones.

No merchant abroad would lend unless he could prosecute a debtor in that court where he had the best chance to recoup his investment. Whatever the home laws might say about Florentines not suing their compatriots for debt in foreign courts, if a member of the Ruspi family in Provence borrowed from another Florentine, he would probably have to promise his submission to the court of the apostolic camera at Avignon or to the civil courts at Montpellier. It was in those areas that this family had the wealth from which legal recompense might be expected in case of default. Florence was far away.[25]

A variant on this procedure was the *obligatio in forma camere apostolice*.[26]

23. Y. Renouard, *Les Relations des Papes d'Avignon et des Compagnies Commerciales et Bancaires de 1316 à 1378* (Paris, 1941); Davidsohn, *Storia*, VI, 690–726.

24. Becker, *Transition*, I, 89.

25. An example: When Jacopo Corbizzi died in Avignon in 1336, the Acciaiuoli refused to repay 500 florins of an outstanding debt to the remaining associates of the Girolami-Corbizzi company, for fear that Jacopo's estate would later make a claim. In order to have the sum, Filippo Corbizzi "mi ne ubrighai a la chamera del papa, al sugielli di Mopolieri, ad ongni chorte in avere i persona" to defend the Acciaiuoli if such a subsequent claim were ever made (M. Chiaudano [ed.], *Il Libro Vermiglio di Corte di Roma e di Avignone del Segnale del C, della Compagnia Fiorentina di Jacopo Girolami, Filippo Corbizzi e Tommaso Corbizzi [1332–1337]* [Turin, 1963], pp. 128–131).

26. See A. Campitelli, *Precetto di Guarentigia e Formule di Esecuzione Parata nei Documenti Italiani del Secolo XIII* (Rome, 1970), pp. 135–142. I thank Domenico Maffei for

By such an obligation in a contract, the debtor promised *in curia* or before a curial commissioner that if he failed to meet the terms of the contract, the apostolic camera was to execute the contract by penal procedures which foresaw the excommunication of the debtor and the automatic institution of the papal camera as the recipient of the fruits of the debtor's property up to the amount of the debt involved, plus costs. The peculiarity of this form of security was that it used spiritual penalties, and that it was international in scope. For the institution of the camera and the excommunication of the debtor were commonly carried out by the local collector and the local bishop. Thus the bishop of Florence and the Tuscan collector executed in Florence a decision of the auditors of the camera in Avignon.[27]

The third case in which merchants might be immune from home courts occurred when, as was so often the case, Florentine merchants at the papal court were legally members of the papal household, and thus subject to the Roman Curia. These merchants *curiam romanam sequentes* often used the curial courts as courts of first instance for the collection of loans rather than the distant *Mercanzia* or court merchant in Florence.[28]

Thus beyond the sketch of institutionalized securities of the commune, we have offered elements of the external securities involved. First of all, the security of the commune was intimately tied to the financial potency of its great families with the papacy and to the power of these same papal bankers in communal councils. Secondly, the international merchant was

---

this reference. The notarial formula can be read in most early printed notarial formularies. For many quattrocento cases involving Florentines, see *Archivio Arcivescovile, Firenze, Atti Straordinari, ser Domenico da Figline,* filza 2, fols. 200r–201v *et passim* (1469); hereafter cited as *AAF.* See also G. Holmes, "How the Medici Became the Pope's Bankers," in Rubinstein (ed.), *Florentine Studies,* p. 362.

27. For a case of an excommunication in the diocese of Florence of a citizen who had accused in Florentine secular court one Florentine of suing another in Avignon, see *Archivio Segreto Vaticano, Instrumenta Miscellanea,* 2064 (Nov. 5, 1356), 2095 (June 28, 1357); hereafter cited as *ASV.*

28. On this problem of the judiciability of followers of the Roman Curia, see G. Levi, "Bonifazio VIII e le sue Relazioni col Comune di Firenze," *Archivo della Società Romana di Storia Patria,* V (1882), 400 f, 455–458; G. Tellenbach, "Beiträge zur Kurialen Verwaltungsgeschichte im Vierzehnten Jahrhundert," *Quellen und Forschungen aus Italienischen Archiven und Bibliotheken,* XXIV (1933), 165, 180 f.; G. Mollat (ed.), *Lettres Secrètes et Curiales du Pape Grégoire XI (1370–1378) intéressant les pays autres que la France* (Paris, 1956–65), nn. 827, 829; G. Mollat, "Les Conflits de Juridiction entre le Maréchal de la Cour Pontificale et le Viguier d'Avignon au XIVe Siècle," *Provence Historique,* IV (1954), 11–18. For a form letter claiming cameral jurisdiction over a merchant citizen of Florence because he was a courtier following the curia, see *ASV, Diversa Cameralia,* 20, fol. 77r (Feb. 10, 1438).

commonly active in foreign courts in the defense of his interests vis-à-vis other Florentines. The same group which secured communal institutions secured itself by extracommunal means.

An example of this triangle of interests is afforded by a loan arrangement through which the commune financed an alliance with Venice against the Scaglieri of Verona in the years 1336–1338. The law instituting the loan reveals at the same time the contours of the crisis of faith which would arise in 1345 in the securing of the commune from abroad.

Giovanni Villani tells us that in the wake of the treaty, the commune took steps to fulfill its financial obligations for the coming war.[29] A commission of ten merchants from the leading companies in the city was elected to find the necessary money, and it was given power to assign up to 300,000 florins of future gabelle income to cover repayment. That is, the commission could secure loans it would obtain by promising that certain gabelle incomes up to 300,000 florins would be used exclusively to repay loans and interest. There was, however, one difficulty. The commune had already stipulated 100,000 florins of future gabelle income to previously incurred debts. This meant that the security which the gabelles offered to potential creditors was not as strong as might be desired. The ten would have to reckon with lenders who, in Villani's words, "would not want to believe in the commune on the basis of the said gabelles."[30]

Given the commune's lack of credibility, there was no alternative but to use securities external to those the commune could offer. Representing as they did the leading companies in the city, the ten called in "other merchants wise and subtle in these matters," and counseled together in search of a solution. The decision was to place the burden of raising the money squarely on the backs of the companies: "One found a method in which the companies and the merchants of Florence took upon themselves the task of furnishing the money for the said undertaking."[31]

29. *Croniche*, XI, 50. The treaty was signed July 15, 1336.
30. "Chi non vollese credere al comune sopra le dette gabelle" (*ibid.*).
31. "E' Fiorentini elessono dieci savi cittadini mercatanti, e delle maggiori compagnie di Firenze, con piena balía a trovare moneta e fornire la detta guerra; e assegnarono loro trecentomila fiorini d'oro l'anno sopra certe gabelle, raddoppiandole gran parte. E per cagione che 'l nostro comune in questo tempo, per le guerre e spese fatte per addietro, si trovò indebitate le gabelle e l'entrate del comune per lo tempo a venire in più di fiorini centomila d'oro, e danari bisognavano maneschi per fornire la detta impresa; i detti dieci oficiali sopra i fatti di Vinegia, col consiglio d'altri mercatanti savi e sottili a ciò fare, e in ttra' quali noi fummo di quelli, si trovò modo, che le compagnie e' mercatanti di Firenze prendessono sopra loro lo 'ncarico di fornire di moneta per la detta impresa ..." (*ibid.*).

In raising the initial loan of 100,000 florins, the companies themselves promised to loan one-third of the total. The rest was to be raised from other wealth in the city. Three lending eventualities were foreseen in the raising of the latter two-thirds. First came the case of lenders who "believed the commune," and would loan to it on the strength of its assigned gabelles. They were to receive 15 percent interest. Then came the citizens who had the money to loan, but who "non volesse credere al comune sopra le dette gabelle." The merchants decided to give these individuals the security of the companies themselves. Such lenders would earn interest of only 8 percent, while the companies securing the loan would in turn imburse 5 percent from the commune for such loans. Thus the commune carried a total interest burden of 13 percent on such loans secured by its merchant-bankers. Evidently in 1336 these private securities were superior to those of the commune, even though the companies themselves were already showing signs of the financial vulnerability which within a few years would bring the whole economy to the brink of ruin. The security the commune had to offer required a high-risk interest of 15 percent. The companies were safer, and the lender received only 8 percent. Finally, a third contingency was used for lenders who did not have the cash to lend under either security arrangement. These had to find a merchant willing to assume the obligation, but then also imburse the creditor's interest. This was the most attractive arrangement for the banker: he stood to gain 20 percent per annum on such assumed obligations.[32]

Bernardo Barbadoro, the historian of Florentine finances until mid-trecento, did not miss the significance of this procedure. The tightening of available credit had created a situation in which "the mercantile companies became the intermediaries between the contributors and the commune. . . . With this finance plan the capitalistic class showed itself as almost the only supporter of the public fisc."[33] It was not new, of course, that the companies furnished security. What was new was that their intermediary function was institutionalized.

What may seem to us a striking innovation appeared less imposing to contemporaries. For Villani it was simply a sagacious business arrangement. Why should he be struck by an arrangement which put this segment of communal finances on an overtly "businesslike" basis? Did he not assume as natural a civic order in which the financial power of the great

32. For future reference, note this particular on those loaning at 15 percent on the gabelles: "avesse di guiderdone *libero e sanza tenimento di restituzione* a ragione di quindici per cento l'anno" (*ibid.*; italics mine).

33. Barbadoro, *Finanze*, pp. 579, 581. See also Sapori, *Crisi*, pp. 109 f.

houses dominated the town councils, whose credit was that of the houses of the papal court?

Let us summarize what has been said on financial securities up to the crisis of the 1340s. In securing its laws, the commune used penal clauses levying fines payable to the commune of Florence and, at times, to other hurt parties within the commune. The coercion could be internal because those making and breaking precise laws were generally of the same social strata of the population. The penal threats themselves were not prohibitive. In addition, the international merchants in practice used foreign courts against compatriots. This *gentle paideia* functioned as long as foreign profits from the great houses were steady and could subvent war budgets at home. Faith in the Florentine merchant abroad and at home mixed with a homogeneity between political and financial power in the commune to produce Villani's euphoric description of Florence in 1338.[34]

Armando Sapori and Barbadoro are those historians who have given extensive attention to the financial crises of the forties. Barbadoro concentrated almost exclusively on public finance, Sapori on the bankruptcies. These emphases have caused one important aspect of the crises to go unnoticed: The government which emerged from the disasters of the early forties had as one of its most difficult tasks the creation among the citizenry of a faith in government.[35]

There was a radical change in office-holding patterns. Gene Brucker has shown that between 1343 and 1348, fully two-thirds of the seats held in the *Signoria* were retained by individuals whose families had not previously been represented in communal office.[36] These "new men" of property were faced with significant social agitation from below. Because of a lack of experience in communal affairs and because of property interests, these men allied themselves with the older families. It is thus Brucker's contention that "no single group or class controlled the communal government" in the early years of the regime.[37]

The problems facing this new regime were formidable. In 1342 foreign creditors had started to demand their credits from the faltering banks, and the credit Florentine merchants abroad had enjoyed quickly turned to

34. *Croniche*, XI, 94.

35. Barbadoro, *Finanze*, pp. 654–666; Sapori, *Crisi*. Gene Brucker alludes to this problem: the regime survived "because it had won the allegiance and support of large and important segments of the citizenry" (Brucker, *Politics*, p. 387).

36. Brucker, *Politics*, pp. 105 f.

37. *Ibid.*, p. 106.

poco fede.[38] The government had to correct this situation with all due speed, and its instrument was the passage of laws guaranteeing a percentage of real debt to all creditors.[39] From the first, however, the commune was forced to grant preferential treatment to the papacy, the college of cardinals, and to certain key Italian political figures.[40] Equal treatment of creditors remained a pious sentiment.

Every florin paid to a foreign creditor was that much less paid to domestic creditors. If more money left the companies for abroad, less remained to finance the costs of government. Thus the government had to balance the imperative need for faith in its international merchants with its own immediate needs at home. For the regime to survive, it had to insure that potential lenders to the commune had the liquid wealth necessary to loan. Since the regime was new, and different in social structure from previous governments, the diffidence of older families had to be conquered. As for the newer families, not so thoroughly wedded to the commune as their social superiors, they had to be convinced of the merits of throwing in their financial lot with that of the commune.

The creation of faith in communal institutions was not easy under these conditions. We have seen that the security which the commune could offer lenders in 1336 was already insufficient. By 1341, the government was complaining that it could not farm its gabelles at a just price. And when it did sell them, it soon had to prosecute the buyers, who were negligent in paying for them.[41] The income from the gabelles gives every indication of being in decline in these years.[42] If we find the gabelle farmers indifferent in 1341, we may imagine that the gabelles offered little security for potential lenders in 1345.

Another security was also in crisis. This was the lands of bankrupts. One might suppose that the flood of bankruptcies starting in 1342 would have released a large amount of immobile wealth which could be used by the commune not only to clear the debts of the merchants, but to guarantee loans to the commune. Such was not the case. The glut of lands drove their price down. A part of the trouble was simply financial—supply exceeded

38. *Ibid.*, p. 7.
39. Sept. 17, 1344; Sapori, *Crisi*, p. 164.
40. *Ibid.*, pp. 198 f.
41. *Ibid.*, p. 138.
42. See the fundamental article of C. M. De La Roncière, "Indirect Taxes or 'Gabelles' at Florence in the Fourteenth Century," in Rubinstein (ed.), *Florentine Studies*, pp. 160, 176 (Tables I and II). M. Becker has argued that the years after 1342 saw an upturn in gabelle receipts, and that this is a sign of "adjustment and growth" (Becker, *Transition*, I, 188 f., 197). For De La Roncière's criticism, see *op. cit.*, p. 171, n. 2.

demand. But just as critical was a lack of faith in title. How could buyers be sure the new titles or usage rights would stand? The suspicion is mirrored in the prologue of a law of March 11, 1345. A commission established the previous fall to sell these lands had accomplished practically nothing: "The public had such little faith in the actions of these officials, and was so uncertain about the limits of the authority they possessed *and the responsibility that they had assumed,* that it was hard to find anyone either to buy the lands or willing to accept them in restitution of credits."[43]

These traditional securities being compromised, the commune could not hope to tap the available capital in the commune for loans without some spectacular new type of guarantee. Without it, the citizens would not loan.

The condition of the communal debt did not stimulate the patriotic sentiments of potential investors. Until February, 1345, the debt was considered at least in law something to be paid back. While those involved in government realized that the enormous war debts met by loans would not soon be restituted, the obligation of the commune remained, in flagrant conflict with the real potential of the commune to repay. A compilation of the debt made in 1344 showed that the commune owed more than 800,000 florins.[44] There being no possible way of paying this, a regime which desired to stay in power chose the only road which could be traveled. The sums necessary to absolutely guarantee interest payments on the debt would first of all have to be set aside from gabelle receipts which were still unobligated. The commune would have to draw a legal distinction between past and future debts if it ever hoped to borrow in the future from creditors with the promise of repayment of capital. To make this amortization acceptable, it would have to legalize the negotiation of titles in the debt. Finally, the commitment of the commune to this course of action would have to be sealed with a security eternal in time and infallible in practice.

In October, 1344, buying and selling shares in the public debt was legalized.[45] On February 22, 1345, the debt was officially declared amor-

---

43. Sapori, *Crisi,* pp. 163 f. (italics mine). A law of Feb. 14, 1345, states specifically that the faith of the commune was in question because of the unreliability of their assignation; *Archivio di Stato, Firenze, Provvisioni Dupplicate,* 5, fol. 12r; hereafter cited as *ASF, Provv. Duppl.* All dates of laws are those on which the bill entered the Council of the Popolo.

44. Barbadoro, *Finanze,* pp. 630 f.

45. *Ibid.,* p. 632.

tized. A perpetual interest of 5 percent on the book sum was ordained, and measures were taken to guarantee the interest on the debt through assignment of funds from the gate gabelle.[46]

But what of the necessary security? How could a government of new men guarantee shareholders that it would not from one day to the next repeal this law? How could shareholders be sure that perpetual income from the debt, perhaps exceeding the capital amount even during the lifetime of the lender, would not involve usury on their part, and that a needy commune might not claim it had been usured, and cancel holdings of creditors in the *Monte*?

Obviously this law would have to be written in a perpetual precise form. But the old penal clause would no longer suffice. For in that clause, as will be recalled, the financial penalties threatened had been stipulated to the commune itself. The oath taken not to attempt to change precise laws, as well as the bond posted with the oath, had been taken and stipulated to the commune. But quite clearly, the commune of 1345 could not offer as security to its creditors penalties which reverted to the commune itself. That had been possible only in a time when the companies were stable and when their members managed the government of Florence. In 1345, creditors would only regain confidence if a third-party security were offered them. To defend their investment, they would insist that penalties go to someone other than their debtor the commune, and that the third party have the juridical and financial potential to reimburse them if the commune did not honor its commitment. If the commune were to avoid bankruptcy, it would have to create a penal system whose penalties would be automatically effectuated by a foreign power, and thus it would have to surrender judicial authority over its creditors.

The new *clausula penalis* which was to play such an important role in Florentine legislation for the next thirty-two years was first utilized as a rider on the law of February 22, 1345, which funded the *Monte Comune*.[47] Once its utility had been proven, it was attached to a number of different types of legislation all concerned with the administration of government. Its text underwent development until it reached a classic form in the 1350s. It was used for the last time on October 18, 1376.[48] After a long generation during which it remained the standard precise form, it became useless when Florence and the papacy went to war with each other. By 1376 the

---

46. The text is preserved in the *ASF, Provv. Duppl.*, 5, fols. 23v–26r and *ASF, Capitoli*, 18, fols. 133v–136r.

47. *ASF, Provv. Duppl.*, 5, fols. 25rv.

48. *ASF, Provv.*, 64, fols. 154v–157r.

commune, under the aegis of the church, had reached that point where its regained strength allowed it to war with its erstwhile protector.

Before describing the new penal clause, let us record at once its most noteworthy feature. Penalties or forfeited bond levied against those who would attempt modification of the basic law of the *Monte* (and all successive laws which came to be secured with this rider) were payable half to the commune of Florence, and half to the apostolic camera.[49]

As in the previous clauses, the priors and *gonfaloniere*, with or without their colleagues, might not undertake anything against the preceding law. Neither the *podestà* nor captain could summon his respective council if such a modification was to be proposed. The first penalty was against any official responsible for calling one of the legislative councils. He was to be deprived of his authority and office the moment the illegal proposition was brought forward, and to suffer a fine of 1,000 florins, payable to the commune.

The priors and *gonfaloniere* were then prohibited from being present at any such council. The penalty was privation of office and official immunities. They were automatically to be considered infamous, and as banished from the commune; as such they could be offended by anyone. By their presence in that council they were convicted of barratry and considered corruptors of the commune, and fell into the penalty of 2,000 florins, "comuni Florentie applicandis pro una dimidia, et pro alia dimidia applicandis camere domini pape."

Having fined the notary who would record the acts of such a transaction in council, the clause banished and removed from the protection of the law any councilor present and counseling or speaking against the contents of the precise law. The financial penalty was 1,000 florins, no recipient of this penalty being specified. Speakers in council attacking the illegal proceedings were to be rewarded financially for defending the constitutions.

Whatever the proceedings, they were declared null and void, and no one could be bound to obey a law which abrogated or modified the law secured by this clause.

From a delineation of penalties, the clause then turns to bonding the priors and *gonfaloniere*, the sixteen *gonfalonieri* of the administrative subdivisions of the city, and the twelve *buonomini*, thirty-seven in all (*tre maggiori*). Each was required to post bond of 2,000 florins as security for their oath: they would obey the secured law and not attempt to abrogate

49. The description which follows is of the classical penal clause given in the Appendix (see pp. 213–15).

or modify it under the same penalty of 2,000 florins, to be applied half to the commune and half to the papal camera.

The notary who as a public person was the recipient of the oath and promise was required, under a penalty of 1,000 florins, to represent himself as receiving oath and promise half in the name of the commune and half in the name of the papal camera.

The *podestà* and captain, the captains of the guilds, and the members of the two legislative councils were all held to take the same oath and promise—that is, subject themselves to the same eventual fines distributed in the same way—without, however, being required to post the 2,000 florins in bond.

The classical penal clause ends by requiring the *esecutore della giustizia* to examine the executive's actions to determine if they had violated the secured law. If so, he was to punish and condemn them to the penalties above, "applicandis pro dimidia camere domini pape, et pro alia dimidia comuni Florentie, ut dictum est." [50]

These features comprised the classical *clausula penalis*. In the law instituting the *Monte*, however, and in certain other laws of the years 1345–1347, this rider contains two additional paragraphs. The first required the presently constituted priorate to take this oath within three days of the passage of the law.[51] A second paragraph helps clarify the legal obligations being undertaken, and is worth quoting *in extenso*:

And also, desiring to proceed to contractualizing the said, and to the end that it will be irrevocable, they constitute and make ser Niccolò di ser Ventura Monachi the syndic of the said commune to obligate by public document (and who is required and ought to obligate within eight days of the passage of the present provision in the Council of the lord *Podestà* and Commune of Florence) the commune of Florence to the observation of the aforesaid to someone receiving [this obligation] for the creditors of the commune; [and he will obligate] future priors, *gonfalonieri della giustizia*, twelve *buonomini*, *gonfalonieri* of the societies

50. For the sake of clarity, note that a penalty of 2,000 florins is referred to four times: (1) as a penalty for violating the law (in some later riders, this penalty is payable to the commune and not to the papacy); (2 and 3) in connection with the oath; (4) in connection with syndication. I believe that all four references are to the same sum. The change in the first in later years would seem to mean that the bond money, once forfeited, was payable to the commune, to be then divided with the papacy. For an example where the first is payable to the commune, see *ASF, Provv.*, 47, fols. 193r–195r (May 20, 1360).

51. *ASF, Provv. Duppl.*, 5, fol. 25v.

and each one of them in the said penalty of 2,000 florins gold for each of the aforesaid [to someone] receiving and stipulating as vicar and in the name of the camera of the lord pope for half, and the commune of Florence for the other half.[52]

What are the salient legal and historical points of this clause, used at this point in time? First of all, the penalties were substantially increased. We are dealing with penalties six times higher (previously L1,000 or approximately 335 florins, compared to 2,000 florins). Secondly, the apostolic camera acting as a tribunal became the creditor of any Florentine perjuror who would attempt to modify this law. The latter was subject to these amends since he was guilty of barratry, corruption of the *res pubblica*, and of perjury. Third, this money in bond was received by a public person representing to one-half the apostolic camera. Thus in the act of transgression the money became the legal property of the apostolic camera.

The additions to the rider cited above help us to determine future salient features. The consolidation of the *Monte*—and other laws sealed by these additions—were conceived as a formal contract binding "the commune of Florence" to creditors of the commune, and obligating the persons of present and future members of the *tre maggiori* to the commune and to the apostolic camera. Thus a strict reading suggests that the commune was obligated not to the camera, but to the creditors of the commune. Individuals were bound not to the creditors, but as felons to the judicial entities of the commune and the apostolic camera. Secondly, there can be no doubt that these additions reflect the pressing financial and political needs in a city where faith required that the relative oaths be taken immediately. Since the office of the priors, for example, lasted only two months, one might have expected that the creditors would see no point in the present colleges and *Signoria* swearing to the law and posting bond. Certainly there was little chance that those in office would undertake anything against the law, at least not in their two months in office.

---

52. "Ac etiam volentes ad contractum super et de predictis transire et ut inrevocabilia sint, fecerunt et constituerunt ser Niccholaum ser Venture Monachi sindicum dicti comunis ad obligandum, et qui obligare teneatur et debeat infra octo dies a die qua presens provisio firmata fuerit in consilio domini potestatis et comunis Florentie ad observationem ipsorum, comune Florentie alicui recipienti pro dictis creditoribus, et futuros priores, vexilliferum justitie, duodecim bonos viros, gonfalonieros sotietatum et quemlibet eorum in dictam penam 2,000 florenorum auri pro quolibet predictorum collegeorum et cuiuslibet eorum, recipienti et stipulanti vice et nomine camere domini pape pro dimidia et pro alia dimidia comunis Florentie per publicum instrumentum" (*ibid.*).

Yet the oath had to be taken within three days by those then in office. The solemnity of the promises, the submission of the office-holding class to the penal authority of the universal church, were the "arduous obligations" which could conceivably pacify the creditors and restore faith in the public thing.

Once introduced, this new penal clause quickly replaced the older. While the latter was applied to the law immediately preceding the *Monte* law,[53] the arduous new rider was used a second time no later than August, 1345 (the lacunae in the law registers of this year do not allow one to follow the process precisely).[54] Subsequently it came to be applied to a series of law types. They cover loans made by the citizenry, the basic *divieti* laws regulating the foreign officials, the law outlawing the re-entry of those banned for certain torts, laws favoring the *Parte Guelfa*, and certain others. Before examining these subsequent developments, however, it will be well to understand the place of this security arrangement within the history of medieval securities, especially those involving the spiritual authority.

The peculiarity of this arrangement is that the commune, which the lawyers of the period were saying had the same *imperium* in its dominion as a king had in his,[55] secured the inviolability of certain crucial segments of its legal *corpus* by stipulating a penalty and/or bond levied against members of the government to a *dominus* outside its dominion. That that authority was the papacy which could and, as we shall see, did at times "grace" communal officials by absolving their oaths, completes what, as far as I can determine, was most unusual, perhaps unique.

The splitting of penalties in medieval laws was, of course, common enough. In Florence, for example, it was not unusual in laws separating a weaker from a stronger segment of a clan to contain penalties payable half to the commune and half to the weak party.[56] This half to the harmed party was not, at least in the Roman law, considered recompense—which could be additionally required—but pure *pene*.[57]

Moving from the private sphere to the semipublic, one finds that in pacts between *dominationes* each party commonly secured the treaty in

53. *Ibid.*, fols. 22r–23v.
54. For the August usage, see below, pp. 138–40.
55. For a compendium of statements on Florentine sovereignty by trecento and quattrocento jurists, see D. Tuscus, *Practicarum conclusionum iuris in omni foro frequentiorum ... tomus III* (Lyon, 1634), pp. 558 f. My thanks to Domenico Maffei for this reference.
56. See for example *ASF, Provv.*, 58, fols. 156rv (Dec. 23, 1370).
57. A. Bozzi, *op. cit.*, p. 216.

respect of the partner by promises stipulated to third dominions, which acted as depositories of the promised object and judge of a potential treaty violation.[58] This might be as straightforward as an agreement of two parties that if one broke a pact, the third party would militarily aid the damaged party. Or the third party, on determining that one of the obliged had broken the pact, might be held to award the damaged party hostages, sums of money, etc.

The use of the spiritual authority was common in pacts between dominions and in those between private persons. Pertile gives an example of a treaty which stipulated that if it were broken, any pope, archbishop, or bishop was held to excommunicate the violator and interdict his lands.[59] In the realm of private contracts, the *obligatio in forma camere apostolice*, originally intended to guarantee for the papal camera debts owed it by clergy, had developed to a generally accessible security arrangement used by lay parties. The papacy would act in the case of contract violation with an *executio parata* by which the debtor, having fallen *ipso facto* into the state of excommunication by his violation of the contract, found his stipulated estate passing *ipso iure* to the camera, which used its income to satisfy the debt and the costs of both creditor and camera.[60]

The Florentine *clausula penalis* certainly involved an obligation to the papal camera. Just as surely the penalty was considered as *ipso iure* passing to the camera by the nonfulfillment of the oath. But there the similarity to the *obligatio in forma camere* and to the use of the papacy as an intermediary in international affairs ends. In the Florentine arrangement there is no hint of spiritual penalties, though the papacy did act as a spiritual agency having the power to absolve from oaths and perjury.[61]

58. This practice was of course closely related to similar procedures in private commercial law. On the penal clause in modern Italian law, see the summary with bibliography in N. Distaso, *I Contratti in Generale*, Vol. II (Turin, 1966), 772–791.

59. A. Pertile, *Storia del Diritto Italiano*, Vol. V (Rome, 1892), 502 f.

60. Campitelli, *loc. cit.*

61. "Viso quomodo ecclesia debet se praecipue de temporalibus intromittere ut inter suos filios valeat pacis foedera reformare, videre restat quando postremo debet hoc facere quando talia foedera sunt iuramento firmata. Dicemus enim quod fractio iuramenti dicitur esse crimen ecclesiasticum, quia ad iudicem ecclesiasticum spectat iudicare de periurio sive de fractione iuramenti" (Aegidius Romanus, *De ecclesiastica potestate*, iii, 6, p. 178, cited in M. Wilks, *The Problem of Sovereignty in the Later Middle Ages* [Cambridge, 1964], pp. 313 f.). For *absolutiones iuramentorum* during the Avignonese period, see the indexes of the papal *Lettres* published by the French school in Rome. There is no reason to believe that the Florentine commune in the interest of continuity now used the papal right to absolve oaths for the first time. The old *clausula penalis* may contain an allusion to such a usage. At its end, one reads the following: "Nec aliquo modo, iure, causa vel

The history of this clause may now be taken under consideration. The following summary of stages will help to light the way:

1345–1376	laws rendered precise through use of the papal clause
1345–1376	financial laws secured by the rider
1349–1357	introduction of the rider to cover other key areas of communal law, subsequently in effect until 1380
1350	introduction of the formal disclaimer
1371	modification of the disclaimer
ca. 1373	beginning of the decline in the use of the rider
1378	papal absolution of all debts owed its camera on the basis of the precise laws
1380	abolition of the rider from all the laws of Florence

Finally:

1345–1361	wide use of the rider by legislators and finance officials
1361	introduction of solemn procedures to limit its use and its "arduous obligations"

The stability of the 5 percent *Monte* after its institution was what prompted Matteo Villani's eulogy to faith, the first, if not the greatest, of the three theological virtues. Not until the year 1370 do we encounter pressures in communal councils to withhold interest payments, and those pressures were resisted.[62] Faith, Villani implied, came in part from the papal *clausula penalis* which covered the 5 percent *Monte* into the late seventies. By law the gabelle incomes to meet the interest on this and other debts could not be diverted, and we often find the communal bursars instructed to protect these incomes so that no penalty to the pope will be created.[63]

---

ingenio possit absolutio ab ea vel eius observatione concedi, sed sit precisum, ita quod a verbis et tenore ipsius recedi non possit, non obstantibus in predictis aliquibus privilegiis vel beneficiis indultis vel indulgendis Prioribus et Vexillifero iustitie ac eorum scribe" (Caggese [ed.], *Statuti*, p. 97). What is new is the stipulation of financial penalties and its fusion with oaths, as well as the omnipresence of references to the apostolic camera in the law books of the commune.

62. Brucker, *Politics*, p. 95. Here is the opinion of one counselor in the debate: "Comune servet fidem suam. Quia deficiente fide comunis, deficit comuni" (*ASF, Consulte e Pratiche*, 11, fol. 88r [Sept. 10, 1370]; hereafter cited as *ASF, CP*).

63. See below, pp. 184 f. The relevant statements of Matteo Villani: "La fede, utile sopra l'altre cose, e gran sussidio a' bisogni della repubblica, ci dà materia di non lasciare

In 1345 there was no such confidence. Whether or not the commune would be able to keep faith was not yet determined. And in light of the enormous financial pressures being exerted on the commune and the companies in the 1340s, it was to be expected that the commune would use every available security, every conceivable promise, to buy time for creditors at home and abroad. One of the most important commissions or *balìe* dealing with this financial crisis in the coming years was that handling the debt to the Veronese Scaglieri. By following their activity, we can get a feel for the crisis atmosphere of these years and the expedients chosen to deal with that crisis.

The Scaglieri of Verona had sold Lucca to Florence for some 180,000 florins, itself a substantial part of the total public debt.[64] In the end the bargain gained the citizens nothing but debt, and they became embittered by the fiasco. Tempers were not cooled when in June, 1345, the *Signoria* sent a number of hostages to Verona as bond for the debt. "Scandals and inconveniences" were the result, and it became politically imperative that the hostages be returned. But this meant settlement of the debt.[65]

Since forced loans were out of the question at this time, the priors of August, 1345, chose the path they would regularly use in the next few years to meet the extraordinary expenses of the commune: voluntary loans at high interest with the promise of integral return of capital and interest. In the *balìa* given to the Officials for the Settlement of the Debt Owed the Scaglieri, the key financial commission of these coming years, the priors on August 13, 1345, authorized a loan of up to 50,000 florins from those *sponte mutuare volentes* designated by the officials. The sum borrowed was to be used only to repay the Scaglieri; the creditors loaning this commission were to be integrally repaid.[66]

The loan mechanism is of considerable interest, since it represents another innovation in communal funding practices, one used repeatedly

---

in oblivione quello che seguita. Il nostro comune . . . fecene un monte . . . ; e ordinò con certe leggi penali, alla camera del papa obbligate, chi per modo diretto o indiretto venisse contro a privilegio e immunità ch'avessono i danari del monte . . . . E cominciato questo gli anni di Cristo 1345, sopravvenendo al comune molte gravi fortune e smisurati bisogni, mai questa fede non maculò: onde avvenne che sempre a' suoi bisogni per la fede servata trovava prestanza da' suoi cittadini senza alcuno rammaricamento" (*Croniche*, III, 106).

64. D. Velluti, *La Cronica Domestica di messer Donato Velluti* (Florence, 1914), p. 181.

65. *ASF, Capitoli*, 18, fol. 89*v* (Aug. 13, 1345). The names of the hostages are found in *ASF, Provv.*, 34, fols. 42*rv* (Apr. 21, 1346).

66. *ASF, Capitoli*, 18, fols. 82*r*–88*r* (Aug. 13, 1345). For a summary of this complex law, see *ASF, Provv.*, 33, fols. 59*r*–60*v* (Nov. 4, 1345).

thereafter in the forties.[67] It also sheds light on the confidence of the lenders: under what conditions would investors loan to the commune in the period immediately after the institution of the *Monte?* First of all, lenders were to receive back from the commune double the amount they had loaned. At the same time, however, they were to release the commune from an amount they held in the *Monte* equal to the amount they now loaned.[68] Thus if the real value of their *Monte* holdings had been equal to the face, the loan would have carried no interest at all. But values had careened downward after February.[69] Thus if a citizen loaned 300 florins in cash, he was guaranteed a cash payment of 600 florins (the time of repayment was to be established by the *balìa*, with some loans being repaid within a year).[70] At the same time, however, he wrote off 300 florins he held in the public debt. If the market value of that *Monte* holding was half the face, it meant he wrote off the 150 florins which he could have realized by selling his shares in the market. Thus his net income on a 300 florin investment was 450, or a 50 percent profit if we assume the debt was repaid within the year. If on the other hand we consider the lender to have invested 450 florins (300 plus the real value of *Monte*), then the 600 received would represent an interest of $33\frac{1}{3}$ percent. There are enough variables involved to prohibit an exact computation of interest. But the interest was high, usuriously so.[71]

The risks were correspondingly high, evident at once in the repayment methods chosen. The borrowing party was the *balìa* for the Scaglieri debt, and the commune was thereby obligated.[72] But the party held to actually

67. The last reference to this type of loan is in *ASF, Provv.*, 45, fols. 195r–197r (June 5, 1358).

68. Therefore the lenders at least in law had to already be creditors of the *Monte* in the amount they now loaned. For the violation of this requirement, see below, p. 149. Both Giovanni (XII, 49) and Matteo Villani (III, 6) describe this loan type in their *Croniche.*

69. Brucker, *Politics*, pp. 19 f.

70. See for example *ASF, Provv.*, 41, fols. 69v–75r (Sept. 12, 1354). Giovanni Villani stated that the repayment period was two years for the loans of 1345 and 1346. But the payment schedule might be on a monthly basis starting in the second year (Villani, *Croniche*, XII, 49; *ASF, Provv., loc. cit.*).

71. Matteo Villani said that it was at least 15 percent (*Croniche*, III, 6). The computations here are meant to show how the method worked. The actual value of *Monte* holdings was actually much less than half, perhaps from one-quarter to one-third (Brucker, *Politics*, p. 19).

72. "Insuper teneantur ipsi domini priores et vexillifer et duodecim, gonfalonierii et capitudines . . . curare ita et taliter quod predictis sic mutuantibus integre solvantur . . . . Et ipsi . . . teneantur in subsidium post dictos emptores, fideiussores, approbatores . . ." (*ASF, Capitoli*, 18, fols. 86v–87r [Aug. 13, 1345]).

return the *dupplum* to the lenders was not the commune, but the persons who had bought the gabelle which had been assigned to repay the loan. The gabelle farmer in question, that is, did not pay the commune for the gabelle he had bought, but rather communal lenders for the Scaglieri debt. The farmers were those who were legally obligated to the individual lenders.[73]

The fluctuating value of *Monte*, and this hand-to-mouth repayment scheme show how difficult the financing of expenses was, and how much risk the lender assumed. But not only was the interest high, the lenders *were being permitted to liquidate their paper for cash.* This is the most important aspect of this lending arrangement. Immediately after the amortization of the public debt, many lenders were not so much demanding high interest as they were seeking to escape participation in the debt. Their favored position was clear: they were in effect being allowed to liquidate their paper and realize cash without undergoing the loss on the shares which would have been involved if they had forthrightly sold those shares on the open market. Even if the value of their existing *Monte* shares had been at par, it meant realizing cash rather than paper, all while acting for the *bene comune*. Clearly, there was no faith in the public debt at this point. Many of those who had cash to lend wanted out, and the commune had to let them, even if it meant creating extremely high short-term debts.

To meet the risks involved in this arrangement, an elaborate security system was established. We have noted already that two parties were obligated: commune and farmers. This was not enough. The apostolic *clausula* was appended to this lending bill of August, and would be used each time the Scaglieri officials' *balia* was enlarged or elaborated during the some five years it existed. Since this *balia* soon became the authority through which much of the commune's extraordinary financing was done during this period (its borrowing came to extend far beyond the purpose of repaying the Scaglieri), it can be said that most of the loans authorized through the communal councils before the Black Death were precise or unalterable, with the security of the papal camera.

If our emphasis here is on the use of the *clausula penalis*, it would be remiss not to stress that it is but one aspect of the security offered. All possible means were induced to safeguard creditors during this period. Offering hostages, as was done to secure the debt to the Scaglieri, was a spectacular example.[74] The new cameral clause was equal in import,

73. *Ibid.*, fol. 86v. See also *ASF, Provv.*, 33, fol. 59r (Nov. 4, 1345).
74. "Nulla est cautior quam clare obsides" (*ASF, CP*, 1, fol. 168r [Mar. 10, 1354 *stilus florentinus*]; hereafter dates using the Florentine style will be followed by *sf*).

binding as it did the members of the government to the papacy. In the Scaglieri officials' loan bills, we again find the commune as a corporation required to commit itself to its citizen-lenders within the week. Still a fourth means was used, one which would remain a feature of this *balia* until its demise. This was the direct obligation of individual members of the government to the lenders. In an insert to the rider, it was specified that if the government either ceased to repay, or modified repayment, the members of that government personally became debtors to the lenders for the integral repayment of the whole debt.[75] In short, to become a member of the *tre maggiori* during this period when the Scala debt was outstanding involved assuming a personal obligation toward the creditors.

A century later, this latter type of security, called the *Monte penalia*, became the preferred means for attaching gilt-edged security to the most crucial communal loans.[76] In the trecento, however, this insurance made only a brief appearance during the crisis of the late forties.

An important payoff of the August accord with the Scaglieri was the prospect that the hostages would be released. Determined to prevent such a disgrace in the future, the communal councils followed up the enabling law on the financing of the Scaglieri accord with one providing that no one of the Dominion could be sent or be forced to go as a hostage, to Verona or anywhere else. Any communal official foreign or domestic who attempted to force anyone to present himself as a hostage, stood to suffer amends of 3,000 florins. To whom was this penalty to be paid? One half was to go to the papal camera, and the other half to the Inquisitor.[77]

75. "In ipso casu et casibus et quolibet eorum teneantur ipsi priores ... quorum tempore in predictis contrafieret vel fieri cessaretur quod fieri debebit predictis omnibus et singulis quibus restitutio et solutio predicte fieri debent ... ad integram restitutionem et solutionem eius in quo fuerit cessatum" (*ASF, Capitoli*, 18, fol. 87r [Aug. 13, 1345]). More striking was the *ipso facto* debt incurred by any legislator who spoke against this bill: "Intelligatur et sit obligatus predictis qui sic mutuarunt vel mutuabunt, et cogi possint personaliter et in rebus ac si dictos mutuos per publica instrumenta guarantigie confessi fuissent se habuisse, et ac si ad eorum et cuiuscumque eorum mutuorum restitutionem se effectualiter obligassent et preceptum guarantigie recepissent" (*ASF, Provv.*, 33, fol. 59v [Nov. 4, 1345]).

76. *Monte* officials during the quattrocento took an oath that they would meet particular types of debts during their term. The list of debts thus sworn to was the *Monti penali*. To place a debt on this list was to furnish it with gilt-edged security; see L. F. Marks, "Development of the Institutions of Public Finance in Florence During the Last Sixty Years of the Republic" (Ph.D diss., Oxford University, 1954), p. 46.

77. "Pro una dimidia applicanda camere domini pape, et pro alia officio inquisitionis. Et nichillominus si venerit in fortiam comunis Florentie caput eidem aspatulis amputetur, nisi postquam venerit in dictam fortiam infra tertiam diem solverit camerario

If splitting amends between the commune and the papacy must be considered evidence of a weak government, how much more so when the whole penalty was assigned to outside spiritual authorities! The regime which had offered hostages could not be the assignee of a penalty for future hostaging, and political forces within the city forced the externalizing of the penalty clause to better assure the law's inviolability. Using the Inquisitor's office to attack citizen's estates was an old communal expedient.[78] But that the commune would agree to the eventuality of that office prosecuting ex-officials for perjury is a striking sign of how far governments needed to go to assuage mistrust among the citizenry.[79] To give this law on hostages precise form, the government added the apostolic rider, with the standard division to camera and commune.[80]

Throughout the negotiations with the Scaglieri, a key role was played by Marchese Opizzo d'Este, who in 1345 became the binding arbiter between the Scaglieri and Florence.[81] His relations with the commune bring out a key element of the financial crisis of these years: foreign creditors of the bankrupt banks were potential allies in the solution of the economic crisis.[82]

When in the fall of 1344 Este had been informed of the low bankruptcy settlements decided on by Florentine officials, he threatened to retaliate against Florentine merchants and goods in his lands. The *Signoria* was quick to yield, and in September of that year carried through a law allowing its officials to settle with him at a higher rate, up to 50 percent of true debt.[83] We find him acting as an arbiter the following February. He played an important role in the August, 1345, accord. But that did not

---

camere comunis Florentie pro ipso comuni recipienti florenos auri duo milia" (*ASF*, *Capitoli*, 18, fols. 89v–90r [Aug. 13, 1345]). This is one of the rare times during the whole regime when decapitation was prescribed. The only other one I have encountered was stipulated at the end of the regime, when the security system was in disorder; see below, p. 201.

78. This is an aspect of church-state relations which needs examination. One historian has noted the seeming complicity between commune and Inquisition in a sentence of the 1330s (B. Gerolamo, "Inquisitori ed Eretici a Firenze [1319–1334]," *Studi Medievali*, N.S. VI [1933], 172).

79. This was at a point, also, at which the Inquisitor in Florence was not on the best of terms with the city's citizens (Brucker, *Politics*, pp. 132 ff.). See also below, pp. 160 f.

80. *ASF*, *Capitoli*, 18, fols. 90rv (Aug. 13, 1345).

81. *Ibid.*, fols. 121rv (Feb. 4, 1344sf).

82. This is part of a more significant truth: creditors of any type were elements which could contribute to the solidification of the regime.

83. *ASF*, *Capitoli*, 18, fols. 34v–35v (Sept. 17, 1344).

end his usefulness, for this agreement had been made under great pressure, and the *Signoria* continued to seek a better, longer term settlement. By November a new pact had been signed, one which apparently allowed the commune longer terms of repayment in exchange for a substantial hike in the amount owed: from the 50,000 florins of August, the debt had increased now to 65,000. In the eyes of the legislators, the hero of this more acceptable accord was, after God, the Marchese d'Este.[84]

By the terms of the new agreement, the Scaglieri received 10,000 florins on the spot. This meant that the Florentine *balìa* for the Scaglieri debt would have to raise another 5,000 florins. This seemingly minor sum required the same elaborate security arrangements as had the August bill prohibiting hostages,

> since in the treasury of the said commune of Florence there is not at present nor is there hope of there being the money to effect the said payments and a number of other eminent necessities toward the expedition of this negotiation. This is so especially because almost all the incomes of the aforementioned are deputated and assigned to certain and special uses through ordinances of the said commune. . . .[85]

In numerous loans floated by the commune in the coming years, the cluster of securities in the August, 1345, law were used, including of course the papal rider. Thus in a loan of March 12, 1347, the *cautele* were not spelled out, but included "as if" they had been.[86] This practice of using this security system without spelling it out continued into the mid-fifties, at which time each loan authorization sealed with this penal clause came to include the clause, word by word.[87]

Thus the penalty clause directing fines and stipulating bonds to the apostolic camera quickly became the form par excellence with which to secure citizens' investments in the commune. The great majority of voluntary loans raised by this regime and formalized in law carry the rider. Interest on forced loans was guaranteed. Beyond the formal documents we meet with in the *Provvisioni*, however, the papal *cautela* was

---

84. *ASF, Provv.*, 33, fols. 59*rv* (Nov. 4, 1345); see also *ASF, Capitoli*, 18, fols. 56*v*–57*v* (Oct. 25, 1344).

85. "Et quia in camera dicti comunis Florentie non est ad presentem nec esse speratur pecunia pro dictis cambiis faciendis et quampluribus necessariis ad expeditionem ipsius negotii eminentibus, ea precipue ratione quia quasi omnes redditus comunis predicti sunt in certos et speciales usus deputati et assignati per ordinamenta dicti comunis" (*ASF, Provv.*, 33, fols. 59*rv* [Nov. 4, 1345]).

86. *ASF, Provv.*, 34, fol. 113*v*.

87. Examples: *ibid.*, fols. 114*r*, 117*r*; 35, fols. 38*v*, 93*v*, 128*rv*; 38, fols. 2*v*–3*v*; 39, fols. 150*v*–151*v*.

commonly given in the *balìa* of varied commissions. Sometimes a commission's right to use it was spelled out; [88] more generally, officials were empowered to bestow whatever securities they thought necessary. Consequently, the utilization of this security was not limited at all to formal laws. It extended down to the administrative level of many tax commissions. Until 1361, these "arduous obligations" were undertaken with a minimum of hesitation. Until that date the commune could not see its way clear to limit the papacy's involvement in securing the state.

What were the lending forms covered during this thirty-two year period?

First came the 5 percent *Monte* and all the forced loans amortized into it. A new consolidation was carried out in 1347 which specified exactly which citizens were to receive interest. This law's penalties were so arranged that half went to the commune, but the other half to the creditors of the commune rather than to the pope. [89] Thus as a result of this law, the situation in the 5 percent *Monte* seems thereafter to have remained as follows: The right to negotiate shares, the duty of the commune to set aside 2,704 florins each month to meet the interest on the amortized debt, and the inviolability of these assignments were all covered by penalties and bond half of which was to go to the papal camera. By the law of June, 1347, however, the penalties against those not paying due interest on this basic *Monte* to defined individuals were to be kept in escrow for eventual claimants whose names had—unjustly—not been recorded in the 1347 books of the 5 percent *Monte*. Could such damaged creditors still seek redress in the Roman Curia? We will address ourselves to this question at a later point.

Next came the *dupplum* form of lending, all negotiated with *sponte*

88. "Et pro predictis et circa predicta et predictorum omnium et cuiusque eorum expeditione, efficacia vel effectu, ac etiam pro securitate et cautela omnium et singulorum eorum quorum interesset vel interesse posset, facere et componere semel et pluries et quotiescumque illas provisiones et illa ordinamenta que volent, et ea vallare quibuscumque penis, et etiam camere domini pape seu cuilibet alteri applicandis quibus volent" (*ASF, Provv.*, 46, fols. 71r–72r [Dec. 11, 1358]; see also *ibid.*, 48, fols. 67r–68v [Oct. 23, 1360]).

89. "Et quod presens provisio, quantum ad omnia et singula suprascripta, contineat et continere intelligatur omnia et singula beneficia, ligamina, penas et cautelas de quibus continetur et fit mentio in reformatione consiliorum populi et comunis Florentie edita de mense Augusti MCCCXXXXV pro satisfaciendo ... Scale .... Hoc tamen mutato quod pena que ibi apponitur commictenda et applicanda camere domini pape pro dimidia, in ea parte qua ipse camere applicatur ibi, hic applicetur creditoribus dicti comunis, de quo in presenti provisione fit mentio. Ita quod per presentem provisionem vel contenta in ea vel aliqua sui parte, nullum ius ipsius camere domini pape in aliquo acquiratur" (*ASF, Provv.*, 34, fol. 155v).

volentes. It was used from August, 1345, until 1358.[90] Sometimes the cash reimbursement was something more or less than double. A loan of July–August, 1354, for example, guaranteed a 150 percent pay back, while requiring the standard write off of the same amount as loaned from the lender's existing credits in the *Monte.*[91]

Still another lending form covered by the cameral penal clause was the inscription in separate books of amounts which were multiples of the actual amount of cash loaned to the commune.[92] The stated interest was 5 percent, but since it was computed on a book sum, actual interest earned amounted to 10 percent where two florins were recorded for every one loaned in cash, 15 percent for the *Monte uno-tre* and so on. The discoverer of this approach, ser Piero di ser Grifo, was lionized by contemporaries as a financial wizard.[93] Its beauty was that it offered potential creditors a high, yet secure long-term interest, all under the fictional interest of 5 percent, a more or less acceptable rate among the official consciences of the time. This practice was used from 1358 until 1378. Originally, lenders had a limited time in which to enter the new *Monti.* By 1372 there was no time limit on one such arrangement. A law of that year stated that from then on, those investing in the commune would be inscribed at a rate of 100 florins for each 45 loaned.[94]

A common lending form was the straight loan *spe rehabendi,* with assignment of gabelles to repay capital and interest, where a fixed rate of interest was either stated in the enabling law or left up to the loan commission in charge. The laws in question contain an obligation of the commune to the acts of the *balìa,* so that the attached rider, used in the overwhelming majority of such enablements, in effect guaranteed the payment of interest. The interest rates, when stated, run between 10 and 15 percent.[95]

In its incessant search for revenues, the commune came up with another

90. The last reference to this type is in *ASF, Provv.,* 45, fols. 195r–197r (June 5, 1358).

91. *ASF, Provv.,* 41, fols. 69v–70v (Aug. 27, 1354).

92. *Monte nuovo* or *del uno tre: ibid.* 45, fols. 217r–220r (June 16, 1358); fols. 239r–241r (July 13, 1358); 46, fols. 4r–6r (Aug. 9, 1358). *Monte del uno due: ibid.,* 46, fols. 71r–72r (Dec. 11, 1358); fols. 79r–82r (Jan. 11, 1358*sf*).

93. Brucker, *Politics,* p. 60.

94. A perpetual rather than a limited subscription of two florins for one in the regular *Monte* books was ordered Aug. 29, 1372 (*ASF, Provv.,* 60, fols. 72r–74r). This did not attract investments, and the rate was changed to 100 for 45 loaned, again a perpetual subscription (*ibid.,* fols. 91r–94r [Nov. 5, 1372]).

95. One of dozens of examples, this one at 15 percent: *ASF, Provv.,* 40, fols. 97rv (Apr. 24, 1353).

lending arrangement in 1371, and dutifully sealed its institution with the apostolic rider. This was the perpetual rent, earning 10 or 12 percent *inter vivos*, with the capital finally becoming the possession of the commune.[96]

All of these types involved loans made by citizens. But the cameral clause was also a welcome security for foreign lenders depositing extensive sums of money in the Florentine *Monte*.[97] Besides loans, foreign creditors insisted on the clause when they sold lands to the commune, in order to better guarantee the financial arrangements.[98]

There seems, in short, to have been no lending arrangement which was not secured through these penalties. The clause represents the major legal security offered both foreign and domestic creditors during the life of the regime. An occasional law does not have this clause. For example, a law allowing the priors of the commune to loan to the commune was not so insured.[99] On the other side, the *cautela* was used for many transactions which never appeared on the law books at all. It is not until 1375 that one encounters a consignment of *balìa* which specifically excludes the use of penalties payable to the papal camera.[100] And this exclusion was contemporary to the last use of the rider on a standard loan bill.[101] By this time, the commune was plotting the dissolution of the papal authority in the states of the church.

The penalties and bonds in the majority of these cases is standard. Even though the reasons for slight modifications remain a mystery, certain of these should be mentioned. We have already mentioned the single case in which the penalties were divided between papacy and Inquisition, as well as the unique law which divided them between the commune and its creditors. There is one case in 1372, to be examined later, in which penalties were to go completely to the apostolic camera.[102] Finally, there were four financial laws in the mid-fifties in which the division of forfeited bond was to be between the apostolic camera and the creditors of the commune.

The first of these came in the wake of an uproar over the imposition of a direct tax in the city. The displeasure of the citizens soon forced the

96. *Ibid.*, 59, fols. 170v–172r (Nov. 24, 1371).

97. *Ibid.*, 54, fols. 45r–46r, 153r; 58, fols. 127v–129r, 129r–130r.

98. *Ibid.*, 54, fols. 43r–45v; 62, fols. 47r–48r. The foreigners involved in these negotiations were north Italian nobles plus the Genoese Grimaldi.

99. *Ibid.*, 45, fols. 180rv (Apr. 23, 1358).

100. "Cum illis roborationibus et penis, non tamen camere apostolice, et capitulis et articulis quibus volent" (*ibid.*, 63, fols. 70v–71v [July 12, 1375]).

101. *Ibid.*, fols. 174r–176r (Dec. 11, 1375).

102. See below, p. 175.

commune to convert the tax to a loan and inscribe it in the *Monte* books.[103] Then in May, 1353, another piece of legislation regulated the restitution of these sums. This was covered by a rider with bonding half to the creditors and half to the apostolic camera. As an earnest of the lenders' anxiety, the priors in office had to swear to the law.[104] A second instance is found in a straightforward loan bill, but with one wrinkle. If the commission could not raise the sum authorized with *spe rehabendi* from voluntary lenders, they could force lending, but not from anyone they did not believe to have a worth of at least 1,000 florins.[105] Two other cases are of a like nature. These laws list those Florentines by name who had loaned the commune money at *dupplum* or at 150 percent at specific times, noting their loan and the amount they were to be repaid. They then spell out the repayment schedule. These are the only two laws in which these specifics are given.[106]

It is not clear why this division of the bond was necessary. It can only be said that all four bills occur in the period of years after the abortive direct tax or *sega* of 1352. And the arrangement indicates that the commune represented an unacceptable coercive agency for these negotiations.[107]

Much of the lack of clarity caused by these fine distinctions arises from uncertainty as to the actual role of the papacy in this whole system of securities. How did Rome become involved? What advantages were there for its participation in the scheme? Just how did a loan in which oaths and bond were posted to the Holy See contribute to encouraging the lender to subvent the commune? To answer these questions we must first pose and respond to a more basic question: What were the reflections of the potential communal creditor during this period? What risks did he run, or better, how might the commune not keep faith?

There was of course the possibility that a needy commune might generally suspend payments either of interest or of capital. That it did not

103. Security was to be given, "etiam in perpetuo duratura" (*ASF, Provv.*, 39, fols. 150v–151v [June 9, 1352]).

104. *Ibid.*, 40, fols. 108rv (May 20, 1353).

105. "...A quibuscumque sponte mutuare volentibus." If the officials could not raise it in this fashion, they might force, "dumtaxat non debeant ... cogere ... aliquem quem non credant ... habere in bonis valentis saltem 1,000 florenorum de auro" (*ASF, Provv.*, 41, fols. 133r–134r [Jan. 19, 1354sf]).

106. *Ibid.*, fols. 74r–75r (Aug. 27, 1354); 42, fols. 103v–106v (Aug. 13, 1355).

107. Matteo Villani spelled out just how severe the repercussion of the *sega* or direct tax had been. He saw in its conversion to a loan a strengthening of the communal temper. Thus this externalization of forfeited bond is certainly in part explained by a crisis of confidence over the *sega* (*Croniche*, IV, 83).

do so during our period was what brought on Villani's enthusiasm.[108] Secondly, it might force creditors to liquidate their holdings in the debt. If they were inscribed in a *Monte* paying 15 percent interest this could be a most disadvantageous turn of events, since this was a high and fairly secure investment. The commune might, however, not only force the creditor to sell, but at the market price of the shares rather than the book value, or even at a rate below the market price.[109]

A third risk was that in correcting the books of the *Monte*, the commune might act against creditors. If, in the periodic re-examinations of the books, a creditor was determined to be incorrectly entered, he could be prosecuted for the interest he had taken from the republic. He could be prosecuted, that is, for what amounted to theft.[110] No one doubted that the books needed revision on a regular basis, but the suspicion was always alive that the appointment of a commission for such a purpose might also have as a motive the reduction of the debt by any possible means. The commune, that is to say, under its mantle of morality, might break its faith without running the risk that the damaged creditors would seek recourse. We must pursue this eventuality further, for it leads straight to the problem of usury, and therewith to the spiritual authority of Rome.

What were the chief means by which creditors "defrauded" the commune? A law of 1372 sums them up: citizens had had written into the books holdings which they did not possess, or higher shares than they were entitled to; some had sold more shares than they were permitted to; others had had themselves fraudulently inscribed as heirs of deceased creditors; "and some there are who have received *pro donis, dampnis seu interesse* [sums] from the bursar of the *Monte Comune* beyond that which was owed."[111]

---

108. Marvin Becker has argued that interest on the *Monte* was in fact suspended from 1349 to 1351. His evidence is a statement in Donato Velluti's *ricordanze* which is irrelevant (*Transition*, II, 168 ff.). We have seen that Matteo Villani, whose expertise in *Monte* matters is pointed out by Becker, stated that "mai questa fede non maculò" (see above, p. 138 n. 63).

109. When each *Monte* was established, any rights of the commune to buy up these shares were carefully stipulated. For example, they might be limited to purchase at the book value, or it might be said that *Monte* X could not be liquidated until *Monte* Y had been, and so forth. For an example of this, see *ASF, Provv.*, 60 fols. 72r–74v (Aug. 29, 1372). In 1367 a law was passed requiring holders of *Monte del uno tre* to sell their shares on demand to the commune at L28 on the 100; *ibid.*, 55, fols. 34rv (July 21, 1367). Opposition quickly arose to this forced selling; *ibid.*, fols. 98v–99v (Dec. 4, 1367).

110. See below, pp. 150, 154.

111. "Et aliqui qui pro donis, dampnis, seu interesse receperunt a camerario montis comunis predicta ultra debitum rationis" (*ASF, Provv.*, 60, fols. 15rv [May 29, 1372]).

One other fraud must be mentioned which was apparently widely practiced in the early years of the regime. It will be recalled that in the *dupplum* loans of the regime's first decade the lender was held to release the commune from an amount in the *Monte* equal to the amount he loaned. This limited the number of potential investors in such an arrangement to those who in fact had at least that sum already inscribed in the *Monte*. What of those, however, who either had not been caught in the mid-forties with extensive holdings, or who had disposed of them on the open market? What of those who did not have equivalent sums already invested? Were they to be prevented from helping their commune? Could the commune turn away from such a source of revenue?

Despite its desire to liquidate old debt (a purported rationale of these *dupplum* loans), it could not. Investors forced this decision upon the commune by the simple expedient of loaning at *dupplum* and either avoiding the cancellation from the *Monte* of that amount,[112] or alternatively not having that amount in the *Monte* to start with. In 1347 the government excluded those sums from the 5 percent *Monte* which should have been cancelled by such *dupplum* lenders.[113] But not until 1350 did it take steps to stop the fraud at its roots. In a *dupplum* enabling bill it added a derogatory clause which effectively prevented a lender from advancing more to communal agents than he had in the 5 percent *Monte*.[114]

The loan *balia* soon found that such strict adherence to the law made its job of raising money much more difficult, for it excluded those who did not have the necessary holdings in the 5 percent *Monte*. The commission petitioned the *Signoria*, and the derogatory clause was struck.[115] This meant that the commune subverted its own lending practices because of its need for funds. It was willing apparently to pay back two hundred florins on a loan of a hundred without accomplishing any diminution of the old debt. Subsequent *balie* were established to insure that the required cancellations had in fact been made, but their effectiveness was doubtless dependent on the state of the finances. A commune driven to negotiate these *dupplum* loans was weak per se. It was but one more step backward to avoid seeing the fraud before its eyes, if that was necessary to float a quick loan.

112. *Ibid.*, 40, fols. 102r–103r (May 10, 1353).

113. *Ibid.*, 34, fols. 154rv (June 20, 1347).

114. "Pro duplo et usque ad duplum eius quantitatis quam sic mutuabunt, dum modo nemini assignare possint seu concedere ultra quam pro duplo eius in quo pro creditoribus comunis Florentie scripti reperientur" (*ibid.*, 38, fols. 2v–3v [Mar. 20, 1349*sf*]).

115. *Ibid.*, fols. 75v–76r (June 21, 1350).

When the commune did react against this fraud, it put itself forward not only as the guardian of the *res pubblica*, but as the custodian of its citizens' state of grace. These practices "issue not only in damage to the said commune, but issue and can issue in damage to the true creditors of the aforesaid *Monte Comune*, and *in danger to the souls of these deceivers*."[116] Here was a great danger to the creditor: the commune might determine that he had gone beyond reason; that he owed money to the commune for fraud; that he had to "restitute." And it could do that in the name of God.

Subsequent events would show that these creditor suspicions were well founded. The law books of the sixties and seventies are dotted with hints that the commune was experimenting with self-liquidating *Monte* holdings.[117] Liquidation by testators of holdings was made attractive, one may suspect, by assurances the commune would renounce any rights or interest in the estate. At the same time, successive governments encouraged testators to leave to the commune anything they thought they had taken in usury, and one such restitution of usury shows up in the law books.[118] Citizens were asked to leave illegal interest in a basket in the cathedral, with the government vaguely promising that such an anonymous act

116. "Et nisi opportune provideretur deciperent verisimiliter in futurum. Quod non solum cedit in dampnum dicti comunis, verum etiam cedit et cedere potest in dampnum verorum creditorum montis comunis predicti et in ipsorum decipientium periculum animarum" (*ibid.*, 60, fols. 15*rv*).

117. One of the first of these was mentioned above, p. 146.

118. The Franciscan Fra Francesco di Tommaso di Dino di Ricciardo de' Bardi in his testament "comuni Florentie reliquit et legavit LXX florenos de auro per eum, ut dixit, habitos et receptos indebite pro dono, dampnis, seu interesse sui crediti montis veteris comunis predicti." Bardi's heirs had renounced the inheritance, "propter quod comune predictum non potest consequi nec totum nec partem legati predicti" (*ASF, Provv.*, 54, fols. 159*v*–160*r* [Apr. 23, 1357]). The law in question does not use the word "restitution," and in general the communal approach is that testators left free legacies. But that there was a communal *quid pro quo* is suggested by a law of 1371 which ordains that monies left to the commune in testaments go to the Officials for the Diminution of the *Monte*. "Et quod ut predicta legata et relicta commodus et habilius habeantur," the *tre maggiori* were given authority to legislate, "etiam penalis." This would seem to indicate that the authorities could guarantee heirs against further communal action against the estate (*ibid.*, 59, fols. 203*rv* [Dec. 23, 1371]). That this encouragement to leave money to the commune was directly related to *Monte* profits is clear from the following: the same *Monte* diminuators were to receive "omnis pecunie quantitas que ad comune predictum seu ad aliquem dicti comunis pro ipso comuni recipientem quandocumque perveniet de quibuscumque vel pro quibuscumque legatis seu relictis quomodocumque factis vel fiendis, pro eo quod dixisset vel dicent se a dicto comuni vel alio pro dicto comuni dante recipisse pro dono, dampnis seu interesse dictorum debitorum montium vel alicuius eorum vel propterea se dicto comuni teneri vel dari velle . . ." (*ibid.*, 60, fol. 15*v* [May 29, 1372]).

would absolve such men from their debt "in the eyes of conscience, God, and the world."[119]

As our potential lender thought his way through these risks, he came to see that the greatest risk of all was that he as lender might make himself a debtor "in the eyes of conscience, God, and the world." Through the right to correct the books of the debt, his debtor the commune could, as a sufficient moral authority defending the creditor's soul, avoid the interest it owed him by claiming that it had been usured, or at least it could cease paying interest, confident that the creditor would not risk prosecution by the commune or the spiritual authority for the "excessive" interest he had taken.[120]

Faced with this hazard, what assurances did communal lenders require? Of course they would insist on gabelle assignations and the like. But what assurances could be found to counter the dangers portrayed here? The creditor took three separate technical steps to insure himself.

First, he would carefully consider the moral quality of the loan. Certain types of voluntary loans might be safe from usury prosecution; others might not be. Certainly one of the most questionable types would have been a *Monte del uno tre*, by which the investor was paid 5 percent on a booked sum three times greater than the sum actually loaned. And it is in fact at this juncture, in 1358, when the creditors first forced the commune to rewrite its voluntary loan bills. Let us review what happened.

In June, 1358, the commune authorized a repayable loan of 30,000

119. "In quibus capssis et qualibet earum poni et micti possit per quamcumque personam illa pecunie quantitas in qua ipse vel ille cuius fuerit heres secundum suam conscientiam putaverit se teneri vel esse obligatus ad restituendum comuni Florentie in aliqua pecunie quantitate vel rebus ipsius comunis ad eius manus vel cuius heres fuerit perventas quoquomodo illicito seu licito et inlicite retento, quas ob verecundiam restituere cessaret. Et quod quilibet inmictente, vel cuius nomine inmissa fuerit, aliqua pecunie quantitate modo predicto, ipsa commissione facta, esse intelligatur et sit liberatus a comuni Florentie ac si soluisset camerariis camere comunis Florentie" (*ASF, Provv. Duppl.*, 5, fols. 14rv [Feb. 14, 1344sf]). This custom was followed for many decades thereafter.

120. It may be that at an earlier time a partial restitution of interest on communal loans was practiced. Barbadoro mentions nothing of the sort; yet we have noted Giovanni Villani's reference to a 15 percent interest "sanza tenimento di restituzione" (see above, p. 127 n. 32). Matteo Villani described the debate on the licitness of speculation "sanza tenimento di restituzione" (*Croniche*, III, 106). As late as 1383 the commune insisted it had no rights to restitution from the 5 percent *Monte*: "Nullatenus ad restitutionem aliquam teneatur, etiam quoad conscientiam vel ad Deum" (*ASF, Provv.*, 72, fols. 71r–72r [June 12, 1383]). At the very least, we must say that the possibility the commune might recall usury was a very real one.

florins from *sponte volentes, dupplum* to be returned in exchange for a cancellation equal to the sum loaned.[121] On July 13, the commission for the loan gained a revision of their mandate: anyone loaning to them from that point until August 15 was to have their loan inscribed in a multiple of the actual sum loaned, and the booked sum was to earn 5 percent interest. No cancellation of previous credits was foreseen.[122]

Obviously the *balia* was encountering difficulty. We do not have to wait long to determine its source. For in August the officials again appeared before the *Signoria*. Despite their best efforts, they had been able to collect less than the half of the 30,000 florins required. Why? "Many Florentine citizens are held back by pangs of conscience from making the said loans spontaneously. If they were forced, they would avoid the danger of sin." The commune decided to oblige. It authorized the officials to designate those who were to loan the remaining amount, with no one to be named to lend less than 50 florins. They might force collection by all appropriate means. Those lending were to be booked at an amount three times that actually loaned. This meant 15 percent interest on the actual loan.[123]

We must, I think, take these statements at their face value: the conscience of many Florentines did not allow them to freely loan within this scheme. But we must also accept the assizement of the tax collectors: if the law read that the loan was to be forced, it would salve consciences, even though the force spoken of might be no more than a legal fiction. This "force" clause was subsequently introduced into other loans, but its fictional character is clear in these laws' stipulation of a substantial minimum amount to be loaned.[124]

The licitness of these and subsequent loans of this type was seriously in question. Matteo Villani opined that creditors had loaned willingly to the *uno tre* fund not because of charity, but because of the cupidity for profit. And that, as anyone knew, was precisely one of the conditions for determining that a profit was usurious.[125] A few years later, we find the *Signoria* seeking out the opinions of Dominican and Augustinian canonists and

---

121. *ASF, Provv.*, 45, fols. 195r–197r (June 5, 1358).

122. *Ibid.*, fols. 239r–241r.

123. "Quodque multi cives florentini retrahantur ex conscientie stimulo a dicto mutuo spontanee faciendo, quod faciendo cohacti, peccati periculum evitarent..." (*ibid.*, 46, fols. 4r–6r). This bill formalized the *Monte del uno tre*.

124. These "force" clauses are especially prominent in the period right after the rewriting mentioned above. See for example *ibid.*, fols. 79r–82r (Jan. 11, 1358*sf*).

125. M. Villani, *Croniche*, VIII, 71.

theologians so that, if it were determined that certain loans were illicit, the Florentines could avoid falling into further sin.[126]

A second assurance the lenders sought was that, whatever the nature of the loan arrangement, they would under no circumstances be subject to prosecution for having accepted interest from the commune. Of course, the commune itself could not, on its own authority, assure them that the spiritual authority, either local or Roman, would not prosecute them. Nevertheless, the creditors demanded the greatest formal assurances the government would commit to paper. Without them, the commune would be unable to borrow.

The commune satisfied this demand by issuing its creditors chits containing a truly imposing promise. The first record I have found for such *Monte* chits is in 1354, contemporary to an extensive debate in Florence over speculation,[127] and shortly before the misgivings over the *uno tre Monte*. By this law syndics were to be appointed by the Council of the Commune for one year

> specifically and namely to pardon, terminate, and remit both as far as God, as far as conscience and as far as the world is concerned, all those who up until now . . . or during the said year . . . receive any of the money of the aforesaid commune *pro dono, merito provisione, usuris, seu interesse* on whatever money of the said commune of Florence.

And they were to record such pardons, terminations, and remissions in public instruments for any such creditor asking for one.[128]

We may quickly summarize the subsequent history of this "liberation" formula. What officials were in charge of this? At first specific syndics were appointed as above. In 1360 the task of liberating was in the hands of the Officials for the Diminution of the *Monte*, as well as a group of

126. *ASF, Missive*, 13, fol. 45r (May 23, 1365). On a Franciscan chapter general which discussed usury, probably in part upon the solicitation of the brothers' Florentine hosts, see J. Kirshner, "A Document on the Meeting of the Chapter General in Florence (1365)," *Archivum Franciscanum Historicum*, LXII (1969), 392–399.

127. *ASF, Provv.*, 41, fols. 35r–36r (June 20, 1354); M. Villani, *Croniche*, III, 106. M. Becker says that this was practiced in the 1330s and before (*Transition*, II, 48). He believed that the procedure had been discontinued, and takes this as a sign of a "new ethos."

128. "Specialiter et nominatim ad perdonandum, finiendum, et remictendum et quo ad Deum et quo ad conscientiam et ad mundum . . . omnibus et singulis qui hactenus . . . seu . . . recipient durante tempore dicti anni aliquid de pecunia comunis predicti pro dono, merito provisione, usuris, seu interesse cuiuscumque pecunie dicti communis Florentie. . . . Et ad faciendum . . . de perdonantia, fine, et remissione instrumentum et instrumenta cuilibet petenti . . ." (*ASF, Provv., loc. cit.*).

syndics. Syndics were functioning in this role in 1367, and the diminution officials in 1372. In the meantime, however, the commune had added a statement to the bills containing this *balia* that the creditors were, by the terms of the bill itself, *ex inde liberati*.[129]

There were slight shifts in the verbiage of these provisions which are of great interest. After the first bill of 1354, the word *perdonare* is not found, and the terms *indulgendum, liberare, finire, absolutio, terminare,* and *remissio* were used. In addition, the striking phrase according to which certain creditors owed "usury" to the commune seems to have been used for the last time in 1360.[130] After that the remission is always from *dono, dampno et interesse.* Finally, verbiage indicating that the creditors actually did owe something to the commune crept into these provisions. Thus in 1357 it was said that anyone receiving such a chit was understood to have been liberated and absolved from any sum he had received from the commune as part of a loan transaction, through which he had become obligated to the commune.[131]

These developments in the *balia* given for the chits suggest that they slowly became less necessary. Furthermore, as time went on the hint that the creditor owed the commune for the interest he had taken was emphasized. This indicates a shift from a buyer's to a seller's market in shares in the debt. The new communal confidence is reflected in a recommendation made by a communal counselor in 1372. On the problem of diminishing the interest paid on the *Monte,* he suggested that the payment of interest to certain lenders be postponed in exchange for a promise to spare them "if they incurred some sin for an undue acceptance [of interest]."[132]

129. "Et quod nichilominus ex nunc etiam absque absolutione predicta fienda, ut dictum est, intelligantur esse et sint liberi . . ." (*ASF, Provv.,* 45, fols. 11*v*–12*r*). In 1360 the Officials for the Diminution "possint . . . ad remictendum omnibus et singulis cum quibus concordaverunt, pepigerint seu transegerint, ut est dictum, totum et quicquid dicto comuni tenentur pro usuris, provisione, dampno, donis seu interesse quod vel que ipsi creditores . . . habuissent seu recepissent de pecunia comunis predicti . . ." (*ibid.,* 47, fol. 119*r* [Jan. 30, 1359*sf*]). See *ibid.,* fols. 190*rv* (May 4, 1360); 55, fols. 68*v*–69*r* (Oct. 27, 1367); 60, fol. 73*v* (Aug. 29, 1372), fols. 91*r*–94*r* (Nov. 5, 1372).

130. *Ibid.,* 47, fol. 119*r*. The shifting use of words reflects a legal problem. If the word *usury* was not used, then it could be said that the commune had not intended to remit usury. If it was used, then the sin might be said to be manifest. This could only be hedged by using the conditional mood ("if usury were taken").

131. "Ad finiendum . . . omnibus et singulis illis qui hactenus quandocumque aliquid a comuni predicto . . . pro usuris . . . sibi comuni vel alteri pro decto comuni ratione mutuate" (*ASF, Provv.,* 45, fols. 11*v*–12*r* [July 28, 1357]).

132. "Dominus Jacobus de Albertis consuluit quod hinc ad kalendas Novembris proxime venturas officiales monete deliberent qui creditores montium debeant, non

In the early years of their usage, these chits were extremely important. What could be clearer than this prologue to the law appointing the chit-syndics for 1360–1361:

Noting that it is useful to the commune of Florence to ascertain who would subvent with money the said commune at opportune times in exchange for a competent recompensation, and [noting] that if the following law and others like it were not made and had not been made up until now, men would not have been disposed and will not be disposed to loan money to the said commune. . . .[133]

In the simplest terms, this means that the commune had difficulty raising voluntary loans between 1354 and 1372 unless it furnished lenders a document promising them it would not prosecute them for usury. Voluntary lenders would not come forward unless the lending arrangement and the renunciatory promises of the commune were such as to protect them from falling under the suspicion of usury. Conscience and good sense dictated both. This is a very different picture of lending practices than has been presented by other students of this period. They have usually mentioned Villani's passage indicating that the Florentines were troubled in conscience, but then have gone on to consider these arrangements from a purely secular point of view.[134]

How do we explain the commune's claim to "pardon," "absolve," and "remit" usury? Sapori and Becker have gone so far as to say that the commune was remitting *sin*, but such a formulation raises more questions

---

tamen simul sed divisim, supersedere acceptationi interesse. Et qui a quantitate declaranda infra habebunt, si volunt supersedere acceptationi interesse, primis et secundis parcatur si incurrissent in aliquid peccatum acceptationis indebiti" (*ASF, CP,* 12, fols. 11v–12r [Mar. 18, 1371*sf*]).

133. "Advertentes quod utile est comuni Florentie invenire qui dicto comuni de pecunia subveniant temporibus opportunis, recompensatione habita competenti, et quod nisi infrascripti provisio et ei similes fierent et facte fuissent hactenus, non fuissent dispositi nec disponerentur homines ad mutua dicto comuni facienda . . ." (*ASF, Provv.,* 47, fols. 190rv [May 4, 1360]). Cf. Becker, *Transition,* II, 48.

134. A particularly noteworthy example is: "Few were sufficiently troubled as to the licitness of this trade in the eyes of God to refuse *Monte* interest payments or to make restitution to the treasury" (Becker, *Transition,* II, 175 and *ibid.,* n. 63, discussing *Monte* speculation). It is hard to ignore the *Monte* official and chronicler Matteo Villani, with his open concern for "contaminated consciences" (*Croniche,* III, 106). And it is just as difficult to bypass the significant numbers of restitutive legacies to the commune indicated by the laws cited above.

than it answers.[135] All canonical and theological implications of this term aside, certain observations are in order to put these promises into perspective.

In the first place, such promises were a common means in private documents by which lenders sought to secure their estates from raids for the return of purported usury. They would receive from borrowers "pardon" from any usury the lenders might have taken, and a promise not to prosecute the lenders' estates for restitution of usury.[136] Thus this method was common in the private realm. Indeed, the merchants' guild in Florence required that such absolutions be carried out by its members at regular intervals.[137] Secondly, absolutions "quoad Deum, Conscientam, et ad mundum" were not limited to matters of usury, but were used to syndicate ex-officials of the commune. For example, in 1375 a Cistercian lay brother who had terminated his office as a bursar of the communal camera told the *Signoria* that at different times during his term of office he had received money from government officials for clothing and the like. Wishing now to visit the Holy Land "with every purity of conscience," he requested that he "be understood to be and to be *quoad Deum et conscientam et ad mundum* totally liberated and absolved from all and everything . . . of which he could be said to be obligated."[138]

Contemporary and subsequent canonists wrote extensively on this clause, asking if it excused the communal creditor from the necessity of restitution, and if it further liberated him from the stain of sin.[139] It is unnecessary to pursue this argumentation, however, for we are only interested in the creditor, who had to decide whether to loan or not. And we can say with some confidence that such a chit must have encouraged

---

135. A. Sapori, "Il Taccamento dei Panni Franceschi a Firenze nel Trecento," in his *Studi di Storia Economica*, 3 vols. (Florence, 1955–67), I, 262; "Arti e Compagnie Mercantili Toscane del Due e del Trecento e il Principio della Pubblicità per Registrazione," *op. cit.*, II, 828; M. Becker, "Church and State," p. 513.

136. For a person going from parish to parish collecting these chits, see *ASF, Notarile antecosiminiano*, G 106 (1319–25), fols. 14v–19r: hereafter cited as *ASF, not. antecos.* For several examples at Avignon, see Chiaudano, *Libro . . . Corbizzi*, pp. 7 f, 15, 25.

137. Sapori, *Studi*, II, 828.

138. "Quare . . . supplicat quatenus dignemini opportune providere . . . quod ipse frater Laurentius intelligatur esse et sit quo ad Deum et conscientiam et ad mundum totaliter liberatus et absolutus ab omni et toto eo ad quod quomodolibet diceretur vel dici posset ipsum fratrem Laurentium aliqualiter teneri . . ." (*ASF, Provv.*, 62, fol. 280v [Feb. 12, 1374*sf*]).

139. For the views of the Florentine canonists Lapo da Castiglionchio and Lorenzo de' Ridolfi, see St. Antonino, *Summa Theologica* (Paris, 1521), Part 2, title 1, cap. 11, Introduction and sec. 3 (col. 48r).

the lender to believe that he would be safe from prosecution for usury from the commune (*mundum*), from the spiritual authority (*Deum*), and be under no necessity to restitute in the forum of internal conscience (*conscientam*).

Perhaps, however, his confidence had deeper sources. Perhaps he knew that this chit-promise was made in the light of an understanding with the commune and the Roman Curia that they would not prosecute for usury. This brings us to the third assurance the potential lender might require of the commune. Though he might shape the lending arrangements to avoid the suspicion of usury (forced rather than voluntary loans), though he might insist on chits, though he might obtain canonistic opinions vouching for the licitness of loan types, he knew that the final word on whether a loan was usurious lay with the papacy. And as we have stressed, he feared not only that the spiritual authority might attack him, but that under the guise of morality, the commune itself, perhaps in liaison with Rome, might damage him. What was needed, consequently, was assurance from Rome that it would not only not attack creditors of the commune, but would defend them from the commune if it defaulted. In short, what was needed was the papal *clausula penalis*.

The papacy was ideally constituted for such a role. As a spiritual lord, it could prosecute the perjuries of city officials if they failed to meet their obligations. As the defender of Christian peace, it could prosecute for barratry and corruption, the crimes into which defaulting officials fell by the terms of the *clausula*.

From a historical point of view as well, the papacy was well suited to give such guarantees. It is in the Avignonese period that the papal bureaucracy becomes a central penitential agency for absolving all comers from uncertain usury, increasingly bypassing the local church courts and assuring merchants immunity from prosecution.[140] The papacy, having established its right over the local churches in this matter, was thus in a position to deal with the local secular authorities from a position of strength. The right it had obtained it could give up. And in fact, we find that sometime before 1365 the papacy had reserved to the bishop of Florence the disposition of cases involving usury and *incerti*.[141] And given

140. In the *Collectores* records of the apostolic camera during the Avignonese period, the receipts from this activity were separately handled; see for example *ASV, Collectores*, 245, fol. 119*v* (1348). The commissions of the collectors authorized them to publish letters notifying one and all that they were inviolate from further prosecution for *incerti*; see the case of a Panciatichi who had procured such an absolution, in *ASF, not. antecos.*, L 37 (1373–75), fols. 4*rv* (Aug. 3, 1373).

141. "Processibus supra facta usurarum et incertorum, quorum dispositio episcopo

the balance of forces in the commune, this meant in effect that the episcopal curia could prosecute for usury only after seriously considering the communal will in the matter.[142]

The period 1345–1378 was one in which the papacy and the commune worked together to the advantage of both. In 1344 or 1345, I shall argue, the papacy and commune agreed to a pact by which the papacy agreed to protect communal creditors both from the commune and the papacy, and assured the commune that its lending institutions would not come under attack from Rome. For such promises, I believe, a weak commune agreed to give preferential treatment to the papacy and cardinals who had been in danger of losing large sums of money as a result of the bankruptcies of the forties. This understanding, I believe, persisted into the 1370s. The papacy during this period was a guarantor of communal laws.

It would be optimal if one could reproduce the text of such a striking agreement, but alas it has not turned up. This is not surprising, though, since this agreement would have been of such a secretive and questionable nature as to preclude its circulation. One could argue that the whole arrangement may have necessitated no formal agreement: the papacy may have functioned as such a guarantor without ever formally agreeing to do so. But the circumstantial evidence for a pact is strong enough that one must posit it. This evidence may be summed up in the following fashion: first, the state of relations between Rome and Florence in the forties and fifties suggests some basic understanding; second, the papacy to my knowledge never disclaimed the role the *clausula penalis* spelled out for it; third, in 1378 the commune requested that the pope renounce any sums due him because of violation of the cameral clause, and Urban VI specifically did so renounce.[143] Thus, even though I have been unable to discover in the records of the apostolic camera any actual reception of such funds—again not surprising, given the delicate nature of the accord—the fact remains that the papacy had to have accepted its right to penalties in order to renounce them in 1378.[144] Fourth, there is an abundance of direct

---

florentino per bullam apostolicam reservatur" (*ASF, Missive*, 13, fol. 25*v* [Jan. 10, 1364*sf*]; Brucker, *Politics*, p. 137, n. 141).

142. See my *Synodal Law in Florence and Fiesole, 1306–1518* (Vatican City, 1971), pp. 145–46.

143. See below, pp. 206 f.

144. There are several payments to the apostolic camera *in foro conscientie* with the money stipulated for the crusade; see L. Mohler (ed.), *Die Einnahmen der Apostolischen Kammer unter Klemens VI* (Paderborn, 1931), pp. 359 *et passim*. In connection with this it may be pointed out that when the papal penitentiaries absolved from perjury, penalties

evidence showing that the papacy intervened actively in its role as guarantor of other types of communal laws sealed with the apostolic rider. For at the request of the *Signoria*, it often absolved individuals from the danger of prosecution for perjury. That is, the papacy at times renounced its rights when it considered a modification of a law thus sealed to be in the interest of the *bene comune*. All of this evidence, to be presented in what follows, would seem to dictate some basic understanding between mother Rome and daughter Florence.

What evidence in the history of the 1340s and 1350s suggests such a view? Certainly it is not orthodox. Most historians have seen this regime as generally antagonistic to church interests. The source of its anticlericalism has been found in the changed social composition of government. The old elite was in this view high Guelf, rich in ecclesiastical benefices and offices. Its interest-taking was moderate and not usurious. Small usurers in the recent past, many of them resented the official conscience of Rome, while being jealous of their social superiors' privileges. The effect of this antagonism, so goes this view, were the antiecclesiastical laws of the 1340s: the law forbidding access to benefices without communal letters patent, the violent dislike of the Inquisitor in office in Florence, and the accompanying laws of 1345 and 1346 against those impetrating or declining the jurisdiction of the commune. There can be no doubt that relations between Rome and Florence were tense between the expulsion of Walter of Brienne (1343) and the Black Death. Nonetheless, there are other aspects of this period which suggest a great measure of accommodation. Without pretending to present a balanced picture, I would mention the other side of the coin.

If we remember just how important the Florentine bankers were to papal fiscal arrangements, a natural question comes to mind. With enormous sums of papal collections in the hands of the Florentine banks, which transferred them from the dioceses of Europe, through the camera, to their destination to support the wars of the papacy, with the papacy dependent on these banks for its own solvency, would it not have been all important for Rome to maintain continuity in these operations? If it could not successfully continue its working arrangement with these bankrupt houses, would it not at least have been anxious to avoid sharp breaks with

---

were given to the apostolic camera for the crusade; see the penitential formulary of Walter of Strassburg in *Biblioteca Apostolica Vaticana*, MS. *Vat. Lat.*, 2663, fol. LV; hereafter cited as *BAV*. There is a chance that the cameral payments are related to perjury.

these banks? If that happened it could throw its collection machine and therewith its liquidity into chaos.

This was the need of the papacy. It could not indiscriminately attack the commune and its citizens. A traumatic transition in its collection business had to be avoided. The papacy needed the commune too much to indiscriminately demand its rights. And as we have seen, the commune certainly was not in a position to recklessly insist on its own rights. Ignoring all other questions, such as their mutual diplomatic and military interests, we can see that in the forties, the road was open for a *modus vivendi* of significant proportions.[145]

The history of church-state relations in the subsequent period needs reinterpretation in the light of the complex of mutual security described in this paper. It is true that the years 1344–1346 were marked by the passage of some three laws against ecclesiastical privilege. And it is just as true that the generation of Florentines with which we are dealing was exposed to interdicts at various times. In 1346, in 1355, again in 1361, and in 1367 the commune was faced with ecclesiastical strictures. But two of these were not imposed by the pope, but by lesser officials.[146] And most important, there is apparently no case during this period where the papacy seriously considered enforcing the interdicts. There seem to have been no seizures of the goods of the Florentine colony in Avignon by the apostolic camera, and no attempt to enforce an economic boycott of Florentine goods and merchants by other communes or states. The pope at no time ordered the clergy of Florence to leave the city during any of the interdicts. No one could expect the relations between two such vulnerable and inter-

145. Renouard has argued that the papacy followed a shortsighted, purely egoistic policy, and brutally abandoned the companies (*Relations*, pp. 198 f.). Brucker adds that this precipitate abandonment nullified any possibility that the companies might weather the storm, something not soon forgotten by the merchants (*Politics*, p. 133). I can find little to suggest such a view. There being practically no evidence of cameral action against these banks for its credits (for example, no seizure of Florentine possessions in Avignon), and no evidence of a settlement, as well as no evidence of Florentine bitterness toward the papacy on this score, one can suppose that a compromise was struck, with the papacy receiving preferred treatment. It is true that these companies' names disappeared from the ledgers. But the same can be said for the Alberti bank at the time of the later war with the church. Yet this bank was conspicuously absent from the list of Florentines who had their goods seized by the papacy in 1376. There had obviously been a settlement, and the Alberti stepped right back into its role as papal banker when that war was over. These *argumenta ad silentium* suggest that the papacy acted reasonably, and not egoistically; see my *Interdict*, pp. 34 f, 40.

146. The 1346 interdict was imposed by the Inquisitor (see below, p. 161). That in 1355 was laid by the bishop (*ASF, Provv.*, 42, fols. 15v–16r [Mar. 6, 1354sf]).

dependent powers to be smooth. But it is a testament to the essentially pacific nature of these relations that the papacy did not insist the interdicts be enforced, couched its objections to the Florentine laws against ecclesiastical liberties in the mildest terms, and not only relieved the Inquisitor who laid the interdict of 1346, but promptly tried him for excesses, and immediately transferred the bishop who imposed the interdict of 1355.[147]

On the other side, a close examination of communal policy toward the local church will show that its policy was cautious and ameliorative: few impositions, general recognition of judicial immunity, and so forth. The period from 1345 to 1375 is, as Marvin Becker has pointed out, one of great importance in church-state relations.[148] The laws of 1344–1346 were important landmarks. But the lid remained on during this period. As in so many other areas of Europe, it was the period of the Great Schism which represented the apogee of communal power over the local church. The years 1345–1375 were generally peaceful.

There are certain aspects of the settlement of Florentine debts *in curia* during the forties which suggest that the commune and papacy were working within a general understanding. Sapori has shown that almost from the beginning, the commune had been ready to accord preferential treatment to certain clerical creditors of the Acciaiuoli.[149] A law of September 17, 1344, authorized communal agents to pay up to ten shillings on the pound to Opizzo d'Este and any other foreign creditor. This was to be in cash; the possibility of repayment of additional amounts by other means was left open.[150] A law of 1347 lists the pope and other clerical creditors of the Acciaiuoli.[151]

It must remain a matter of speculation if one of these additional means included inscription in the *Monte*. One certain method was to permit them to imburse the rents from lands of the bankrupt companies. This was one method by which the apostolic camera realized the credits due it. By 1350 the camera referred to this arrangement as traditional. Traditional also, it wrote, was the precedence given the papal camera over other creditors.[152]

---

147. For the trial of the Inquisitor Piero d'Aquila, see M. da Alatri, "L'Inquisizione a Firenze negli anni 1344–46 da un'Istruttoria contro Pietro da L'Aquila" in *Miscellanea Melchor de Pobladura* I (Rome, 1964), 225–49. Bishop Angelo Acciaiuoli had been transferred by March 18, 1355; A. Gherardi and C. Guasti (eds.), *I Capitoli del Comune di Firenze*, Vol. II (Florence, 1893), p. 498.

148. See especially his "Church and State."

149. Sapori, *Crisi*, pp. 183 ff., 193; cf. *ASF, Provv. Duppl.*, 5, fol. 35r (Mar. 11, 1344sf).

150. *ASF, Capitoli*, 18, fols. 34r–35v (Sept. 17, 1344).

151. *ASF, Provv.*, 34, fol. 148v (June 19, 1347).

152. "Non obstantibus traditione huiusmodi per vos facta et quod camera ipsa

The story, however, goes far beyond simple preferential treatment on bankruptcy rates. Sapori and other writers have put a great deal of emphasis on the debt of the Acciaiuoli to Cardinal Sabine, without noticing the strange silence of both Florentine and papal sources on the credits of the papacy itself. The papacy is often listed in the Florentine laws as a creditor, but no laws direct themselves specifically to this subject. Why this silence on that most central of all creditors, the papacy? We see the partial results of the settlement (the farming of lands by the papal camera), but nothing is to be found regarding the settlement itself. It is not going too far to suppose that the financial settlement with Rome formed part of a larger concordat normalizing the papacy's part in the securing of communal loans from its citizens.

The preferential treatment accorded the papacy was most marked in the judicial realm. Who was to decide just how much money was owed to curial creditors? Who was to determine how it was to be repaid? There is no doubt that the commune would have preferred to adjudicate charges against its own citizens. But this was not to be. The Acciaiuoli and the Peruzzi formally submitted themselves to the judicial *dominium* of the papal courts, and the commune agreed to this arrangement.[153]

The *topos* will be recognized, for we saw previously that merchants often submitted themselves to foreign judicial authority in order to provide necessary security. Since the debts of these companies were partly from contracts signed in the curia, they were subject to the auditor of the camera. For the commune to agree to be bound by settlements of the Roman courts in a period of financial strain in affairs regarding companies of the

---

[apostolica] in debitorum suorum utpote fiscalium satisfactione facienda sibi debet aliis creditoribus antiferri, assignare vultis eisdem creditoribus." Do not go, the pope urged the commune, "contra traditionem vestram" (*ASF, Capitoli*, 16, fols. 30*rv* [Aug. 27, 1350]). The receipts from these rents can be followed in the registers of the apostolic camera; see for example *ASV, Collectores*, 245, fol. 2*v* (Nov. 13, 1346).

153. The Acciaiuoli "se et eorum heredes et bona specialiter obligassent, submittendo se et eorum quemlibet specialiter et expresse iurisdictioni et cohertioni curie dictorum filiorum . . . [sic] auditoris nostre camere" (*ASF, Capitoli*, 16, fol. 25*r* [Feb. 28, 1347*sc*]). The Peruzzi "cum super premissis omnibus et singulis debitis, contractus in romana curia initi extitisssent, dicteque societas et singulares persone etiam pro predictis quantitatibus dicto Johanni debitis, se sponte iurisdictioni summisissent eidem [curie camere nostre], ac propterea de iurisdictione auditoris predicti ratione contractuum et summissionum huiusmodi sint effecti" (*ibid.*, fol. 28*r* [Aug. 2, 1349]). When the commune recognized the submission of the Acciaiuoli to the apostolic camera, and promised to live up to the judgment of that court, the interdict on the city of Florence was lifted (*ibid.*, fol. 25*r*).

size of the Acciaiuoli and Peruzzi suggests that a *quid pro quo* was forthcoming from the Holy Father.

Perhaps the most crucial figure in the ordering of debts between Rome and Florence was the bishop of Florence, Angelo Acciaiuoli. Giovanni Villani accused him of being more interested in the fortunes of his family than in his pastoral role. If the bishop of Florence had been a foreigner, said Villani, the local church would probably not have tolerated the antiecclesiastical laws of 1345–1346.[154] But certainly it was no accident that Acciaiuoli was agreed upon by commune and papacy when the see was vacant in 1342.[155] Without his office, one suspects, it would have been more difficult to arrange the outstanding business between curial creditors and the commune of Florence. It was the Acciaiuoli bishop who with one layman determined the rates at which the *soci* of the Acciaiuoli had to pay for bankruptcy.[156] He bore the brunt of papal dissatisfaction with the settlement and payment of debts, being relieved of his post for some years.[157] But the commune reacted to this by passing a law committing it to the defense of Acciaiuoli's and other clerics' benefices.[158] The papacy did in fact yield, and Acciaiuoli was reaffirmed as bishop.[159] When in 1355, with the crisis past, the commune became disenchanted with the bishop, the papacy again responded to the commune's wishes and transferred him to another, lesser see.[160]

I have presented circumstantial evidence to support the argument that there was a general accord between the commune and the papacy which included the right of the commune to secure its loans through the use of the apostolic camera as a third party. The silence of Florentine and papal sources on the settlement of the bankers' debts with the papal camera argues for such an accord, since the debts were certainly sizable, or would have been made to appear so by an opportunistic papacy. We know that two of the three major banks had, with communal approval, subjected

154. *Croniche*, XII, 43.

155. The cathedral canons had elected another Florentine as bishop (Filippo Dell'-Antella); the Acciaiuoli appointment represented the subsequent compromise between commune and papacy (*AAF, filza cartapecore 1321–1389*, fols. 40v–41r). Acciaiuoli took possession of the see Aug. 4, 1342 (*ibid.*, fols. 56r–57r).

156. *ASF, Provv.*, 32, fols. 110v–111v (Jan. 27, 1343*sf*).

157. For references to Fra Matteo, *electo florentino*, see *ASV, Reg. Vat.*, 138, fol. 43r (July 12, 1344), and *Einnahmen . . . Klemens VI*, p. 109 (Aug. 13, 1345).

158. *ASF, Provv.*, 34, fol. 31r (Apr. 4, 1346). Acciaiuoli was not named specifically in this law, but the wording and circumstances make this clear.

159. He is referred to as bishop in 1347 (Gherardi and Guasti, *Capitoli*, II, 488).

160. His new see was Monte Cassino (*ibid.*, p. 498).

themselves formally to the court of the camera, indicating a wider understanding. But there is another piece of evidence which, in my opinion, argues very persuasively for such an agreement. Let me state it as starkly as possible.

In its terrible financial need, the commune, unable to raise forced loans, looked about for means of supplementing its treasury. Its gaze settled on the testamental grants left to the confraternity of Santa Maria in Or San Michele, the most important corporative executor of charitable legacies and inheritances in the city, and on the Franciscan convent of Santa Croce, the most significant clerical recipient of charitable legacies and estates. In the mid-forties, with the agreement of the clerical authorities, the commune started to tap testamental charity.

In one of the most sensitive areas of church-state relations, the disposition of testamental charity, the commune during these years was able to tide itself over with not one word of objection from the papacy. Not only was Rome silent: the see of Florence approved the first "loans" from the confraternity, and certain of the transactions were secured by the apostolic penal clause which is the subject of this article. The massive seizures of church properties during the subsequent war with the papacy (1376–1378) have been traditionally considered as the first major attack on church wealth. But here in the 1340s are to be found the beginnings of a policy of communal supervision of ecclasiastical and paraecclesiastical wealth.

Let us look first at the case of the Franciscans of Santa Croce. The peculiar role which the commune came to play in the management of the incomes of this house and those subjected to it in the Franciscan province of Tuscany flowed from the famous bull *Ad conditorem canonum*, published by John XXII in 1323.[161] This decretal had the effect of making it impossible for procurators of a Franciscan house to sue in secular court for legacies and inheritances left to the convent or church for the necessities of the *frati*. Nor could they request the use of the secular arm to collect such legacies from heirs. This *grande novità*, as Giovanni Villani called it, created an enormous amount of uncertainty as to the status of such legacies and inheritances. Since the Franciscans of Santa Croce were legally poor, and could not own goods in common, and the individual Franciscan had no legal personality, who now would defend their interests? The commune stepped into the void. Already in the *podestà* Statutes of 1325, we find the matter regulated. By petition, but also ex officio, the foreign judges of the commune were authorized to determine by summary process what was

---

161. *Corpus Iuris Canonici, Extra. Joh. XXII*, XIV, c. 3.

owed the Franciscans both for their necessities and for other than their necessities, and could force payment. Since the brothers could not appoint a proctor, the *Signoria* was authorized to appoint a syndic if requested to do so by the guardian or custodian of Santa Croce. In the name of the commune, he would go before the above courts to defend Franciscan interests. Further, this communal syndic was authorized to imburse such legacies and debts and dispose of the sums as desired by the same custodian or guardian.[162]

The city desired to protect its Mendicants from recalcitrant testamental executors. But it is easily seen that this ordinance could be used as a wedge to enforce the commune's interpretation of what was good for the Franciscans. When the city encountered grave fiscal difficulties, it would naturally tend to question whether sizable sums owed to religious houses but not required for the everyday necessities of the friars could not better serve the friars and God if they were, for example, invested in the *Monte Comune*.

Since the *Monte* archive is still not generally available, and the sources for the study of the Franciscans in Florence are so skimpy, it is impossible to follow the process by which the commune came to play an ever greater role in Franciscan finances. There are, however, signs along the way. First, in December, 1349, a new law was passed similar to that in the Statutes of 1325. The one significant modification is that the rights of the communal syndic to act at the behest of the guardian or custodian are spelled out in great detail. The syndic could *petere, exigere, recipere,* and *confitere.* He could sell and cede the goods imbursed, receiving and recognizing the monies imbursed on such sales. He could distribute and expend these monies as deliberated by the custodian or guardian. And, very importantly, he could compromise and settle debts to the Franciscans at a rate lower than the formal debt, a procedure scarcely in keeping with church canons.[163]

This was in 1349. In 1364, Santa Croce was receiving interest on an investment in the public debt which Sapori has calculated to be in the neighborhood of 48,000 florins.[164] Where did such a large investment

162. These syndics were to act "tamquam si essent legittimi procuratores et syndici" Caggese (ed.), *Statuti . . .* , Vol. II (Florence, 1921) (*Stat. uto del Podestà,* dell'anno 1325), pp. 166 f.; see Giovanni Villani's narration in the *Croniche,* IX, 157.

163. "Item ad compromitendum tam de iure quam de facto cum dictis debitoribus" (*ASF, Provv.,* 37, fols. 54v–55r [Dec. 11, 1349]).

164. A. Sapori, "La 'Gabella delle Porte' di Firenze, 1361 e 1364," in his *Studi,* III, 45 f. This may represent the interest from only one holding in one *Monte,* rather than the total investment.

come from? I would hypothesize that it flowed into the *Monte* through the activities of these syndics. It is no accident that the new law was passed in 1349, a period of fiscal need and one in which enormous sums were flowing into the coffers of religious houses as a result of the Black Death. It is worth pointing out that in 1371 the commune silenced by law those who were claiming that the communal syndic was not legally competent to collect grants made to the Franciscans. He could, said this law, act exactly like an heir.[165] Then in 1377, contemporary to a general sequestration of ecclesiastical goods, the commune handed over the rights previously in the hands of the occasionally appointed communal syndics to the regularly constituted court of the *Mercanzia*.[166] The subsequent history of communal influence over ecclesiastical incomes was to remain with this court throughout the quattrocento.

These sparse indications of growing communal influence over testamental charity can be supplemented by the better documented communal intrusion into the affairs of Or San Michele. It is the same commune, desirous of preserving the charitable devotion of its citizens, defending the souls of testators from the sins of their greedy heirs, which attached the wealth of Or San Michele and Sante Croce. And Rome remained as silent on the one as on the other.

Matteo Villani outlined the story of Or San Michele in these years.[167] As a result of the droughts and plagues of the 1340s, the confraternity became enormously wealthy. When whole families died out, the estates often passed through testamentary substitution to this confraternity. For some years, it was like a fiscal state within a state. To be an officer of the confraternity gave one more access to wealth and influence than to be a communal prior. Fortunes were made by many dishonest officials. Villani does not, however, tell us just what role Or San Michele played in communal finances during these hectic years. But it was in fact an important source of revenue for the communal coffers.

Its utility took two forms. The first way in which the confraternity served the commonweal was as a haven for certain funds of the great banks which, because of their pious nature, once located there were exempt from the *corpo* used to satisfy creditors of the banks.

165. "Et quod ... sindici ... possint ... apprehendere omnes et singulas hereditates, relicta ..., et de illis disponere sicut alii legiptimi heredes ..., et in omnibus ... ac si ad ipsas hereditates adheundas, apprehendas, administrandas ... constitui potuissent et possent et fuissent et essent legiptime ... constituti ..." (*ASF, Provv.*, 59, fols. 124*rv* [Oct. 10, 1371]).

166. *Ibid*, 65, fols. 86*rv* (June 22, 1377).

167. *Croniche*, I, 7, 57.

One of the most fascinating aspects of the organization of the Florentine *compagnie* were the accounts carried in their ledgers *pro Deo*. The Lord was a participant in these companies, and his share participated in the profits or losses of the companies. Sapori has characterized these *conti di messer Domeneddio* as caritative, the setting aside of charity by guilt-ridden merchants to assuage the anger of God at their questionable commercial practices.[168] But he noted that only small amounts from God's holdings were actually expended in caritative ends. Why? Because, I would suggest, the accounts had an additional function. Companies were always in danger of being prosecuted for usury, and such sums were a type of insurance: they could be used to settle such claims, and the remainder used caritatively.[169]

When the companies failed, these sums formed a privileged part of the *corpi* of the companies, since they belonged to "the poor."[170] The commune consequently ordered that the *iura* in question be transferred to Or San Michele. This move effectively removed this money from the bankruptcy pool, and put it at the disposal of the commune.[171]

For the commune soon came to rely on the confraternity for monetary sustenance. On the heels of the Black Death of 1348, it cancelled all previous legislation concerning the confraternity and completely reorganized it in such a way as to make it practically a communal institution.[172] Then it moved to regulate the flood of money and goods left to the confraternity. This was done after extensive consultation with ecclesiastics, *and with the license of the episcopal vicar*.[173] First it froze sales by the company to private individuals of any real estate in its possession or due it. It then ordered the captains of Or San Michele to sell to the commune all the real estate it had acquired in the previous two years and any real estate it subsequently acquired through a title originating in

168. A. Sapori, "La Beneficenza delle Compagnie Mercantili del Trecento," in his *Studi*, II, 839–847.

169. *Ibid.*, p. 845. This is hypothetical, since I have not found an actual disbursement of this account to settle usury accounts. But companies also received the absolutions from the Roman see, and *soci* of the companies often stipulated monies in their testaments for the contingency that the company (i.e., the *soci* of the company) would have to pay usury; see for example *AAF*, *Libro di Contratti, 1335*, fols. 160v, 181rv.

170. On the "poor" as the recipients of otherwise unstipulated legacies *pro amore Dei*, see my "The Bishop's Portion," forthcoming in *Traditio*, XXVIII (1972).

171. Sapori, *Studi*, II, 846.

172. *ASF*, *Provv.*, 36, fols. 25v–27r (Nov. 13, 1348).

173. "Cum multis prudentibus viris maxime religiosis, et habita licentia a domino vicario . . . episcopi florentini de infrascriptis omnibus et singulis faciendis" (*ibid.*).

these two years. Provision was to be made to insure that the confraternity retained the property necessary to meet its testamentary obligations to widows and orphans, for the celebration of anniversary masses, and the like. The lands in question were to be sold by the commune to communal creditors as satisfaction for their credits, thereby liquidating some of that pressing debt.[174]

This land was not simply sequestered. Or San Michele was to itself become a creditor of the commune, and be paid a 5 percent interest on the price of the goods taken in. But as with Santa Croce, this amounted to a partial sequestration. Since the communal officials determined the value of lands in a buyer's market (the price had fallen radically), they in fact were buying and selling at cut rates, and only investing this amount in the *Monte*. That was not all. For the value of shares being far below purchase price, the two entities in question doubtless suffered an immediate devaluation of their wealth.[175]

This original incursion of the commune quickly became traditional practice. Soon the commune was not only buying the company's lands, but borrowing cash from it both in amortized form and *spe rehabendi*.[176] By a law of 1352, the different parts of communal activity came together. Communal officials were appointed to see that debts to the confraternity were paid. Then the goods and monies appropriated by these syndics were to be expended by the same communal officials "in urgent necessities of the *popolo* and commune."[177] This too was negotiated as a loan, and the officials were authorized to negotiate repayment through an assignment of gabelles. Significantly, the penalties to be paid if the law was violated were to be divided between the commune and the apostolic camera.[178] What better evidence of a beneficent attitude of the church toward the pressing needs of the commune, even if the practices described here were far from traditional?

By 1363, this regulation of testamental wealth had been extended far beyond Or San Michele. A law of August 23 insisted that some moderation

174. *Ibid.*

175. This situation repeated itself during the later war with the church. In the debate over restitution of church lands in 1379, one can see who had profited and lost by this activity (*ASF, CP*, 17, fol. 48r [July 20, 1379]).

176. *ASF, Provv.*, 37, fols. 70rv (Jan. 9, 1349sf); 39, fol. 5r (Aug. 17, 1351).

177. "Item ad hoc ut pecuniarum quantitates que vigore presentis . . . perveniunt ad ipsos societates . . . possint sine dispendio pauperum et cum securitate dictarum societatum converti in urgentes necessitates dicti populi et comunis" (*ibid.*, 39, fols. 105v–106v [Mar. 9, 1351sf]).

178. *Ibid.*, fol. 106v.

had to be exercised if the desires of testators were to be fulfilled. With this in mind, the government authorized communal imbursement of all the cash which the confraternities of Or San Michele, the Misericordia, and the Bigallo, and the hospitals of Santa Maria Nuova, San Gallo, Santa Maria della Scala, and "other religious and pious places of the city of Florence" collected within the following year on any will written since 1344, as well as all real estate which they were to receive within the same year. Repayment was to follow in a period between two years hence and ten years. The goods which the commune realized were to be used to liquidate communal debt.[179]

There may be an indication in this law that communal creditors were hesitant to accept such goods which, after all, had been left *amore Dei*. The commune authorized the use of force in selling them to its creditors. As security to these creditors, it gave privileged status to the titles of these lands, and then sealed the whole law with the apostolic *clausula penalis*.[180]

Doubtless this activity of the commune could have been attacked by the papacy if it had so chosen. That it apparently did not seems to me very strong evidence that overriding political considerations, perhaps a type of concordat, prevented it from doing so. In fact, it might be suggested that from the very beginning of the fiscal crisis the papacy may have been willing to allow the commune to use Or San Michele as a haven into which the bankrupts could channel monies they ostensibly owed to God for his shares in their companies. These monies could then be borrowed by a needy commune. Be that as it may, the evidence presented here certainly suggests that the roots of this papal tolerance reach back to the middle or late forties, when the commune managed to satisfy the demands of the apostolic creditor, and the papacy managed to preserve the utility which Guelphic Florence and its bankers afforded the Roman see. Such mutual understanding is strong evidence for a formal agreement reached in the early years of the new regime.

The pope had become the guarantor of communal loans and therewith of communal liquidity. In his role as the insurer of the licitness of loans, he was the solace of the individual lender, defending that same lender

179. "Quod nisi debita regula moderentur, verisimiliter minus debite converterentur in causas conformes voluntatibus testatorum .... Possessiones ... vendi, in solutum dari creditoribus comunis Florentie .... Creditores dicti comunis ... cogi possint ... ad accipiendum bon[a] in solutum" (*ibid.*, 51, fols. 7*rv* [Aug. 21, 1363]).

180. "Et ... circa predicta ... componere simul et divisim ... illas provisiones et ordinationes quantumcumque penalia et etiam sub penis camere appostolice applicandis que volent" (*ibid.*).

if the commune did not pay him his due. From the beginning, the jurisdiction of the courts of the apostolic see over questions concerning the public debt and loans was clear enough. A law of May, 1346, made it definitive. Forbidding appeal by Florentines from any judgment of communal courts to a judicial instance outside the commune, the decree specifically exempted those who were or became creditors of the commune.[181] No subsequent law on appeals modified this policy during the period under consideration.[182] Florentine creditors could appeal to Rome if the commune violated the law by not repaying them their due.

Did they actually use this channel? It is impossible to tell, since the archive of the cameral auditors is not extant. In any case, the faith of the commune was kept, as Matteo Villani stressed. Originally the regime had been dissuaded by the apostolic penal clause, but most directly by the simple fact that if it broke faith, its sources of voluntary loans would dry up. But with growing confidence in the *Monte* and its growing attractiveness as an investment, the citizenry came over the decades to have such a significant part of their wealth tied up in the debt that by the 1370s, the option which had been open in the forties—to simply liquidate their investment in the commune—was no longer available. The *Monte* was becoming "the heart of this body we call city . . . [which] every limb, large and small, must contribute to preserving."[183] Growing citizen reliance on

181. No one was to presume "advocare, consulere, seu scribere vel dittare aliquas litteras, instrumenta vel scripturas, monitiones vel sententias contra comune Florentie . . . nec . . . presumat . . . appelare ab aliqua sententia in favorem comunis Florentie . . . nisi dumtaxat ad iudicem appelationis et nullitationis comunis Florentie . . . . Salvis . . . quibuscumque reformationibus consiliorum populi et comunis Florentie, provisionibus et ordinamentis factis in favorem illorum qui mutuaverunt vel mutuabunt comuni Florentie aliquam pecunie quantitatem vel et recipere debent ab ipso comuni, et [salvis] quibuscumque assignationibus et obligationibus factis per comune Florentie vel eius offitialium alicui civi, comitatino, vel districtuali florentino, ab qua ex dictis causis vel alia quacumque quibus per predicta . . . non intelligatur . . . derogatum" (*ibid.* 34, fol. 47*r* [May 12, 1346]). Note well that not only creditors were exempted from the law, but the obligations and financial assignments made to them.

182. See however below, p. 186.

183. L. F. Marks, "The Financial Oligarchy in Florence under Lorenzo," in E. F. Jacob (ed.), *Italian Renaissance Studies* (London, 1960), p. 127. The role of the *Monte*, of public debt, in consolidating communal power has been well brought out by M. Becker, *Transition*, II, 158–164. There are interesting parallels to the debate over the public debt in the United States during the 1790s. On the "integral relation between debts, the power of taxation, and sovereignty," take for example this memorial of 1789: "A certain amount of funded debt is a national blessing . . . . It has been well maintained that, after the revolution in England, a funding system was there encouraged as the best means of attaching the great and powerful body of stockholders to the Government . . . . In short, a debt

the *Monte* meant growing independence of the commune, since by the 1370s the real security on loans made to the commune was the increasingly apparent fact that citizens either loaned to the commune or the commune would flounder, taking private fortune with it. This situation meant that the security of the apostolic camera would become a liability rather than a necessary guarantee.

Common sense will suggest that such an elaborate penal clause, appearing for the first time in the law amortizing the public debt and lasting until the war with the papacy, was more than a gentlemen's agreement. For all that, the reader will want more evidence to show that communal sovereignty was in fact compromised by these penalties. It is one thing to hear Matteo Villani suggest the relationship between the penal clause and communal strength, to hear Donato Velluti narrate how the clause was attached as a particularly solemn commitment to a crucial bill of the year 1367,[184] to note that communal notaries in the forties added an X or the word *pene* in the margins wherever the cameral rider was used in the law books and in the voting registers;[185] it is another to show that the commune was restrained in particular situations by such a penal clause.

There is in fact such evidence. It does not come from the financial realm, but from the use of this clause on other types of legislation. Having examined the origins of the arrangement and its utility in the financial area, let us pass now to its broader application to other types of legislation.

In the period between 1349 and 1357, the commune instituted the use of the papal *clausula penalis* to five standard laws: (1) the laws covering the *divieti* of the foreign officials; (2) those forbidding the readmission to the city of those banished as a result of a conviction for certain serious crimes; (3) laws regulating the communal *balestieri* or militia; (4) a law prohibiting the payment of more than L200 by the commune to any but communal creditors; and (5) laws regulating the corps of government bodyguards or *berrovarii*. The common quality of these laws is that they all touch on the problem of subversion from without. More broadly, they can be

---

originating in the patriotism that achieved the independence, may thus be converted into a cement that shall strengthen and perpetuate the Union of America" (E. James Ferguson, *The Power of the Purse* [Chapel Hill, 1961], pp. 290, 335). I thank Frederic Jaher for bringing this book to my attention.

184. Velluti, *Cronica*, p. 252.

185. See for example *ASF, Provv.*, 33, fols. 59*v et passim*; *ASF, Libri Fabarum*, 24, fols. 82*v et passim*.

characterized as being among those laws which are intended to prevent the subversion of the commune by Florentines dealing with foreigners or expatriots. In addition to these five legal types, whose reissuance and modification during this period were regularly accompanied by the papal clause, the rider was later used for two other significant types of legislation. Let us review these groups, mentioning the essential features of each.

The first *divieto* law governing the foreign officials which was secured by the apostolic rider was made in 1349. It forbade any present or future *podestà, capitano del popolo*, the foreign officials of the guilds (*defensores artium*), and the appellate judges from holding the same office within ten years, and prohibited them from retaining any other communal office within five years.[186] In 1354 this basic law was amended to prevent foreign officials who managed to attain Florentine citizenship from taking office on that basis in fraud of the 1349 law.[187] A law of the following year spelled out which offices were and were not affected by this 1349 law. It added the particular that no foreigner could be elected to an office for a period longer than a year.[188] Finally in 1372 another law ostensibly reaffirming the previous laws was passed. In fact this law contained an important innovation, for it did leave open one possibility for the government to bypass the *divieti*: if thirty-five of the thirty-seven members of the *tre maggiori* agreed to recommend suspension, the government could then take steps to modify the law.[189] Thus in this area as in others, it is in the 1370s that the previous rigor in observing laws sealed by the cameral clause started to ease, and the commune moved toward greater self-sufficiency.

The laws governing the condition of those convicted or banished for serious crimes are extremely complex, and cannot be examined extensively. What made for complexity is simple enough: on the one side, the Florentine commune had traditionally considered perpetual banishment as the only fit punishment for certain crimes. The traditional law foresaw the seizure of the banished's property, and the right of any subject to offend such a person or his goods. On the other hand, however, it was often politically expedient to readmit such persons. A citizen or an influential foreigner might intercede for him; the banned person might be willing to

186. *ASF, Provv.*, 36, fols. 149*rv* (Aug. 12, 1349).

187. *Ibid.*, 41, fols. 111*v*–112*r* (Dec. 17, 1354).

188. *Ibid.*, 42, fols. 101*r*–102*r* (Aug. 13, 1355). All of the above laws have appended apostolic riders.

189. That is, the law had solemn precision, rather than perpetual (*ibid.*, 59, fols. 244*r*–245*r*).

pay for his readmission by a very significant financial concession; again, the plaintiff who had been the cause of his banishment might come to terms with the banned, and even request the readmission. Thus even though by law of April 24, 1354, the commune solemnly re-edited its law *de exbannitis non rebanniendis in perpetuo*, attempts to modify it, and fraudulent circumvention of this law, emerge throughout the subsequent period. Indeed, the modification process was underway even before the bill became law. As introduced in the Council of the Popolo, the bill forbade the cancellation or suspension of a direct sentence or one of contumacy, with or without banishment, for murder, enormous facial wounds, rebellion, invasion, war-making against the commune, rupturing of formal peaces between private parties, the hiring of assassins, kidnapping of children, production of false currency, barratry in office, vendettas, homosexuality, as well as those condemned to death or banished under penalty of death or fined a sum above L500 for rape or adultery. Only if the sentence were served or paid could it or the banishment be terminated. Since the sentences for such crimes were often death, or at least an unrealistically high monetary sum, the law as it left the Council of the Popolo for the Council or the Commune was draconian enough.[190] But in the second council, it could be passed only with the addition of a significant amendment: If the plaintiff or harmed individual made peace with the convicted, and the convicted then paid at least three shillings on the pound plus a quarter of the whole penalty, he might still be liberated from his sentence and admitted.[191]

The third type of administrative law covered by the apostolic rider was that governing the *balestieri* or militia. This body was originally to be composed of four hundred citizens or inhabitants of the city, and a group in each *Lega* of the countryside.[192] This number was gradually enlarged.[193] By law of August, 1356, the salaries were set, and a sum of L19,000 was ordered formally set aside every six months to pay them. For this purpose a *capsa* or safe was created in which this money had to be placed at the stated intervals. The cameral *clausula* was appended to this law.[194] In other words, limits on size and salary were set, a monetary commitment was made, and all three decisions were guaranteed and made precise by the

190. *Ibid.*, 41, fols. 13r–14r (Apr. 24, 1354).

191. *Ibid.*, fol. 20r.

192. *Ibid.*, 41, fols. 48v–50r (Aug. 6, 1354); this law has no rider. On the militia, see S. Salvemini, *I Balestrieri nel Comune di Firenze* (Bari, 1905).

193. *Ibid.*, 43, fols. 57v–58r (Mar. 28, 1356).

194. *Ibid.*, fols. 125v–127r (Aug. 3, 1356). The text, including rider, is printed in Salvemini, *Balestrieri*, pp. 192–197.

clause. This law was subsequently revised to enable modification. Because of the circumstances surrounding this modification, we will consider this at a later point.[195]

The fourth type presents some difficulty. A law of 1357, sealed with the rider, prohibited the payment of more than L200 to any petitioner without the solemn deliberation and vote of the *tre maggiori*. Communal creditors were exempt from the law.[196] What was its intent? I would suggest it was tied to the question of banished Florentines. A subsequent law tells us that one method by which banned individuals could obtain their readmission was by obtaining *intuitu pietatis vel misericordie* a sum of money to be used only for obtaining their release.[197] The early law may have been an unsuccessful attempt to deal with this problem. On the other hand, it may represent nothing more than an attempt to limit influence peddling in the utilization of communal funds.

The last of the five basic types presents no such difficulties. The law *Advertentes* of June 6, 1357, ordained the quality of the *familia* of the communal priors. The salaries and provenience of the ninety-two *berrovarii* were spelled out, as was the quality of the *capitano* of this group.[198] Thus this law limited the size of the personal bodyguard of the *Signoria* and specified the *divieti* of their captain. The law remained unaltered, and subsequent laws dealing with this group carried a disclaimer clause stating that they could not be in conflict with *Advertentes*, and thus incur the penalties to the apostolic camera provided by the attached *clausula*.

Besides these five basic types, there were two other significant circumstances in which the papal clause was used. The first was in laws governing the privileges of the Florentine *Parte Guelfa*. From early January, 1358, this *imperium imperii* was able to exert ever greater influence over admission to public office.[199] Through its ability to designate a potential official as a Ghibelline, and therefore legally excluded from office-holding, the *Parte* became an active competitor for power in the commune. Between 1358 and 1372, a series of *pro Parte* laws were passed which aimed at solidifying and enlarging the role of the *Parte* in the procedures for insuring political orthodoxy. The whole package of growing *Parte* privileges came to be covered by the papal *clausula penalis*. A law of August 23, 1359, reiterated a previous *Parte* law of January, 1358. By

195. See below, pp. 195–97.
196. *ASF, Provv.*, 44, fols. 82v–83r (Mar. 13, 1356sf).
197. *Ibid.*, 65, fols. 61v–62r (June 13, 1377).
198. *Ibid.*, 44, fols. 131v–132v (June 6, 1357).
199. Brucker, *Politics*, p. 171.

attaching the rider to the law, both laws were thus secured.[200] In 1364, another *pro Parte* law informs us that all ordinances edited up to this point in favor of the *Parte* had been sworn to on pain of a penalty to the papal camera.[201] Then in early 1372 a *pro Parte* law which forbade governmental deliberation of legislation affecting the *Parte* without its prior approval involved the apostolic camera in a unique fashion. The law was not sealed with the normal precise clause, replete with bonding requirements and syndication by the *esecutore*; there was no formal rider. But instead of half, all of the financial penalties foreseen by the law were to go to the apostolic camera.[202] This law came in the midst of deep divisions within the city. With so much resentment against the *Parte*, it may be that the *Parte* was unable to win the attachment to the law of the formal precise clause (with bonding) making the law impossible to change, and had to be satisfied with all penalties being assigned to the papacy. This is one of the two cases during our period in which the whole penalty on a law was directed to Rome.

The use of the apostolic clause in *pro Parte* laws is of great importance because it represents an attempt by a coherent political group to use the coercive power of the Roman see in its bid for greater influence in the commune. But events were swift in this struggle between *Parte* and commune, and a law for the *Parte* might be balanced in the succeeding *Signoria* by one restricting its privileges. This is especially true in the late sixties and seventies. In the process, the utility of the apostolic rider as a security and retardant of subsequent legislation declined, for whenever previously legislated *Parte* privileges were restricted, the commune was forced to defy the papal securities attached to laws passed in favor of the *Parte*. Nevertheless, when the commune trod on the past privileges of the *Parte* it attempted to solidify its laws by incorporating the Roman see in the penal segments. In 1366, for example, an anti-*Parte* law had been

200. *ASF, Provv.*, 47, fols. 31*v*–32*r*.

201. "Formam ordinamentorum seu reformationum populi et comunis Florentie hactenus editorum seu que in futurum edentur in favorem partis guelfe . . . que ordinamenta firmata sunt vel erunt iuramento et adiectione pene dicte camere [apostolice] applicande" (*ibid.*, 52, fols. 69*rv* [Dec. 11, 1364]). This law is printed in G. Capponi, *Storia della Repubblica Fiorentina*, Vol. I (Florence, 1875), 586–588.

202. "Et quod quilibet contra predicta vel aliquod predictorum veniens vel faciens quoquomodo, casu, et vice qualibet incidat in penam florenorum auri 2,000 applicandorum camere apostolice"; their illegal action was nonetheless null, and the person culpable became *ipso facto* a Ghibelline (*ASF, Provv.*, 59, fols. 209*r*–210*r* [Jan. 27, 1371*sf*]). See Capponi, *op. cit.*, pp. 586–588. On the city's condition at the time, see Brucker, *Politics*, pp. 246 f.

passed enlarging the number of *Parte* captains and modifying the *Parte*'s method of hearing witnesses. In the following year, this law was re-affirmed, says the diarist Velluti, "with the penalties to the camera of the pope, and against it nothing could be provided except by a certain number of beans."[203] Again in 1372 the commune used the papal rider in this way. A law of April had suspended six members of the Ricci and Albizzi families, all *Parte* stalwarts, from communal offices for five years. In July the commune ruled that anyone seeking to reinstate these six was subject to a series of penalties, one of which was a fine of 2,000 florins to be paid to the apostolic camera "since they are subverters of the liberty, peace, and unity of the city of Florence."[204] This provision, along with the other chapters making up this extensive law, was then sealed with the apostolic rider.[205]

A final type of law which was thus sealed dealt with bondsmen. These citizens posted the bond necessary for individuals to hold offices, escape imprisonment, enter into agreements with the commune, and so forth. For example, the bonding stipulated in the apostolic rider was one case in which *fideiussores* were used. This money could then be sequestered by the commune if faith were broken. A logical development of this situation was for a hard-pressed commune to lay hands on these sums even when no wrongdoing was evident, and to do this in the form of a loan from the *fideiussores*. But of course this was an extremely risky business, for if the integrity of those "swearers of faith" was compromised, not only was the commune dishonored, but in practical terms, it could mean that no bond-ing money would be made available for officeholders. Thus the whole office-holding procedure could be thrown into confusion.

In 1373 a group of bondsmen had liberated the commune from a certain amount of debt in exchange for the usufruct of certain communal lands. But a bureaucratic mix-up had prevented them from receiving any income from these lands. In a second case coming on top of the first, 5,000 florins bond posted for an official was sequestered when that official broke his oath. To escape further responsibility for this official's actions, the bondsmen had agreed with the commune to liberate the commune from 10,000 florins in public debt, which meant that they were themselves responsible for liquidating the debt with the creditors of the *Monte*. The

---

203. "E fece fare una provvisione, per la quale si cassarono tutti i detti ordini della Parte, e fortificossi l'altra riformagione fatta per Uguiccione, colle pene alla Camera del Papa, e che contra quella niente si potesse provvedere, se non con certo novero di fave" (Velluti, *Cronica*, p. 252). See Brucker, *Politics*, pp. 214–220.

204. "Tamquam attentatores contra libertatem, pacem, et unionem civitatis Floren-tie" (*ASF, Provv.*, 60, fols. 48r–51v [July 31, 1372]).

205. *Ibid.*, fols. 49v–50r.

net result of these two operations had been the *infamia dictorum fideiussorum,* their pauperization, and just as important, harm to the reputation of the commune. The ameliorative law of December 23, 1373, directed that the bondsmen be made creditors of the commune up to the amount which would cover their losses, and that they be reimbursed for the useless lands they held. On top of this law came the papal security.[206] Starting in 1345, the commune had used this clause to generate faith. Twenty-eight years later, we see that the retention of faith in the commune could still necessitate this "arduous obligation."

Having now reviewed the full range and use of this clause in Florentine legislation between 1345 and 1373, it behooves us to turn to the dynamics of its use. Keeping in mind that the justification for using this clause was the commune's weakness, its inability to create a sufficient security through a completely internal penal system, we must ask three questions: When did the commune feel itself strong enough to gradually limit the use of the clause? What legal forms did the commune adopt to limit the possibility of claims by the apostolic camera? What steps did the commune take when it was imperative to act against a law whose violation would automatically create rights of that camera? An understanding of the progression of communal practices in these fields will pave the way for understanding the decline in the use of the rider and its open violation in the seventies, as the commune moved slowly but inexorably toward war with its erstwhile protector.

From 1345, the commune had used the rider on its loan laws. Between 1349 and 1357, it extended its use to central laws governing the operation of the commune. All during this period the rider was no more difficult to attach than it was to pass the law itself. There were no particular restrictions limiting its use. And we have seen that it was not only used on formal laws, but was used in wide areas of financial administration; for example, by gabelle officials. The clause was so necessary and so attractive a security that it was used indiscriminately.

This was brought to a halt by the important law of February 19, 1361. "In order to prevent the future burdening of the commune or some officials or citizens of the said by an all too common and inconsiderate facility in taking on arduous obligations," it was decided to limit the presentation to the communal councils of any bill containing the *clausula* that anything had to be done or could not be done under threat of a penalty payable to the apostolic camera or to any spiritual or temporal lord, clerk, or layman. The procedure was now solemnized: the only way to attach this clause was if the *tre maggiori* (the executive of thirty-seven),

206. *Ibid.,* 61, fols. 200r–202r (Dec. 23, 1373).

first held a formal vote and obtained a plurality of twenty-eight beans in favor of using it.[207]

This law remained from then on the basis for the use of the papal security. It had two immediate effects. It became legislatively more difficult to use the clause, and there was a slight decrease in its use. Second, it tended to limit the past practice of giving a general *balìa* to various officials to use the securities they thought necessary. That is, its use came to be limited to specific officials.

With this measure we reach the end of the period when the clause had to be used with little consideration of the risks involved. From early 1361, the commune entered into a period when the securing of loans and communal institutions could, at times, be accomplished without obligating citizens to a beneficient papacy. Some institutional stability and citizen faith had by now been created, and from this point on, alternative securities were more readily available. But the process was slow. The best indication of this is that the very law which limited the use of the *clausula* was itself given precise form by using the same rider.

We would expect that a corollary concern to "cover" the commune and its citizens from unforeseen or injudicious creation of papal claims would make itself felt at about the same time. That is to say, a large number of laws had by now been perpetuated or solemnized by the use of the penal clause payable to the papacy. Having now decided to limit the use of this clause on new laws, it was only natural that the commune would take every precaution to prevent violations of laws already covered by these penalties from giving rise to claims by Rome. How was this done?

The answer must come in two parts. In the first, we will examine the bona fide attempts of the commune to prevent officials from violating a law in such a way as to create such a claim. In the second part, a more difficult phenomenon must be explained. To wit: how the commune, while purporting to act only insofar as it could without creating such claims, was in fact attempting through municipal law to limit previous

207. "Ne nimis vulgari et inconsulta facilitate ad obligationes arduas que comune Florentie vel aliquos offitiales seu cives comunis eiusdem illaquere valeant in posterum procedatur . . . , providerunt . . . , quod deinceps nulla provisio ponenda seu proponenda in consilio seu ad consilia populi seu comunis Florentie fieri possit seu facta vel que fieret, proponi possit in ipsis consiliis vel aliquo ipsorum vel super ea consuli vel aliqualiter reformari in qua contineretur quod aliquid dici vel fieri quoquomodo posset vel non posset seu deberet vel non deberet sub aliqua pena camere domini pape seu sedis apostolice vel romane ecclesie seu alterius domini spiritualis vel temporalis vel clerici seu laici applicanda nisi talis provisio fieret seu facta esset per dominos priores . . . [and colleges] vel saltem 28 ex eis" (*Ibid.*, 48, fols. 142r–143r [Feb. 19, 1360*sf*]).

laws which had been secured by the papal penalties. Under the cloak of respecting their oaths to the papacy, that is, various *Signorie* in the later years attempted to escape from them. Let us look first at the bona fide attempts to prevent a claim originating.

The first such "protestations" or disclaimers emerged in two laws of 1347 and 1350 which adopted the precise penal clauses of earlier laws. These clauses were to be understood to be attached to the new laws as if they were written out word for word. There was only one exception. The penalties payable to the pope were instead to be payable to the commune. Thus, add the laws of 1347 and 1350, no right could be established by the apostolic camera on the basis of these latter laws. These are the first times such disclaimers were filed.[208]

The first of these two laws dealt with the 5 percent *Monte*, and the second with the gabelles. In considering all subsequent disclaimers inserted in bills dealing with communal finances, one must keep a central fact in mind: To state that a bill as written was not understood to create a claim of the apostolic camera was a way of saying that the bill was "in the interest, not the detriment, of the creditors of the commune." This general principle must be kept in mind. Otherwise the use of the disclaimer, which is ambiguous enough in its own right, becomes at times almost unintelligible.

As evidence, consider the following disclaimer:

> Save expressly, in fact, and before all, in the beginning, middle and end of all of the aforesaid, that . . . the said officials . . . cannot do [anything] . . . by virtue or pretext of which the described creditors and those who are described in the said books of the *Monte* would be at all damaged in their rights or in the imbursement of the money which they ought to receive or are owed by the said commune; or because of which the privileges and immunities conceded to [the creditors] would in the slightest be diminished or deleted, and the commune or any of the officials of the said commune or any person at all would or could fall into any penalty, condemnation or fine payable in any form to the Roman church or to the camera of the said pope. But rather the aforesaid rights of the said creditors are understood to be and are strengthened, reaffirmed, and approved.[209]

208. For the text of the 1347 law, see above, n. 88. See also *ASF, Provv.*, 37, fol. 92*v* (Feb. 8, 1349*sf*).

209. "Salvo expresse acto, reservato in principio medio, et fine omnium predictorum quod . . . non possint dicti officiales . . . facere . . . cuius vigore vel pretestu creditores descripti et qui describentur in dictis libris del *Monte* in aliquo ledantur in eorum iuribus

A law of 1371 again brings out this tie between protection of creditors and protestation that a bill did not create a claim of the apostolic camera:

And that the said cede and are understood to cede in favor and not in prejudice of the said creditors [of the commune] or any one of them. *And nevertheless, as an added security:*

Save expressly and declared that by the aforesaid or any part of the aforesaid nothing is understood to have been provided or done, or to be able to be provided or in anyway be done through which or by virtue, pretext, cause or occasion of which any penalty could be demanded or requested from the commune of Florence or from any official of the said commune or from any other person by the apostolic see or Roman church by virtue of some ordinance of the commune of Florence or [by virtue] of whatever stipulation or promise interposed or added by virtue or according to the form of the said ordinance.[210]

Thus the *Salvo* or disclaimer clause, when it occurs on financial bills, *is a security to communal creditors.* Having insisted on this point, let us examine the disclaimer itself. The text given above (from *salvo* to the end) is the classic one, perfected about 1358 after some five years of experiment with various forms. What does it say? Its intended import seems clear enough: it states that the provision or law in question is not understood to have created or to be able to create a claim by the papal camera. That is, the commune does not understand that this law or its execution violates a previous one which had been made perpetual by a precise clause with

---

sive in exactione et perceptione pecunie quas recipere debent sive debebant a dicto comuni, seu propter quod privilegia et immunitates eisdem concesse in aliqua eorum parte minuantur vel tollantur, et comune seu aliqui officiales dicti comunis seu alia quacumque persona incideret seu incidere posset in aliquam penam, condempnationem vel multam romane ecclesie sev camere dicti pape quomodolibet applicandam. Sed potius per predicta iura dictorum creditorum magis roborata, firmata, et approbata esse intelligantur et sint" (*ibid.*, 40, fols. 103rv [May 10, 1353]). For another example, cf. *ibid.*, 51, fol. 155r (June 20, 1364).

210. "Et quod predicta cedant et cedere intelligantur in favorem et non in preiudicium creditorum predictorum vel alicuius eorum. Et nichilominus etiam ad cautelam:

Salvo expresso et declarato quod per predicta vel aliquod predictorum non intelligatur aliquid provisum vel factum esse, seu provideri vel quomodolibet fieri posse, per quod seu cuius vigore, pretextu, causa, vel occasione, aliqua pena per sedem apostolicam vel romanam ecclesiam possit exigi seu peti a comuni Florentie vel ab aliquo officiali dicti comunis, seu alia quacumque persona vigore quorumcumque ordinamentorum comunis Florentie, sev cuiuscumque stipulationis vel promissionis interposite vel secute vigore seu secundum formam dictorum ordinamentorum" (*ibid.*, 58, fol. 163v [Jan. 15, 1370sf]). Italics are mine.

penalties or forfeited bond payable to the apostolic camera. Now, the clause "or to be able to be provided" goes beyond a statement of intent or understanding. For by this phrase, the commune implied that the law or its execution would be invalid if it could engender a claim by the apostolic camera; by definition, of course, a law violating a precise law was irregular and unenforceable.[211] This implication was subsequently translated into an explicit formula in 1371, which was thereafter attached to and became an integral part of the classic disclaimer quoted above. The new addition read:

> ... of the said ordinance. And that if in this law or within the words of this law something would be contained or included in any way, or could in the future by any process result by which or by virtue, or occasion of which any [such] penalty could [result] according to or by virtue of the said ordinances or of any stipulation done or interposed, as has been said, this [law] is understood to have been and to be null and void, and is to be considered and to be totally infected and inapplicable.[212]

What could be more straightforward? At all costs, communal promises had to be respected. If perchance a law gave rise to a claim by the papacy, it was null and void.

Here we may make two points: first, this disclaimer was a security to communal lenders (and further to all citizens) that communal obligations were being met. Secondly, it placed the commune on record as disputing any rights of the apostolic camera originating in the execution of the law in question.[213] There is only one trouble: can it be assumed that the commune in fact passed no laws which were in violation of previous precise laws secured by the apostolic camera? Of course not. What then did it

211. See above, p. 132.

212. "... Secundum formam dictorum ordinamentorum. Et quod siquid in ipsa provisione vel sub verbis ipsius provisionis contineretur vel includeretur quoquomodo vel posset exinde aliqualiter resultare per quod seu cuius vigore, pretestu, vel occasione aliqua pena posset secundum seu vigore dictorum ordinamentorum seu alicuius stipulationis facte vel interposite, ut est dictum, illud intelligatur fuisse et esse irritum et inane et pro infecto et non apposito totaliter habeatur et sit" (*ASF, Provv.*, 59, fols. 61*v*–62*r* [July 18, 1371]).

213. There are some cases in later years where a papal rider is followed by a disclaimer. An early example is in *ASF, Provv.*, 55, fols. 101*v*–102*r* (Dec. 4, 1367). Thus an official could fall into the penalty to the apostolic camera if he did not execute the law (rider). By executing it, he was not understood to violate a previous law sealed with the *clausula penalis* (disclaimer).

have in mind? And does it not seem stranger still that in the very years (early seventies) when the commune was definitely loosening its dependence on Rome that it would add a proviso invalidating any law which gave rise to a claim by Rome? Does it not seem strangest of all that the commune would first pass a law which it knew to be in violation of earlier mandates secured by the camera, and then say that its law would be invalid if it were found to create a claim of the Roman see, and then finally proclaim the law as law? Obviously more was being attempted here than a bona fide attempt to limit the extension of papal claims. But before confronting these difficulties, let us return for a moment to this bona fide usage in realms other than the financial. Once having broadened our understanding of this disclaimer, we will better understand the dynamics which shifted its import in the later years of the regime.

In the early years, when the commune was experimenting with the disclaimers, it sometimes made an exception in the general derogatory clause. This is the clause which derogated any previous law not in harmony with the present. It is a typical feature of all municipal legislation. Thus in two cases in 1350 the derogatory clause exempted and preserved any law assigning anything to the apostolic camera.[214]

In general, however, disclaimers protecting legislation with *clausule* were reserved for separate paragraphs in the law. Some examples of disclaimers concerning the various types covered by the papal penalties will clarify the practice.

In 1352, the court of the *Mercanzia* told the commune that because of the drought it had been difficult to find and elect a new foreign official, and asked that the present one be re-elected "as long as they do not elect or reaffirm in such a way that the commune of Florence or any officials or single persons of the said commune or elsewhere effectively incur any penalty payable to the lord pope or to the camera of the apostolic see." The commune agreed to this petition, with a disclaimer that nothing was to flow from the law which could bring on such a penalty.[215]

---

214. "Specialiter derogatis, his dumtaxat exceptis per que pena imponeretur camere domini pape aliqualiter applicanda" (*ASF, Provv.*, 38, fols. 36v–38r, 38rv [May 15, 1350]). This exception to derogation is also found in the law on appeals cited above, p. 170.

215. "Dummodo electionem seu refirmationem non faciant per quam comune Florentie seu aliqui officiales vel singulares persone de dicto comuni vel aliunde cum effectu aliquam penam incurrant domino pape seu sedi apostolice applicandam"; the commune agreed, "Salvo semper reservato eo quod per presentem provisionem vel aliquid quod sequeretur seu sequi posset ex ea vel contentus in ea nichil fiat seu fieri intelligatur vel possit aut debeat per quod seu cuius occasione aliqua pena cum effectu commicteretur

Just a few months later an irregularity in the disposition of the *familia* of the *podestà*, dispositions covered by the precise penal clause, was rectified by the commune, with almost the same proviso.[216] A law of 1357 provided for the election of the *berrovarii* or *familia* of the priors. A specific disclaimer then followed stating that the *divieti* laws covering this office, the violation of which generated a penalty payable to Rome, was not in any way to be violated by the present law.[217]

One of the most common disclaimers was attached to bills providing for the release from a judicial condemnation or a banishment. In the wake of the law concerning *banniti non rebanniendi*, these provisions, after ordering the release, appended a *Salvo* that in no way could such a release violate the basic law of April 26, 1354.[218] Subsequently the classical disclaimer cited above came to be used, and was appended to scores of laws permitting a release. This *Salvo* clause or disclaimer had the effect of halting the release if it appeared that the papacy would press a claim that the release violated the basic law. Such a claim could originate ex officio, or it might be solicited in curia by the party damaged by the condemned or banished.

In certain bills permitting a release from such a condemnation, a particular exception was made. We will simply mention it here, and examine its significance at a later point. In the law regulating the submission of the town of Monte Carelli, whose inhabitants had been condemned for revolt, the commune ordered their release, with the proviso that it could not violate the basic law of April 26, 1354. Even then, the law continues, the releases could still be effectuated if the *beneplacito papale* was obtained.[219] The release of a single person in 1360 gave rise to exactly the

---

per comune Florentie seu aliquam personam camere domini pape seu sedi apostolice applicanda" (*ibid.*, 40, fol. 12*r* [Oct. 29, 1352]).

216. *Ibid.*, 40, fol. 79*v* (Mar. 13, 1352*sf*). For such petitions and responses concerning the wool guild, see *ibid.*, 48, fol. 133*r* (Feb. 4, 1360*sf*), and for the *Mercanzia*, *ibid.*, 59, fols. 61*v*–62*r* (July 18, 1371).

217. "Salvis etiam et in suo robore permanentibus provisionibus comunis Florentie disponentibus de devetis aliquorum officialium seu aliis negotiis quibuscumque per quas seu quarum vigore pena venit seu veniret stipulanda seu comictenda vel danda camere domini pape seu romane ecclesie quoquomodo, contra quas vel quarum aliquam nichil intelligatur per presentem provisionem fieri seu attentari vel aliquid fieri posse" (*ibid.*, 44, fols. 132*rv* [June 6, 1357]).

218. For example, *ibid.*, 41, fols. 90*v*–91*r* (Oct. 14, 1354). There are subsequently scores of such disclaimers.

219. "Nisi quatenus procederet de consensu, licentia, beneplacito, seu voluntate domini summi pontificis vel suas vices in ea parte gerentes. Ita et taliter quod ex ipsa provisione . . . nulla pena possit peti seu exigi quoquomodo per ipsum dominum papam" (*ibid.*, 48, fol. 5*v* [Aug. 27, 1360]).

same verbiage.[220] And finally in late 1360 certain Ubaldini were ordered readmitted. The disclaimer was then added that this could not be done "unless this cancellation and abolition can or could be done without, on the pretext of such a condemnation, . . . falling into or being able to fall into any penalty payable to the said [apostolic] camera."[221]

In addition to this *Salvo* clause which declared laws to be in keeping with previous precise laws and, after 1371, declared them illegal if they were not, the commune would in later years compose powers and limitations of its commissions so as to specifically include within the *nec possint* section of such a commission the protestation that it did not give the *balìa* or commission the right to do anything in violation of ordinances covered by the rider.[222]

A last precautionary measure intended to prevent the commune and its officials from becoming the debtor of the Roman see is encountered in instructions given to communal bursars. This formula appears for the first time in a law of 1366 authorizing the communal bursar to pay a cardinal 1,000 florins from whatever purse and whatever money of the commune, "nevertheless excepting the penal assignments to the camera of the lord pope."[223] In a law of 1369 ordering payment to another foreigner, we find the variant: from whatever money, "with the exception of the deputations or assignments . . . against which nothing can be done without fear of or incurring of a penalty payable to the apostolic camera."[224] These occasional uses of this particular stipulation are supplemented by its use in one general category of directives to the bursar. Between 1367 and the end of the regime, whenever the bursar was ordered to pay to the emperor part of the money owed him as *cens* by the commune, the following cautionary directive was added: from whatever money,

> Save expressly and declaredly that by the said, no derogation is understood to the assignments made up until now from the income and monies of the commune of Florence against which nothing can be

220. *Ibid.*, fol. 24r (Aug. 29, 1360).

221. "Nisi quatenus ipsa cancellatio et absolutio fieri posset vel poteret absque eo quod pretextu talis cancellationis . . . commicteretur vel commicti posset in penam aliquam dicte camere applicandam" (*ibid.*, fols. 114rv [Dec. 30, 1360]).

222. For an example, see *ibid.*, 64, fols. 41rv (June 10, 1376).

223. "Salvis tamen assignamentis penalibus camere domini pape" (*ibid.*, 54, fol. 55r [Oct. 2, 1366]).

224. "Salvis deputationibus sive assignamentis . . . contra que provideri . . . non potest absque metu vel incursu pene camere apostolice applicande" (*ibid.*, 57, fols. 21v–22r [June 14, 1369]).

undertaken, done, or provided without fear of some penalty payable to the apostolic camera, which assignments remain in force.[225]

It is not clear just what these assignments were. Perhaps the reference is to monies set aside by law for the reimbursement of communal creditors. These assignments had been traditionally secured by the papal penalties. Yet the language "penal assignments to the lord pope" seems to suggest something else. Perhaps these "assignments" refer to the bond money which had been posted by communal officials to insure that they observed the penal ordinances, and which belonged *ipso iure* to the apostolic camera if these were violated. The difficulty with this hypothesis is that I have been unable to find any indication that this bond money had to be kept on deposit or could not be used by the commune during a term of office. One other possibility suggests itself from a strict reading of the term "assignments made to the papal camera." Since the term *assignment* means an actual sum which was directed by law to some party, it may be that this phrase refers to an actual sum of money owed the apostolic camera. Perhaps sums of money regularly passed to Rome as payments for violations of precise laws. But why then is this directive used particularly with sums owed to the emperor? I do not know. Here, as in so much else concerning the papal rider, only a close examination of the cameral records of the commune will throw light on the technical operations in play.

We have, however, almost without being aware of it, moved from an examination of bona fide disclaimers and directives designed to prevent debt to the apostolic camera to that more difficult area where the disclaimer was actually being used to cancel existing rights of the papacy. Let me try to describe in a few words what the goal of communal policy was in the later years of the regime. In the beginning, the rider had been extensively used, even indiscriminately. In 1361, the use of the rider was limited to prevent unnecessary "arduous obligations" to Rome. In the following years, the commune was often faced with the necessity of modifying laws secured by these obligations. At the same time, it gradually came into the position where its independence from Rome could be reasserted. And yet those obligations had been undertaken. Finally, those obligations continued to be an assurance to the citizens that its wealth and communal

225. "Salvo expresso et declarato quod per predicta . . . non intelligatur . . . derogari assignamentis hactenus factis de introytibus seu redditibus vel pecuniis comunis Florentie contra que veniri, provideri, vel fieri non potest absque metu alicuius pene camere appostolice applicande, que assignamenta in sua remaneant firmitate" (*ibid.*, 55, fols. 141*rv* [Mar. 6, 1367*sf*]).

administration would be predictably attended to. This is the problem complex within which the regime had to act.

Consequently, disclaiming the intention of violating a precise ordinance was intended to build up in the municipal law a tradition excluding the papacy from claims on Florentine officials. Even when the disclaimer was fraudulent, and the law in question did in fact violate a precise law, its insertion could serve a purpose. For if the papacy did not prosecute, it was prima facie evidence that the law was legal.

The *Salvo* disclaimer was then always ambiguous. There is no better way of illustrating this than to revert to that touchy situation when the Officials for the Correction of the Books of the *Monte* decided that some particular holding in the *Monte* was fraudulent. On the one side, the commune acted as a moral agent in correcting the books: the soul of the citizen was damaged when he imbursed dishonest interest. On the other side, we know that communal creditors had the right to appeal to the Roman see when the commune failed to live up to its obligations.[226] Yet this very right was destructive of administrative continuity. In the forties, this cession of sovereignty had been essential. But the stronger the commune became, the less essential this appeared. At the same time, increased investment by the citizens in the *Monte* resulted in less capacity to defend this right of appeal.

In a law of 1353, these officials were given authority to decide on fraudulent claims.

> And from the said condemnations or declarations there can be no appeal, nor can they be opposed on the grounds that they are null or iniquitous, nor can a complete restitution [of investment] be impetrated, nor can anything else be said or opposed.[227]

So much for the right of appeal, one might think. The only appeal permitted was to the communal priors. Yet immediately thereafter one reads that by none of the previous were these officials authorized to do anything on the basis of which they would fall into a penalty to the apostolic camera for having violated laws secured by the penal clause.[228]

This legal contortion was infrequent in these early years, and it is only in the seventies that an attempt was made to disembowel the obligations.

---

226. See above, p. 170.

227. "Et a dictis condempnationibus vel declarationibus non possit appellari vel de nullitate seu iniquitate opponi, vel in integrum restitutio impetrari vel aliquid aliud dici vel opponi nullo modo" (*ASF, Provv.*, 40, fols. 178v–179r [Dec. 12, 1353]).

228. *Ibid.*

Take for example the addition to the basic disclaimer made in 1371 according to which if a law was found to be capable of engendering a claim of the apostolic, it was to be considered null.[229] Remembering that this magnanimous attitude of respect to the Roman see was not made when the commune was weak, but when its independence and maneuverability were growing, the kenner of Florentine affairs or the student of church-state relations will not be deceived. What this addition really amounted to is a miniature declaration of communal independence. A comparison will clarify this point.

When the commune passed a law which it knew to be against ecclesiastical liberty, it was acting in defiance not only of the canon law but of its own, for the communal statutes explicitly stated that laws against the faith, Inquisitor, or church liberty were void and unenforceable.[230] Consequently it would often add as a disclaimer to an anti-ecclesiastical law that it was not understood to be against ecclesiastical liberty and if it was, it was null in that part.[231] In short, it was left to the church to react. If the commune were strong, the law remained on the books and it was enforced. If the papacy were in a position to forcefully object to a law it felt completely unacceptable, the commune might have to yield.[232] In the meantime, communal lawyers would argue before the pope that his contention that the commune had laws against the church was false; anyway, they could not be obeyed, for a derogatory clause at the end of the statutal compilation stated that laws that were or could be against church liberty were null and void.[233]

The similarity to our problem will be apparent. The canonist Giovanni d'Andrea might assert that such disclaimers had no standing in the law. But the Florentine canonist Lapo da Castiglionchio stated the obvious: disclaimer or no disclaimer, "it is a law and is also observed."[234] The disclaimer stated that they were not understood to be against church

229. See above, p. 181.
230. See my *Synodal Law*, pp. 23 f.
231. *Ibid.*, p. 22.
232. For examples, see *ibid.*, pp. 23 f., 142, 144.
233. "Et si appareret aliquam factam fuisse, quod negatur, ipsa lex non fuit observata nec ad praticam deducta, nec de iure ipsa lex potuisset observari; et maxime secundum formam statutorum civitatis Florentie in quibus ordinibus expresse cavetur in fine per clausulam derogatoriam quod omnia statuta facta vel fienda per civitatem Florentia in quibus continetur quod esset vel esse posset contra libertatem ecclesie non valeant nec teneant, et nullius sint efficacie vel momenti, prout in dictis statutis latius et plenius continetur" (*ASF, Atti Pubblici a Quaderno*, Mar. 12, 1376).
234. Trexler, *Synodal Law*, pp. 25 f.

liberties. It remained for the papacy to prove otherwise. The same can be said of our disclaimer. It tended to define as legal a law which was not. It remained for the papacy to prove otherwise.

Thus the 1371 addition to the basic disclaimer was a sign of strength, and not of weakness. The more insistent the claims of faithfulness to the precise laws, the less effectively they were being observed. This is most evident in the laws concerning the *Parte*. It is well known how swiftly the balance of force between *Parte* and commune shifted in the late sixties and seventies. And when it shifted toward the commune, the latter had to show concern for the privileges of the *Parte*, which were protected by the papal security.

A striking case is offered in the law of December 11, 1371, by which the commune reformed the process by which the *Parte* probated witnesses in cases against alleged Ghibellines. This was a law indubitably against the privileges of the *Parte*, but one would never know it from the introduction. The procedures followed by the *Parte* in hearing witnesses, says this prologue, is incautious and even improvised. This should be corrected. But *before* the action section of the law, the communal lawyers inserted this long and unprecedented disclaimer:

All these [priors] prefix by way of protestation that by the following or any of it they have not done, provided, or ordained or deliberated, nor have they intended (or wanted to)[235] provide, ordain, or deliberate in any way anything on the pretext, or by cause or occasion of which these [priors] or any one of them or any person at all could fall into or incur any pecuniary penalty applicable to the apostolic camera or Roman church by virtue of or according to the form of any statutes or ordinances of the commune of Florence or of some stipulation in reference to this interposed or done. And that if in the present provision someting would be contained through which or on the pretext of which it would appear that one could fall into or incur the said penalty, this [aspect] is to be considered totally nonapplicable and as not made, unless insofar as, if and to the extent that it would be put forward, deliberated, and approved in the Council of the *Podestà* and Commune.[236]

235. Inserted in the text.

236. "Et premissa per eos omnes protestatione quod per infrascripta vel aliquod ipsorum non faciebant, providebant, vel ordinabant vel deliberabant nec providere, ordinare, vel deliberare seu quomodolibet facere intendebant (vel volebant) aliquid seu pretextu, causa, vel occasione possent ipsi vel ipsorum aliquis aut alia quecumque persona commictere vel incurrere in aliquam penam pecuniariam camere apostolice seu romane ecclesie applicandam, vigore seu secundum formam aliquorum statutorum seu ordina-

There then follows the action which clearly violated the *Parte* privileges. And the closing derogatory clause (*non obstantibus*) goes so far as to list the laws *pro Parte* (some of which were sealed with the papal rider) which were not to stand in the way of the present law. But just one month later, the *Parte* was able to force through a bill very much in its favor, one whose penalties were payable entirely to the apostolic camera.[237] And thereafter any law remotely touching the privileges of the *Parte* was fitted out in the following fashion: first came the classical disclaimer, then the addition to that clause, and then the following:

> ... is held to be and is. And also this having been provided and expressed, that if in the present provision would be contained or would be that which would be against the law effected in the month of January 1371 in favor of the *Parte Guelfa* of the city of Florence, it is to be understood to be and to be totally null and void, as if it had not been deliberated, effected, or registered.[238]

Compared to the economy of the security clauses in the first decades of the regime, this growth of disclaimers must be termed baroque. And as with the art style, so here the true meaning is obscured. Once the dynamics of politics are grasped, however, the situation is clear: as the effectiveness of the papal rider was increasingly compromised, the greater the legal ingenuity employed to compromise papal claims. The greater the irreconcilability between *Parte* and commune in Florence, the more desperate the attempts of the *Parte* to preserve its privileges (for example, laws *pro Parte* with all penalties payable to the papacy, and none to the commune), and the greater the distance between asserted and actual continuity of communal legislation respecting citizen rights (in this case the *Parte*'s).

In describing the methods the commune chose to limit papal rights,

---

mentorum comunis Florentie seu alicuius stipulationis circha id interposite seu facte. Et quod siquid in presenti provisione contineretur per quod seu cuius pretextu videretur seu posset commicti vel incurri in dictam penam, illud habeatur et sit totaliter pro non facta, nisi si et prout et quemadmodum reformata, deliberata, seu approbata fuerit in consilio domini potestatis et comunis predicti" (*ASF, Provv.*, 59, fols 187r–188r [Dec. 11, 1371]).

237. See above, pp. 25 f.

238. "... Habeatur et sit. Et etiam eo acto, proviso, et expresso quod siquid in presenti provisione contineretur vel esset quod foret contra provisionem firmatam de mense Januarii proxime preterito in favore partis guelfe civitatis Florentie, illud intelligatur esse et sit totaliter iritum et inane et pro non deliberato et non apposito vel descripto" (*ASF, Provv.*, 59, fols. 221rv [Feb. 19, 1371*sf*]).

we have been forced to look at the problem over the whole life of the regime. The emphasis placed on the ambiguity of the disclaimers must not, however, lead us to think that legal subterfuge was built into the system from the beginning, or that it characterized the whole of a paper institution. Nothing could be further from the truth. In the early years of the regime, the commune was saddled with these obligations whether it desired them or not. Legal subterfuge is in fact quite isolated and random until the seventies. Certainly the commune would have preferred to run its own affairs free of papal tutelage. But the simply enormous attention given to the apostolic *clausula* in the law books of the commune is proof enough that it was for a long time incapable of doing so. We do not have to rely on simple bulk, however, to demonstrate this factual dependence on Rome. For the documents at our disposal show incontrovertibly that the commune, far from being able to cancel potential papal interference by legal manipulation, was forced to rely directly on the "grace" and *beneplacitum* of the papacy, to beg papal "indulgence" when circumstances required a modification of precise laws. It could, therefore, by no means ignore or avoid the papacy when the good of the commune required a retraction of a precise law. The commune could act only if the papacy judged that a modification was in the interest of the public good. Thus this paper argues not only that the threat of papal interference forced the commune to keep faith with its creditors and maintain its central administrative laws. Communal sovereignty was structurally affected not only in a passive way. The papacy was a dynamic third party, judging when and to what extent it would permit the commune to modify its laws and procedures.

The key to the papacy's influence lay first in its right as a court to hear appeals. More specifically, it had the right to absolve members of the *tre maggiori* and communal legislators, who had sworn oaths to an agent of the papacy to obey all precise laws.

What then did the commune and citizens do when political necessity required modification, but the penal clause threatened unacceptable penalties?

Let us look first at those affected by the laws concerning *banniti non rebanniendi*. It will be recalled that communal releases from condemnations regularly contained disclaimers to prevent claims by the Roman see. In some cases, where the release was clearly in violation of the precise law of 1354, it was stated that it could not be effected unless with the *beneplacitum* of the pope.[239] How was this obtained? Obviously, either the commune or an individual was forced to deal with the Roman pontiff.

239. See above, p. 183.

The first evidence of supplications to Rome is contained in a letter of May 2, 1355, from Innocent VI to the commune. It concerns the case of the Florentine citizens ser Geraldo, Bernardo, and Vincenzio Chele, Bindo Corsi, and Angelo di Paoli de' Bordoni—all of whom had been convicted of murder. The pope wrote that according to Florentine law, outside of Florence they had no hope of "being reconciled to your community," nor could any penalty, financial or otherwise, be remitted. According to this same law, the pope continued, any official or private person who would step in to obtain the modification of this law was subject to a penalty, "half of which is to be paid to the apostolic and the remaining half to your camera." Innocent pleaded that the murder in question had been done in anger, and advised the commune that the reconciliation of the murderers with the commune would be "in the public interest of this city and *patria*." Moved by piety "and by considerations of public interest," the pope asked the commune to take steps to readmit them "notwithstanding any penalty, for we will not concern ourselves with that part which pertains to us." [240]

The salient features of such letters do not need great elaboration. First of all there is the fiction according to which the pope had his information from the *fidedignorum assertio*, rather than from some named supplicant. Because of the law, said Innocent, "there was no one who would dare to promote their reconciliation." Thus the Florentine laws had required the papacy to choose a supplication formula which left the actual supplicant anonymous, and thus safe from prosecution in Florence. Second there is the fact that the pope based his decision on the "public interest," as well as on considerations of piety. His willingness to permit the introduction of a bill to liberate these self-confessed murderers into the legislative councils of Florence was based on his judgment of what would be utile for the communal *res*. Third, it seems clear from this letter that the interested party was the banished themselves. The pope was in effect permitting the

240. "Habet fidedignorum assertio quod inter alia statuta vestre civitatis est unum statutum in quo summarie continetur quod nulla persona que aliquem civem florentinum occiderit possit reconciliari communitati vestre perpetuo, nec pena pecuniaria vel alia illi propterea inflicta remitti, et quod si aliquis officialis vel alia privata persona civitatis ipsius pro reconciliatione occisoris vel remissione pene illi propterea institerit, certa pecuniaria pena multetur, cujus medietas apostolice et reliqua medietas vestre cameris applicetur . . . . Non sit qui reconciliationem eorum promovere audeat, quamquam utilitati publici civitatis ipsius et patrie videatur admodum expedire; nos, pietatis intuitu et huiusmodi publice utilitatis consideratione suasi . . . , non obstante pena huiusmodi, de qua prout ad cameram apostolicam pertinet, non curamus" (P. Gasnault and M. H. Laurent (eds.), *Lettres Secrètes et Curiales du Pape Innocent VI (1352–1362)* (Paris, 1959–), No. 1484 (May 2, 1355). On Angelo de' Bordoni, see Brucker, *Politics*, p. 63.

colleges and legislators of Florence to come to the aid of the convicted without incurring this fine. The potential influence which the pope could enjoy by determining who among the banned and sentenced could return to Florence will be immediately clear. The pope possessed an instrument to aid or weaken the regime.

The next extant letter of this type was addressed to the commune by Pope Urban V on August 18, 1364. Like all subsequent letters here described, it is preserved in the *Atti Publici* of the Florentine State Archives. The description of its contents on the reverse of the parchment is significant: "Privilegium Urbani Quinti continens quod Pazzinus de Donatis possit rebanniri," one reads in a contemporary hand. The chancery thus described these letters as papal privileges.[241]

The language of lordship is still more explicit in the letter itself. The *Signoria* had supplicated the pope "to deign to concede," "de speciali gratia," "license . . . to abolish the condemnations" of Donati. The supplication was successful:

> We . . . impart plenary license, remitting every oath which you have taken, and totally [remitting] to you this time, by the grace of apostolic munificence, whatever pecuniary penalty owed to the said camera, which you will therewith incur. Notwithstanding the said laws and oath previously taken, and also whatever stipulations, received in the name of the aforesaid camera, of the said penalty promised to this camera.[242]

We possess two further letters of the same year to the *Signoria* with the same formula. The "Privilegium Urbani Quinti quod Antonius Foresi de Sacchetti possit rebanniri, non obstantibus aliquibus statutis" was a response to a supplication of the government.[243] That which aided Giovanni di fu Tedici Manovelli was in response to the convict's supplication.[244]

241. *ASF, Atti Pubblici*, Aug. 18, 1364.

242. "Nos . . . licentiam plenariam . . . impertimur, omne iuramentum per vos prestitum et quamlibet penam pecuniariam dicte camere debitam, quam propterea incurreretis, hac vice de apostolice munificentie gratia vobis totaliter remictentes, non obstantibus predictis ordinamentis, iuramento ut premittitur roboratis, seu etiam quibusvis stipulacionibus nomine prefate camere recepte, de dicta pena eidem camere applicanda" (*ibid.*). The same Pazzino de' Donati had been readmitted years before through the intercession of Cangrande della Scala of Verona (*ASF, Provv.*, 41, fols. 19v–20r [Apr. 18, 1354]).

243. *ASF, Atti Pubblici*, Sept. 10, 1364. See Brucker, *Politics*, p. 63.

244. *ASF, Atti Pubblici*, Sept. 25, 1364.

In these latter letters there is no talk of public utility. One notes further that the supplicants were specified individuals or the commune, rather than the anonymous *fidedigni* of the 1355 letter. Further, the wording of these latter papal letters indicates that the supplicators in any case incur a fine. The pope munificently returns to the communal officials in advance a penalty which will be incurred in law despite his remission of the oath. Thus legally the commune through its supplication and then by its future legislative action activated the sum stipulated to the camera. It became the camera's property, to be then graciously returned by the pope.

The reason for this change in formula can be found in a law passed in the city councils on April 12, 1359. It forbade the impetration from the pope or any of his authorized agents of a remission or rescript. Even if it were obtained, it might not be used as a basis for suggesting the modification of a law secured with the *clausula penalis*.[245] This meant in effect that the only possible way to use the grace of the pope was to incur the penalty only if assured in advance of its remission. Thus the modification of the papal formula.

The incessant concern of the communal lawmakers with impetration to the Roman see will be documented shortly. Here it is enough to affirm that continued objections to impetration of such rescripts suggests that there must have been hundreds of them. But the remains are scant. The Florentine documents record one other case, this in 1368. Sentenced in May of that year for wounding the well-known lawyer Tommaso di Marco degli Strozzi, Berto and Lamberto de' Frescobaldi subsequently obtained from the commune the possibility of a release from this sentence. Following the standard procedure, such a release was made contingent on no papal claim arising as a result. The two had then succeeded in obtaining a letter of grace from Urban V. This

> gave and conceded license to the officials of the commune of Florence and to anyone of them to consult, provide, and deliberate licitly and with impunity regarding the cancellation and abolition of the condemnations and sentences made up until the present of the said Berto and Lamberto; to cancel and abolish their condemnations and banishments; and to absolve them and restitute [their estate] to them. And it remitted the oath sworn by the commune of Florence or by its officials as well as whatever pecuniary penalty owed to the apostolic camera.[246]

245. *ASF, Provv.*, 46, fols. 119r–120v (Apr. 12, 1359).

246. "Data et concessa fuit offitialibus comunis Florentie et cuilibet eorum licentia de cancellatione et abolitione condempnationum et sententiarum hactenus factarum de

On this basis, the two had been released from their condemnation, and the government had instructed a communal scribe to abolish the records of their condemnation and banishment. When it was discovered, however, that there was a variance between the names as recorded in the sentences and as inscribed in the papal concession, the Frescobaldi were forced to petition the government to proceed despite the clerical mix-up. The government agreed, "*Salvo* . . . that nothing is to be understood to have been ordained . . . in case that license has not been conceded by the said high pontiff or [in case] the penalty payable to the camera of the apostolic see [has not been conceded]."[247]

It is not surprising that this impetration continued. What is to be stressed is that the commune of Florence did not simply decide to readmit some and keep others out, but that it sought the necessary agreement of the papacy before acting. The verbiage of the documents is no less striking: privilege, grace, apostolic munificence, concession, remission were what the commune sought from the pope in order to legislate in certain areas.

We have given examples which illustrate the practical steps citizens and commune took to circumvent the precise laws regarding sentences and banishments. These examples make clear that the authority to modify a precise law rested with the papacy. Of course it is not suggested that the commune in an absolute sense was unable to violate its own laws, but that it assumed, at least into the 1370s, that it did not have the necessary power to do this without unpleasant internal repercussions, not to mention the eventual claims of the camera. It had bound itself to the papacy in order to obtain the confidence of its citizens. The time had not yet come when it would *per forza* have to secure itself from within.

It might be argued that to show that the papacy used *exbanniti* to strengthen its hand in dealing with the commune is to prove no more than the research of previous scholars has made clear. The response would be that this misses the point: the ability or inability of the commune to admit or refuse an *exbannitus* was mediated by the authority of a third power, the spiritual leader of Christendom, who could bind and loose

---

dictis Berto et Lamberto, licite et impune consulendi, providendi, et deliberandi et eos cancellandi et abolendi quibuscumque condempnationibus et bampnimentis et eos a predictis absolvendi et in integrum restituendi, et remissentur iuramentum per comune Florentie vel eius offitiales prestitum et quelibet pena pecuniaria camere appostolice debita, prout . . . in licteris summi pontificis continentur" (*ibid.*, 56, fols. 49r–50r [Aug. 19, 1368]).

247. "Salvo . . . non intelligatur aliquid provisum . . . in casu quo licentia concessa non esset per dictum summum pontificem nec per ipsum pena applicanda camere sedis appostolice, ut supra narratur remissa" (*ibid.*).

from oaths. This technical arrangement had been chosen by the commune as a means of stabilizing its institutions.

The direct effects of this "voluntary" limitation of sovereignty are by no means evident only in the area of the commune's judicial authority. The real import of this arrangement can best be measured by considering three further impetations whose political implications are truly formidable.

The first of these concerned the hiring of *balestrieri* or militia. The *Signoria* wrote to the papal legate and Grand Penitentiary Egidio Albornoz informing him that for the public good the commune had in the past established *divieti* provisions concerning the militia's recruitment, pay, size, and so forth. While this law had at the time redounded to the public interest, now, because of the *malitia temporis*, it was "seen to effect evident harm and enormous scandal." Though the law had been "secured with oaths and the insertion of diverse penalties," the commune insistently asked the legate to deign to provide some remedy.

Albornoz's reply, written in the nearby town of Scarperia on December 19, 1358, met the needs of the city. "If and in so far as the observation of the aforesaid ordinances redound to the detriment of your *res pubblica*," the commune was conceded the faculty for one month to modify, correct, and change the lesive statutes. The oaths, promises, and obligations, as well as the penalties to the apostolic camera, "by which you could be in any way impeded or also molested by the aforesaid camera and church" would not stand in the way. The oaths were "relaxed," and the commune was "absolved" from the penalties and obligations.[248]

248. "Sane pro parte vestra fuit nuper nobis expositum, quod olim . . . nonnulla ordinationes et statuta circa electionem fiendam de balistariis recipiendis, cum expedit, de civitate et diocesi florentinis ac solutiones fiendas eisdem et consignationes seu monstras faciendas per ipsos, ac circa quorumdam reddituum et pecuniarum quantitates . . . pro utilitate et favore rei publice civitatis predicte facta et edita ac iuramentis et diversarum penarum adiectionibus vallata fuerunt. Verum quia malitia temporis faciente ordinationes et statuta huiusmodi sicut tunc in dicte vestre rei publice atque vestri redundabant utilitatem, ita ad evidentem lesionem ac enorme scandalum nunc cedere dinoscitur. Propter quod pro parte vestra fuit nobis cum instantia supplicatum ut providere vobis super hoc de oportuno remedio dignaremur. Nos igitur considerantes quod *iuramentum iniquitatis vinculum esse non debet*, ac civitatis vestre predicte utilia procurare et dampnosa excludere paternis studiis affectantes, vestris supplicationibus inclinati, vobis si et in quantum in vestre rei publice predicte detrimentum predictarum ordinationum observatio redundet, usque ad unum mensem proxime futurum per vos seu consilia vestra ac rectores, officiales et alios quos ad hoc duxeritis deputandos, ipsisque consiliis, rectoribus, officialibus, et deputatis huiusmodi proponendi, consulendi, ordinandi, et disponendi super premissis, eaque revocandi, modificandi, reformandi, corrigendi, et mutuandi, et alias circa ea providendi in totum vel in partem, prefatis iuramentis et penis, etiam si pene ipse camere apostolice et romane ecclesie in casu quo eisdem

Furnished with the legate's permission, the commune acted swiftly. The following January 11, it brought a bill before the councils to modify its previous law. It was necessary to change the law, said the prologue, notwithstanding the fact it had been sealed with an oath and with penalties payable to the apostolic camera. Taking note of the "gratia" by which the papal legate had relaxed the oath, remitted the financial penalties, and conceded to the government the faculty to modify the statutes insofar as they redounded to the detriment of the republic, the priors affirmed "that it was evident that the observation of the aforesaid ordinances redounded *totally* to the detriment of the *res pubblica*." [249]

Having cleared the ground for a revision, it proceeded to reclaim the right to change the wages of the militia. Further, it modified the perpetual nature of the previous law. Whereas that had foreseen no possibility of modification, this prohibited change unless the *tre maggiori* voted two out of three with a minimum quorum of twenty-eight present to recommend modification to the legislative councils. The modification thus carried through, the following disclaimer was added:

> This also expressed and declared, that the aforesaid should have place and effect and ought to and can be observed and ought to be done, provided and ordained . . . if and in so far as it flows out of a concession of the aforesaid grace and a relaxation of the said oath and a liberation from penalties, which [concession, relaxation, and liberation] are efficacious to the extent that these penalities . . . cannot in

---

premissis contrafieret stipulatione per vos promisse fuissent vel aliqualiter deberentur, ac quibuscumque promissionibus et obligationibus quibusvis solennitatibus et muniminibus roboratis, per quas super hiis a camera et ecclesia prefatis possetis aliquatenus impediri vel etiam molestari, que iuramenta videlicet relaxamus, et penas, obligationes, et promissiones predictas vobis ex nunc remictimus, vos ab eis totaliter absolventes devotioni vestre plenam et liberam, auctoritate qua fungimur, tenore presentium concedimus facultatem" (*ASF, Atti Pubblici*, Dec. 19, 1358; italics mine). The motivation for absolving from the oath is to be found in the gloss on the Sext; see W. Ullmann, *Medieval Papalism* (London, 1949), p. 74, n. 3. See also S. Kuttner, *Die Kanonistische Schuldlehre von Gratian bis auf die Dekretalen Gregors IX* (Vatican City, 1935), pp. 291–333.

249. "Ac etiam actendentes gratiam nuper factam per . . . dominum Egidium . . . legatum ipsis dominis prioribus et vexillifero et ipsi populo et comuni circa relaxationem iuramenti predicti et circa remissionem dictarum penarum, obligationum, et promissionum, et concessionem libre facultatis modificandi, reformandi, corrigendi, et mutandi dicta ordinamenta et provisiones . . . et affirmantes sibi totaliter videri observantiam predictarum ordinationum in detrimentum dicte rei publice redundare" (*ASF, Provv.*, 46, fols. 83*rv* [Jan. 11, 1358*sf*]).

any way be requested or demanded from anyone by the Roman church or its camera or that of the lord pope.

Protesting, that if because of the aforesaid, anything has been said or could or ought to have been said by which . . . any penalty could be in any way demanded from anyone by the Roman church . . . they have not intended to thus provide . . . ; nor is anything related to this understood to be proposed, counselled, or also enacted, nor to have been proposed, provided, ordained, deliberated or done; rather it is understood to be and is as if not done. It exists only insofar as no penalty can in any way be demanded from any person by the Roman church by pretext of the aforesaid.[250]

The peculiarity of this absolution in comparison to those privileges we have already examined is that whereas in the latter an exception was made to a general law which remained otherwise in force, here a general law itself was being cancelled through impetration. That the law cancelled was one dealing with the size of the militia retained by the republic sustains with *force majeure* the argument presented here: the pope had his hands on the stabilizing levers of the Florentine republic.

The most striking instances of impetration, however, and thus our best insight into the extent of the communal obligation to the apostolic camera, deal with the office of the *podestà*. For in two cases, the commune was forced to request a papal privilege which would permit it to re-elect that highest communal judicial official.

The first case occurred in 1359. Details are not forthcoming, but, the outline is clear. The *podestà* for the semester October 30, 1358, to April 30, 1359, was one Tizio di fu Bartolommeo del Fiesco of Genoa. The available information on his office is this: on January 30, 1359, the priors were authorized to seek his successor.[251] Then in an anti-impetration bill

---

250. "Eo quoque expresso et declarato quod predicta locum habeant et effectum et observentur et observari possint et debeant et fieri provideri et ordinari . . . si et in quantum constet de concessione gratie antedicte et relaxatione dicti iuramenti et liberatione penarum adeo efficacibus, quod ipse pene . . . per romanam ecclesiam seu eius vel domini pape cameram a quoquam peti seu exigi nequeant quoquomodo, et non aliter. Protestantes quod siquid per predicta . . . aliquid diceretur . . . vel dici . . . posset seu deberit, per quod . . . pena aliqua per romanam ecclesiam . . . a quoquam posset exigi quoquomodo, illud non intendunt providere . . . nec super eo aliquid proponi, consuli, vel etiam reformari, nec quod propositum, provisum, ordinatum, deliberatum, vel factum esse intelligatur vel sit, set pro non facto . . . esse intelligatur et sit. Sit solum quo ad ea quorum pretestu . . . nulla pena posset aliqualiter exigi per romanam ecclesiam . . . ab aliqua persona" (*ibid.*).

251. *Atti del Podestà del Comune di Firenze. Inventario*, Vol. I (Florence, n.d.), p. 210.

brought to the council of the *popolo* on April 12, the commune exempted from the force of that law the following two letters of impetration. First:

> If letters of grace have been or would be impetrated or have been or would be conceded by the apostolic see . . . in favor . . . of Tizio del Fiesco da Genova, in which it would be ordained that it could be provided, proposed, enacted or however done with impunity that this [*podestà*] for the period of six months for which he had been re-elected as *podestà* of the city of Florence might . . . keep and retain with him in office . . . those officials whom he has had with him until now in the office of the *podestà* of the aforesaid city.²⁵²

Second, the letters of grace conceded to the city by the cardinal penitentiary Francesco degli Atti by command of the pope, dated February 23, 1359.²⁵³

The reconstruction I would offer of these events is that by his letters, the penitentiary had allowed the commune to re-elect the *podestà* without fear of a penalty. At the time of this law, the commune was awaiting a second letter of grace permitting a second evasion of the precise law on the *divieti* of the foreign officials: the limited term of the *familia* of those officials.

252. "Si que lictere gratia, privilegium vel rescriptum impetrata essent vel impetrarentur vel concessa essent vel concederentur per sedem apostolicam . . . in favorem Tedisii de Flisco de Janua, seu in quibus disponeretur quod provideri, proponi, seu reformari vel quid fieri posset impune quod ipse tempore sex mensium, pro quo reelectus est in potestatem civitatis Florentie, potuerit secum habere et tenere in offitio . . . aliquos ex offitialibus quos hactenus secum tenuit in offiitio potestarie civitatis predicte" (*ASF*, *Provv.*, 46, fols. 119r–120r [Apr. 12, 1359]).

253. "Lettere gratie iam concesse per Franciscum cardinalem S. Marchi, penitentiarium pape, de mandato pape" (*ibid.*). It is significant that this cardinal had been bishop of Florence in 1355–56, and according to F. Ughelli was called the cardinal of Florence (*Italia Sacra* [Venice, 1717–22], III, col., 149). He was the author of a tract on bishops' canonical portions; see my "The Bishop' Portion." The anonymous penitential formulary in BAV, MS. *Barberini Latini*, 1533, has been thought to stem from the time when Atti was penitentiary; E. Göller, *Die Päpstlichen Pönitentiarie von ihrem Ursprung bis zu ihrer Umgestaltung unter Pius V*, Vol. I (Rome, 1907), part 1, pp. 36 ff., 92 f; part 2, pp. 9 ff. A formula in this manuscript reads: "Franciscus Dei gratia episcopus florentinus . . . , auctoritate domini pape cuius penitentiarie curam in absentia reverendissimi in Christo patris domini Egidii maioris penitentiari . . . gerimus . . . "; BAV, *op. cit.*, fol. 91v. Thus Atti was papal penitentiary while still bishop of Florence, and again in 1359. These circumstances: the bishop of Florence and then "cardinal of Florence" absolving Florentine individuals from oaths not to violate precise laws, must have been very satisfactory to the *Signorie*.

Tizio was the first *podestà* to serve more than a six-month term.[254] It was not a route the commune enjoyed taking; circumstances forced it upon the city. A decade later the situation came up again, and the attempted re-election of the *podestà* at this juncture has provided us with a documentary insight into the role the papal *clausula* occupied in the communal scale of precedence.

Despite several offers, the government had been unable to elect a *podestà* and *capitano del popolo* for the second semester of 1369. Consequently the government had decided that it was imperative to re-elect the present *podestà*, one Piero della Marina of Recanata. However, "one cannot go ahead, since the ordinances of the commune of Florence regulating the *divieti* of rectors and foreign officials of this commune stand in the way. One cannot violate them without fear of a penalty applicable to the apostolic camera."[255] A deliberation of the *tre maggiori* (thirty-two of thirty-seven in favor) sent to the councils a bill designed to meet this administrative crisis. Upon passage, it authorized the priors and *gonfaloniere* "and anyone else, whatever his condition," to impetrate from the pope

> the privilege, letters of grace, or rescript through which the lord pope would concede license to these lord priors . . . , *gonfaloniere*, . . . and all officials and councilors . . . to provide, ordain, propose . . . , in the colleges or councils of the said *popolo* or commune of Florence the election and reaffirmation of the noble knight [and] lord Piero della Marina . . . , notwithstanding . . . the oaths or penalties payable as well to the apostolic camera . . . , and notwithstanding the promises . . . to observe the said statutes . . . , impetrating liberation and plenary remission from the said penalty.[256]

The very existence in the law books of the commune of such a positive encouragement to citizens to impetrate a privilege from the Roman see

254. *Atti del Podestà, loc. cit.*

255. ". . . Procedi non potest, obstantibus ordinibus comunis Florentie disponentibus de devetis rectorum et officialium forensium comunis eiusdem, contra que veniri non potest absque metu pene camere apostolice applicande" (*ASF, Provv.*, 57, fols. 93*v*–94*r* [Aug. 22, 1369]).

256. "Et quod propterea expedit supplicare domino summo pontifici et, impetrata licentia, procedere ut fuerit opportunum. Habita . . . deliberatione . . . et obtento partito ad fabas nigras et albas per XXXII secundum formam ordinamentorum comunis, . . . providerunt . . . quod domini priores artium et vexillifer iustitie populi et comunis Florentie et quicumque alii cuiuscumque condictionis existerent, possint impetrari [sic] et impetrari facere . . . a domino summo pontifice . . . privilegium, licteras, gratiam, et seu rescriptum

which would permit the commune to re-elect one of its own officials is striking evidence of the dependence of the government on Rome. Note also the date—1369; twenty-four years after the institution of this structural limitation of communal sovereignty. At this late date the commune was far from able to appoint its own officials. Further, the papacy may well have refused this communal request, thereby forcing the commune to come up with a new *podestà*. We know that the reigning *podestà* did not in fact serve another full term.[257]

The commune would not have itself impetrated to Rome for such grace in matters concerning the banished, the militia, and the office of *podestà* unless the stakes had been high and the grace of the papacy an ineluctable part of communal continuity. Such impetration was frowned on by a series of laws passed during the life of this regime, aimed directly against impetration for the purpose of evading the *clausula penalis*. Let us glance at this tradition.

The first such law was passed in 1359. It forbade impetration from the pope or his agents of grace to speak in council without fear of a penalty to the apostolic camera. And it forbade using such a letter of grace even if obtained from the pope.[258] Yet, as we have already noted, this very law contained exceptions for specific rescripts which the commune had obtained.

This general law would have sufficed if it had been enforceable. But

---

per quod seu quam ipse dominus papa concedat licentiam ipsis dominis prioribus . . . vexillifero . . . et omnibus officialibus et consiliariis . . . providendi, ordinandi, proponendi . . . in . . . collegiis seu consiliis dicti populi sev comunis Florentie de eligendo et refirmando nobilem militem dominum Petrum dela Marina . . . , non obstantibus . . . iuramentis vel penis applicandis etiam camere apostolice . . . et non obstantibus promissionibus . . . de dictis statutis . . . observandis, de non faciendis vel veniendis quoquomodo contra ea vel contenta in eis . . . , ab ipsa pena liberationem et remissionem plenariam impetrare . . ." (*ibid.*).

257. Piero did hold office more than the statutory six-month period. His authority had taken effect on May 14, 1369 (*ASF*, MS. *Atti del Podestà. Inventario*, II, 50). He did not yield it until January 11, 1370 (*ASF*, *Provv.*, 57, fols. 152*rv* [Jan. 25, 1369*sf*]). His authority should have expired November 14. On the fifth of that month he was authorized pay for the last two months of his office, despite the fact that he had not been syndicated (*ibid.*, fol. 112*v* [Nov. 5, 1369]). On the twenty-fourth reference is made to his (re)election, which according to the document had not been carried out in statutory form (*ibid.*, fols. 119*v*–120*r* [Nov. 24, 1369]). This would seem to indicate that he had been re-elected despite the precise laws, and then released as soon as an acceptable candidate was found. The reason for this new appointment in mid-semester may have been that the pope refused the request for a full semester re-election, as had been solicited.

258. *ASF*, *Provv.*, 46, fols. 119*r*–120*v* (Apr. 12, 1359). See above, p. 193.

we have seen that it was occasionally bypassed. Consequently it is no surprise to find that new anti-impetration laws were passed dealing with specific laws. For example, in 1360 a paragraph in an election law prohibited an election of the officials in question which would be in violation of the precise clause, even if they were·able to obtain papal rescripts.[259] A law of 1364 specified this prohibition for laws favoring the *Parte*.[260] Finally in July, 1372, this prohibition was articulated in reference to the law of April 5 past, the so-called Ordinances of Liberty, which had established a *balìa* with extraordinary powers (the *Dieci di Libertà*) to unify the city. Persons of "dignity and pre-eminence" had apparently sought to use the papacy to subvert this fundamental law. The prohibition was clear now, and the penalty unusually harsh: if such an impetration were sought, and if gained were used, the penalty was to be decapitation and the sequestration and sale of the estate of the guilty.[261] Here again, in the 1370s solemn warnings aimed at preserving legality suggest not continuity, but the growing ineffectiveness of the system of security involving the papal *clausula penalis*.

It would seem, therefore, that the standard route by which to suspend the rigor of the precise laws was to seek rescripts or privileges from the pope, his penitentiaries, or the legates. Despite the inherent instability this encouraged, even the commune was forced to avail itself of the method. This mechanism could not have been other than amenable to the Roman see, for besides the fact that these impetrations were sources of income to the papal treasury, the mechanism afforded the pope a means with which to significantly influence the course of internal affairs in Florence.

259. "Item quod nullus etiam quantumcumque quibuscumque licteris seu quacumque gratia vel pene remissione a sede appostolica vel alias quomodolibet impetratis vel impetrandis possit contra reformationes seu ordinamenta comunis Florentie penalia camere domini pape seu sedis apostolice vel aliquod ipsorum refirmari, eligi, vel assumi" (*ibid.*, 48, fol. 55*v* [Oct. 21, 1360]).

260. *Ibid.*, 52, fols. 69*rv* [Dec. 11, 1364]).

261. "Item quod nullus cuiuscumque status, dignitatis, preheminentie vel condictionis existat audeat . . . impetrare . . . aliquem rescriptum vel licteras apostolicas vel aliquam licentiam, indulgentiam, seu remissionem a summo pontifice vel . . . potestatem habente . . . per quod vel quas liceat vel possit per dominos priores artium et vexilliferum . . . et . . . [collegia] . . . vel alios quoscumque, seu per consilia populi et comunis Florentie vel per ipsum populum et comune aliquid fieri, provideri, vel ordinari . . . contra provisiones et ordinamenta predicta . . . absque metu dictarum penarum . . . . Nec etiam liceat alicui, eis sic impetratis . . . uti . . . seu . . . aliquam ex eis producere, ostendere, vel allegare . . . . Et quod siquis contra predicta . . . fecerit . . . , pena capitis puniatur et publicatione omnium bonorum" (*ibid.*, 60, fol. 50*v* [July 31, 1372]).

Sooner or later, however, the system was bound to decline. The greater the financial stability of the commune and the more dependent the citizens were on the commune, the less pressing the need for external security. The more often absolution from the oaths of office was sought from Rome, the less valuable was the security itself. This became particularly evident during the late sixties and seventies, when the *Parte* became one of the chief beneficiaries of this papal protection, and both *Parte* and commune used the rider to counter the other's influence. The growing political antagonism between the commune and the papacy during this period helped to encourage this process of decline of the security's utility. Yet we must remember that this tension could now continue to build, and finally end in war, partly because the previous security arrangement between Rome and Florence had proved a successful means whereby the commune was nursed back to financial and political stability, and therewith to a more defensible sovereignty.

The signs of decline first appear around 1370. The laws which could be construed as threatening communal creditors have already been mentioned,[262] as well as the evidence that a *podestà* had (illegally?) served part of a second term in 1369.[263] Laws clearing the priors of illegal acts they may have committed are liberally sprinkled in the registers from 1370 forward.[264] In 1372, a perpetual law concerning *divieti* was converted to a solemn one voidable by an absolute majority of the *tre maggiori*; no mention was made of the cameral rider which was a part of the original law.[265] Then in June, 1373, two laws were carried through which significantly modified the election process for three foreign officials. Absolutely no mention was made of responsibility to the church, and there was no disclaimer clause.[266]

These straws in the wind are substantiated by the important law of May 21, 1375. The prologue points out that in the past, members of the communal legislative councils had not only not been able to state their opinion, but had been forced to accede in matters opposed to conscience. From then on, the government could not threaten councilors with perjury if they expressed their opinions, "onerantes eorum conscientias."[267]

---

262. See above, p. 150 f.

263. See above, p. 200.

264. For examples, see *ASF, Provv.*, 57, fols. 215rv (Apr. 6, 1370); 64, fols. 62rv (June 21, 1376).

265. *Ibid.*, 58, fols. 244r–245r (Feb. 27, 1371sf).

266. *Ibid.*, 61, fols. 67r–68r (June 13, 1373); fols. 73v–74r (June 20, 1373).

267. *Ibid.*, 63, fols. 39r–40r (May 21, 1375).

Though it is impossible to state with certainty the full meaning of the law, it probably refers to the prohibition in the precise clause of any discussion in the councils of perpetual or solemn laws.

By spring of 1375, the commune was well on its way to war with the papacy. And as events moved toward the explosion of December, the effect on the traditional security system became overt. By fall of 1375, the normal disclaimer had ceased to be used on *divieti* laws. In an authorization to communal officials to secure loans (July, 1375), the papal security was excluded by name, the first time such a directive was given.[268] The cameral rider was used for the last time on December 11, 1375.[269]

The problems which would be faced by the commune now that it had decided to war with its past guarantor were perhaps not clearly recognized at first. With dignified euphoria, the government would state that it had found a means to imburse large sums of money with harm to none and utility to many, to wage war without burdening the taxpayer: tax the church and sequester its goods.[270] Let us follow the history of this taxing and sequestration from the point of view of securing and guaranteeing its actions.

In the authorization for the first war loan forced on the local church, we encounter a small but significant modification of *balìa*: The commissioners might insure the loans with penalties "payable to whomever."[271] In short, the commissioners could come to an agreement with the clergy on who would be an acceptable third party guarantor. The papacy was not mentioned as a prospective guarantor, as it had been in earlier formulations. It had now become an unrealistic securer. Still, the commune recognized that it was not credible enough in itself to guarantee its own loans. It remained willing to allow third parties to fulfill that role.

This is to say that the security system had fallen into flux. Other means would have to be found to maintain credibility. But these would take time. In the meantime, the commune would use the apostolic rider twice more to insure faith, but almost in embarrassment. For who could believe that the commune or its officials would actually pay fines to the papacy for the violation of laws when it was at war with the papacy and when the subject of the two laws was the expropriation of the clergy?

268. "Cum illis roborationibus et penis, non tamen camere apostolice, et capitulis et articulis quibus volent" (*ibid.*, 63, fols. 70*v*–71*v* [July 12, 1375]).

269. *Ibid.*, fols. 174*r*–176*r* (Dec. 11, 1375).

270. "Et quod per infrascriptum modum absque alicuius incommodo et cum multorum utilitatibus potuerit haberi pecunia satis magna . . ." (*ibid.*, 64, fol. 138*v* [Sept. 25, 1376]).

271. "Etiam quantumcumque ardua et penalia et sub penis etiam cuicumque applicandis" (*ibid.*, 63, fols. 60*v*–61*v* [June 27, 1375]).

In fact, the commune knew no other way. By the first of these laws, the commune ordered a commission to seize all the long-term ecclesiastical rents of the Dominion and sell them. The titles to the rents were to be privileged and unquestioned. A compensation scheme was set up for clerics hit by these seizures which made them creditors of the commune. Thus the affected parties requiring security were the clergy and the buyers of the rents. The apostolic rider was appended in classic form.[272] Again the question: Was it realistic to expect the commune to honor a potential debt to an open enemy? But the second problem—to buy ecclesiastical properties seized by the commune—was a first-rate moral dilemma, for these lands and rights were God's. And what spiritual authority would assure them they did not sin by acquiring these goods? Many Florentines, of course, were more complex in their business judgments: moral scruples alone might not hold them back. But the most patriotic burgher must have been disturbed by the security offered him: to stipulate a penalty to the Roman see at this juncture was a worthless gesture. Consequently he would have to judge the purchase of such rents from another point of view. Could the commune really maintain its promise to guarantee the titles of these rents? Could it so soundly defeat the papacy as to make the pontiff accept this?

Before all of the implications and difficulties of this first law were fully realized, the second bill in question was carried into law. It bore the last cameral *clausula penalis* ever used by the commune. The ecclesiastical lands of the Dominion were to be sold. The same stipulations found in the previous law were added, guaranteeing title to the buyer and crediting the afflicted clergy with holdings in the public debt.[273] The appended rider raised the same questions as to its worth. The answer remained unsatisfactory. Soon it was evident that laymen were resisting the officials who hawked the lands, even though they were to be had at cut-rate prices.[274] The reasons for hesitation were clear—morality and lack of security.

What could the commune do under these circumstances? Forced sales alienated the citizenry from the war, yet they had to be used. Increased affirmations of the absolute security of title and massive threats against anyone questioning these titles sought to assuage the caution of potential buyers. But the louder the assurances became, the less believable they

272. *Ibid.*, 64, fols. 138r–140r (Sept. 25, 1376).
273. *Ibid.*, fols 154v–157r (Oct. 18, 1376).
274. See references at n. 175 above.

were, especially given the disappointing course of the war and the fragile political position of the war party within the city.[275]

As an earnest of its commitment to guaranteeing title, the commune sought to erase every possible contractual subtlety which could dissuade a buyer. And one such move is of significance to this story. In October, 1377, the commune acted to affirm the actions of the *balìe* which had taxed the church and seized its properties. It especially acted, it said, so that those who buy lands or rents have an absolutely safe title. It provided that

Each and every clause or insertion placed in whatever part of the said law and in whatever other aforesaid laws and provisions or any one of them treating of the office, commission, and power of the said officials or of the business and acts past and future of the said officials or dependent on or connected to their office in any way, which says in substance or effect that it is not understood by these [acts] or any one of them that anything has been provided or done or that [anything] could be in any way provided or done through which or by virtue, pretext, cause or occasion of which any penalty could be demanded or asked by the Apostolic See or Roman church from the commune of Florence or from any official of the said commune, etc., with each and every part attached to the said clause, addition, or *salvum*, however it might be worded, is held to be and is as if truly it had never been placed or added, deliberated or provided.[276]

This action was taken, the law concluded, to strengthen and not to weaken the actions of the past and present officials concerned. That is, it was taken to strengthen the titles on former ecclesiastical lands and not to weaken them.

275. See Brucker, *Politics*, pp. 319 ff.

276. "Et quod omnis et quelibet clausula sive adiectio apposita in quacumque parte in dicta reformatione et in quibuscumque aliis reformationibus et provisionibus ante-dictis vel aliqua earum tractante de officio, balia, et potestate dictorum officialium vel de rebus, gestis, vel gerendis per dictos officiales vel ad eorum officium quomodolibet dependentis vel connexis, continens in substantia vel effectu quod non intelligatur per ea vel aliquod eorum aliquid provisum vel factum esse seu providere vel quomodolibet fieri posse per quod seu cuius vigore, pretestu, causa, vel occasione aliqua pena per sedem apostolicam vel romanam ecclesiam possit exigi seu peti a comuni Florentie vel ab aliquo officiali dicti comunis etc., cum omnibus et singulis ad dictam clausulam, adiectionem, sive salvum facientibus sub quocumque tenore verborum habeat et sit ac si vere num-quam fuisset apposita vel adiecta, deliberata seu provisa" (*ASF, Provv.*, 65, fols. 170r–171r [Oct. 14, 1377]).

Why had the commune stricken the disclaimer from all laws concerning the acts and powers of these officials to tax the church and sequester its lands? The explanation is simple enough. The classical disclaimer always contained the supposition that if the law in question turned out to be in violation of a precise law, or if the execution of the law proved so, the acts and the law were null. But the potential buyer was well aware that by now, so many precise laws had been violated (and thus debts to the apostolic camera incurred), that in strictest law it was doubtful that any act of the government could be called indubitably legal. And if any act were illegal, it would have to be the sale of church lands. The potential buyer would have had difficulty imagining the papacy protecting the buyer's title to church lands. In fact, the use of the disclaimer will in these circumstances have appeared to the buyer a ruse on the part of the commune. Despite the protestations of the commune, any reasonable man could foresee the day when the commune would have to restitute church lands. In this eventuality, the existence of this disclaimer could serve the commune as an escape route. It could claim that the apostolic camera in fact had a claim, that the commune had in fact violated its precise laws. Therefore, it might later argue, the sales were invalid from the start, and the buyers would have to return the lands.

The lifting of the disclaimer clause afforded the buyer greater security than if it had remained. The same clause which had traditionally been meant to protect communal creditors had now proved itself a hindrance to citizen faith.

With this law, we see that the old penal system had nearly exhausted its utility. It was not replaced by new, equally solid articles of faith. The chaos in its system of securities was matched by the growing uncertainty afflicting Florentine society at large. The war, the citizens soon knew, was irrevocably lost. And the Florentines would have to pay. The *sine qua non* of a peace treaty was the restitution of church lands. This having been conceded by the commune, the papacy was willing to show its munificence. Article 15 of the peace treaty (July 28, 1378) reads as follows:

> *Item.* That if the commune of Florence or any citizen or officials of the said city has at any time fallen into a penalty payable to the apostolic camera or Roman church or any high pontiff by virtue of any municipal law or provision made or intended to be made by the commune of Florence, or proposed or brought forward by any citizens or officials of the commune of Florence, or by any other reason, law, method, or cause, from this point this high pontiff named above liberates and absolves this commune and single persons from each and

every obligation and penalty, rights and interests, which this commune or some officials of the said commune or other citizens of the aforesaid city has incurred up to the present day.[277]

We have reached the climax, but not the end, of this institution's history. Before summarizing, it will be best to follow its traces until 1383, when it dropped from sight.

Late summer of 1378 in Florence was marked by civil war between the lower proletariat and possessing classes.[278] Laws came and went as first one, then another group attained and then fell from power. Each change of regime required, of course, the canceling of precise laws. The explusion of the *ciompi* from the streets at the end of August led to a parliament on September 1 to re-create stability. To do this, it took the legal step of annulling all hindrances to the changing of law, specifically including the threat of a penalty payable to the apostolic camera.[279]

Attempts were made during this period to reorient or re-establish the legal securities of the commune. In midsummer the old, pre-1345 *clausula penalis* made its reappearance, with all penalties and bonding done internally.[280] In November an attempt was made to re-establish solemn procedures, including, interestingly enough, the requirement of twenty-eight votes among the *tre maggiori* before suggesting the appending of penalties payable to the pope.[281] This makes clear that the option of returning to the papal bonding system was still open.

But the strains continued. In January, 1379, all perpetual and solemn

277. "Item. Quod si comune Florentie vel aliqui civis seu offitiales dicte civitatis aliquo tempore incurrissent in aliquam penam camere apostolice seu romane ecclesie vel alicui summo pontifici applicandam virtute alicuius legis municipialius seu reformationis per comune Florentie facte seu fieri actentate, seu per aliquos cives seu offitiales comunis Florentie proponite, dictate, seu quacumque alia ratione, iure, modo, vel causa, ex nunc ipse summus pontifex nomine quo supra liberat et absolvit ipsum comune et singulares personas ab omnibus et singulis obligationibus et penis, iure, et interesse, quod et quas incurrisset ipsum comune seu aliqui dicti comunis offitiales seu alii cives civitatis predicte usque in presentem diem etc." (*ASF, Atti Pubblici,* July 28, 1378).

278. See the important article by G. Brucker, "The Ciompi Revolution," in Rubinstein (ed.), *Florentine Studies,* pp. 314–356.

279. *ASF, Balie,* 16, fols. 7rv (Sept. 1, 1378). My thanks to Randolph Starn for bringing this to my attention. For a similar cancellation by the *Ciompi,* see *ASF, Provv.,* 67, fol. 4v (July 21, 1378).

280. *ASF, Provv.,* 67, fol. 12v (July 21, 1378).

281. "Et seu de faciendo vel firmando aliquam provisionem vel reformationem in qua contineatur expresse aliqua pena que camere apostolice veniat applicanda" (*ibid.,* fols. 85r–87r [Nov. 23, 1378]).

laws were again suspended "for the peace and defense of the artisans."[282] And on top of that came the damning admission that, however much the commune ought to keep faith, it was going to be necessary to restitute the lands of the church.[283]

Out of these troubled years and twisted events would come a new, more self-sufficient commune. Two fundamental laws form the last act in the history of the papal *clausula*. On December 7, 1380, the commune suspended the penalties on all laws since 1344 which limited the right to recommend changes in payments on the *Monte*.[284] Having done this, it followed on the twelfth with a law which definitively altered the security arrangements not only on the *Monte*, but on all precise laws. The privileges of creditors of the *Monte* were to remain intact, it said,

> Excepted and declared that in none of these privileges enters or is included or is understood included, placed, or inserted any penalty which in any way would come to be paid to the apostolic camera or to the Roman church. On the contrary, from now on each and every ordinance by virtue of which any penalty could be committed to or come to be paid to the holy Roman church or apostolic camera is understood to be and is null and of no efficacy or effect as far as this penalty and its transferral; as far as this penalty and its transfer, it should be considered totally imperfect.[285]

282. *Ibid.*, fols. 115r–116r (Jan. 22, 1378*sf*).

283. *Ibid.*, fols. 123rv (Jan. 24, 1378*sf*).

284. *Ibid.*, 69, fols. 177r–178v. The chronicler Stefani's narration of this suspension is not free from error, but it shows clearly the continuing relationship between *penali* and citizen faith: "Era dilatata la forma del muovere gli ordinamenti del Comune, non tanto fussero gravi e penali; e questo si vide per li giudici che fanno, e disfanno ogni cosa. Era pena la testa per qualunque parlasse, o proponesse, o mettesse partito di muovere lo interesso, o lo capitale del Monte, nel quale v'erano su danari dal tempo del Duca di Calavria 1327 a ragione di fiorini 5 per 100 l'anno, e fatto legge che pena la testa, chi desse, o pigliasse più che 5 per 100 l'anno." After narrating the origins of the *Monte del uno tre* and *del uno due*, he continues: "Di che questa era incomportabile soma, sì per le spese dei soldati e sì per gl'interessi del Comune del detto Monte; e così il Comune non potea soddisfare alle spese ed alli soldati ed al Monte; e non potendosi del Monte, perchè era penale, muovere, come è detto di sopra, li giudici guastavano, e muoveano ogni cosa; e perchè era nello detto ordine che fusse così penale, ed eglino trovarano modo, che con 25 fave, cioè le due parti de' Priori e Collegi, bastasse a sospendere la detta legge penale; di che in uno mese si potesse parlare ed ordinare, e fare legge sopra lo Monte: e ciò fu vinto a' di 7 di dicembre" (Marchionne di Coppo Stefani, *Cronaca Fiorentina*, *Rerum Italicarum Scriptores, nuova edizione* XXX, rubric 883).

285. "Excepto et declarato quod in huiusmodi privilegiis non veniat nec includatur nec inclusa, apponita, vel inserta intelligatur vel sit aliqua pena que camere apostolice aut romane ecclesie ullo modo veniat applicanda. Set quod omnia et singula ordinamenta

At one stroke, the commune first lifted papal *pene* from the *Monte*, and then from all laws with such penalties. The commune was legally on its own.

Almost. For if we again ask just what needs the apostolic clause had originally been intended to fulfill, we will recall that it provided the creditor not only with security that the commune would meet its obligations, but that his imbursements from the public weal would carry no moral taint. The arrangement with the papacy had insured the creditor that his earnings were not usurious and would not be considered so by the commune or the pope. The rider had never been simply a political instrument; it had also solved conscience problems. And it is remarkable that, as far as is known, no Florentine lending institution from the consolidation of the public debt in 1345 until the end of the regime was attacked by the papacy as usurious.

But now the basis of this understanding was gone. If the commune was to maintain the licitness of its debt payments, licitness would have to be based uniquely on its own authority. Such a step was taken in the law of June 12, 1383, "concerning the relieving of the weight of conscience from the creditors of the *Monte Comune* of Florence." Interest received on any 5 percent *Monte* was a free gift of the commune, the law said. And even though the creditor might ask for the interest, he was not required to make restitution to the commune, "also before God or his conscience." The fact that he asked for this "gift" did not necessitate the chits which had traditionally been given out by communal syndics. "Without any scruple of conscience and without any requirement to restitute," he might retain this mere gift.[286]

It is evident that the commune had retained its self-concept as a moral agent. As it now moved definitively to guarantee its finances to its citizens on its own authority, it sounded almost convincing in its roll as faithful custodian and broker of civic wealth. Almost. For as the potential creditor of the fourteenth century read the fine print of the law before making up

---

quorum vigore aliqua pena commicti posset aut veniret applicanda sancte romane ecclesie aut camere apostolice quo ad ipsam penam et eius commissionem de cetero intelligantur esse et sint nulla et nullius efficacie vel effectus et quo ad ipsam penam et eius commissionem habeantur totaliter pro imperfectis" (*ASF, Provv.*, 69, fol. 190*v* [Dec. 12, 1380]). Stefani does not mention this modification, but tells instead how the multiple *Monti* were eliminated, and of the great murmuring that went with it, since so many Florentines lost money in this reform: "e non credo, che già 100 anni, niuna così gran cosa si facesse colle fave, come questa: perocchè la somma era grande de' denari e la quantità degli uomini e donne era grande" (Stefani, *loc. cit.*).

286. *ASF, Provv.*, 72, fols. 71r–72r (June 12, 1383).

his mind, so must we. And indeed, the conclusion of the law is disconcerting:

> Item. This also saved, excepted, and declared: that by the aforesaid or by virtue or pretext of it nothing is or is understood to be at all derogated or abrogated or any prejudice generated to any right due in any fashion to the commune of Florence, or that could be or is due by virtue or on occasion of any testament or other last will made or to be made in the future.[287]

But testamentary renunciations of *Monte* shares had become a traditional method by which the commune, utilizing the moral anxiety of its creditors, had restrained its debt. Even in these first days of the new order, in which a self-contained commune would control its own debt, the commune could not conceal the two sides of its fiscal character: enricher of the citizenry, endangerer of its wealth. From then on, angry creditors would have to settle their disagreements within the city. And the regime could thank the holy father in Rome for this new-found sovereignty.

The re-creation of citizen faith in the stability of communal institutions was the historic task of the regime which ruled Florence from 1345 to 1378. To engender faith in Florentine government, the *Signorie* had to swear by the faith of its citizens in the Roman see. The apostolic camera came to secure for Florentine citizens first the stable disbursement of the interest and capital of the communal funded debt, and successively the loyal fulfillment by the government of administrative laws guaranteeing the republic against subversion.

The *modus vivendi* between the pope and the commune during the life of this regime was a *sine qua non* for its survival. When necessity required the commune to deviate from its bonded oath to observe these laws, it was able at times to obtain the *beneplacitum* of the pope, for he had become a judge of the *bene comune*, and he decided whether the further observance of a precise law would or would not place the commune of Florence "in iniquitatis vinculum."[288]

By securing citizen loans, the papacy silently fostered an enormous

---

287. "Item. Etiam hoc salvo, excepto et declarato: quod per predicta vel eorum vigore seu pretextu non intelligatur esse vel sit in aliquo derogatum vel abrogatum seu preiudicium generatum alicui iuri competenti quoquo modo comuni Florentie, seu quod competere posset aut competet vigore vel occasione alicuius testamenti vel alterius ultime voluntatis facte et seu in futurum faciende" (*ibid*).

288. See above, p. 195.

incrementation of the public debt. Thus it contributed to citizen confidence in government *per forza*, for the greater the debt, the more unavoidable the reliance on the administrators of that debt. Increasingly sovereign vis-à-vis its citizens in fiscal matters, the commune therewith became more independent in its dealings with Rome. The success of the papal rider was ultimately proved by the war against the papacy. Florence reclaimed its independence.

Certainly this article has raised more questions than it has answered. First of all, what were the antecedents of this technique for securing communal institutions? What was the subsequent history of this practice? Secondly, why was it that certain types of antisubversion and stability laws were very conspicuously *not* secured by the papal *clausula penalis*? Most noticeable in this regard are the *divieti* laws for offices held by citizens, the laws setting up commissions for bankruptcy proceedings, and the clauses in these same laws granting privileged and unassailable titles. Was there in fact a formal agreement between the two parties and, if so, what was its nature? Perhaps with this introductory essay on the institution, previously obscure references in the law and finance will take on new meaning, and the practice will yield up its secrets.

The implications of this security system seem, even with our limited knowledge and tentative hypotheses, to be vast enough. Most important, it throws a new light on the modes of dependence among Italian communes. In order to preserve political order through financial solvency, a structural diminution of the sovereignty of an Italian commune in favor of the papacy was undertaken. Was this practice widespread, or peculiar to Guelphic Florence? Together with Lauro Martines's findings on the power of the papal judiciary in quattrocento Florence, this paper argues for a new look at the question of the extent and nature of the papacy's role in Italian communal history. In a sense, the regime which emerged in Florence from the troubles of the early forties was illegitimate: it could not command credit from its citizens. What was the role of the papacy, and of its camera, in "legitimizing" the communes and tyrannies of northern Italy during these centuries?

This security system has definite implications for the study of the usury problem in connection with public debts.[289] I have argued that the papal

289. J. Kirshner has completed a dissertation on the moral theology of the Florentine public debt; "From Usury to Public Finance: The Ecclesiastical Controversy over the Public Debt of Florence, Genoa, and Venice, 1300–1500" (Diss., Columbia University, 1970). I have been unable to consult this work. His planned book on the subject will help to clarify this complex subject.

rider in effect guaranteed the lender against prosecution for usury taken on *Monte* investments. If this view is correct, it would suggest that the canonical arguments and anguished consciences of contemporaries relate not to fear of persecution but to the internal forum of conscience. Interest from the public debt, my argument runs, was not judicable.

A third implication of this technique has to do with communal power in Florentine history. Doubtless, the commune was dependent on the papacy during this period to an extent and in a way that has not been imagined. But this does not suggest that the commune did not desire its sovereignty. It shows only that that could be achieved under the tutelage and with the support of the Roman church and its camera. Contemporaries did not consider the spiritual authority as the implacable enemy of communal liberty. The papacy needed a strong Florence in the 1340s, and supported the communal debt in order to get one.

One historian has spoken of the Florentine desire for a territorial church. And properly understood, there is much truth in this. But this *and* communal sovereignty could be obtained not by antagonism with the universal church, but *gratia domini pape.*

APPENDIX

The following is the text of a classical penal clause of the period 1345–1376 (*ASF, Provv.*, 59, fols. 189*v*–190*r* [Dec. 11, 1371]). I have paragraphed the text.

Et quod contra predicta vel aliquod predictorum nichil possit provideri, ordinari, stanziari, vel fieri. Et quod domini priores artium et vexillifer justitie populi et comunis Florentie, etiam cum quibuscumque aliis collegiis seu officiis vel sine, non possint ordinare, stabilire, vel facere aliquid contra ipsa que supra proxime dicta sunt, vel aliquod ipsorum. Nec providere vel deliberare utile esse teneri consilium publicum vel privatum contra ipsa vel aliquod ipsorum, seu in eorum vel alicuius eorum abrogationem, derogationem, anullationem, vel preiudicium qualecumque.

Nec pati quod de hiis absolutio vel liberatio per ipsos dominos priores et vexilliferum vel capitanum vel potestatem vel aliquem alium proposita fiat vel aliquod consilium teneatur publicum vel privatum, etiam ad exquirendum de voluntate consilii vel consiliorum.

Nec aliquam baliam vel potestatem recipere vel habere seu procurare, vel consentire quod alii detur cuius autoritate vel pretextu possit quomodolibet provideri vel fieri contra predicta vel aliquod predictorum. Et si aliquam baliam generalem vel aliam per quam posset promissis vel alicui eorum derogari, vel accipere seu consentire quod alli vel aliis daretur, teneantur et debeant omnia et singula suprascripta et que continentur in eis excipere et reservare.

Et quod ex nunc esse intelligantur et sint spetialiter et nominatim, exceptuata et reservata. Nec scriba eorum vel alius huiusmodi deliberationis scribat.

Et quod potestas et capitanus si adessent, vel aliquis alius offitialis populi et comunis Florentie presens et futurus non possit convocare consilium vel consilia populi vel comunis Florentie in quo vel quibus contra predicta vel aliquod predictorum aliquid proponatur. Et si convocaretur, non proponatur vel reformetur aliquid in dicto consilio vel consiliis per quod fieri queat aliquid contra predicta vel aliquod predictorum, etiam ad exquirendum voluntatem, ut dictum est.

Et si proponeretur vel fieret eo ipso quod proponeretur et in ipso

213

propositionis actu intelligatur esse et sit privatus suo regimine et officio. Et insuper condempnetur in florenis auri mille, comuni Florentie applicandis.

⟨Nec priores et vexillifer justitie qui pro tempore fuerint possint vel debeant interesse consilio vel consiliis in quo vel quibus tractaretur vel provideretur aliquid contra predicta vel aliquod predictorum. Et si interessent intelligantur esse et sint privati prioratus et vexilliferatus justitie officio et omni immunitate et privilegio, et sint infames, et habeantur et sint exbanniti comunis Florentie pro mallificio, et impune possint exbanniti comunis Florentie pro mallificio, et impune possint offendi a quolibet. Et insuper tamquam baratterii et corruptores comunis Florentie in duobus milibus florenis auri, comuni Florentie applicandis pro una dimidia, et pro alia dimidia applicandis camere domini pape condempnentur, et condempnati esse intelligantur et sint.

Et quod notarius qui dictam deliberationem, propositionem, vel reformationem scribet puniatur in libris mille florenorum parvorum, et ab officio suo cadat.

Et consiliarii qui dictis consiliis interessent nequeant contra predicta consulere vel arringare, sub pena mille florenorum auri cuilibet arringanti vel consulenti, et sint ipso jure exbanniti comunis Florentie pro mallificio, et tamquam exbanniti comunis Florentie pro mallificio a quocumque impune possint offendi.

Et gonfalonierii sotietatum populi et duodecim boni viri, nec non capitudines vigintiunius artium, et quilibet alius consiliarius populi et comunis Florentie possint, eisque liceat, teneantur et debeant tali consilio contradicere, et propositioni etiam si obtenta esset in consilio populi. Et quicumque ex dictis gonfalonieriis et duodecim et capitudinis dixerint aliquid in aliquo ex dictis consiliis, vel arringaverit contra proposita que fieret contra predicta vel derogationem vel diminutionem, habeat de pecunia comunis Florentie libras quinquaginta florenorum parvorum. Quas camerarii camere comunis Florentie solvere teneantur et debeant absque aliqua apodixa propria habenda.

Quicquid autem contra predicta vel aliquod predictorum fieret non valeat neque teneat ipso jure, nec ad observantiam ipsius aliquis teneatur.

Et quod domini priores artium et vexillifer justitie, gonfalonerii societatum populi, et XII boni viri, qui pro tempore fuerint, teneantur et debeant eo ipso quod iurabunt eorum officium spetialiter et nominatim promictere et satisdare cum bonis et idoneis fideiuxorribus, de duobus milibus florenis de auro, quod predicta omnia et singula observabunt et observari facient, et contra ea non facient vel venient vel permictent ullo modo, tacite vel expresse, directe vel per obliquum, sub pena duorum milium florenorum de auro pro quolibet eorum, applicanda ut dictum est.

Et quod ille qui computaverit juramentum teneatur et debeat spetialiter et nominatim de predictis, ab eis et quolibet eorum recipere juramentum et promissionem, solempni stipulatione vallandam vice et nomine domini pape et sue camere pro una dimidia, et pro alia dimidia vice et nomine comunis Florentie et sue camere, sub pena mille librarum florenorum parvorum.

Et nichilhominus dicta [fol. 190*r*] promissio facta esse intelligatur.

Et quod de predictis omnibus et singulis possit cognosci, procedi, et condempnari, ut dictum est, ad denumptionem cuiuslibet publice vel private persone, et etiam post annum, a die deponiti prioratus et vexilliferatus justitie et scribatus officii computanda.

Et similem promissionem et juramentum faciant et facere teneantur et debeant potestas, capitanus, et capitudines vigintiunius artium et consiliarii consiliorum populi et comunis Florentie tempore juramenti eorum, sine satisdatione eorum. Et ipsam recipere teneatur ille qui dictum juramentum recipiet, sub pena predicta.

Et nichilhominus dicta promissio facta esse intelligatur. Et quod notarius, scriba officii dominorum priorum et vexilliferis justitie teneatur et debeat in apodixis quas micteret de satisdatione et juramento aliquorum ex predictis vel aliquo predictorum in ipsis apodixis inserere quod ipsum juramentum et satisdationem que prestari debent, ut dictum est, recipiat ab eis et quolibet eorum, ut dictum est.

Et insuper quod executor ordinamentorum justitie et quilibet rector seu offitialis comunis Florentie qui sindicabit seu sindicare debebit dictos dominos priores et vexilliferum justitie teneatur et debeat spetialiter et nominatim inquirere de predictis, et repertos culpabiles punire et condempnare penis predictis, applicandis pro dimidia camere domini pape, et pro alia dimidia comunis Florentie, ut dictum est.

Non obstantibus . . .